PEDRO DE ALVARADO, CONQUISTADOR

LONDON: HUMPHREY MILFORD
OXFORD UNIVERSITY PRESS

DON PEDRO DE ALVARADO MESIAS Y CONTRERAS
*From the Jenkins Portrait in Possession of Dr. Fernando Iglesias, Minister
of the Republic of Costa Rica to Guatemala.*

PEDRO DE ALVARADO CONQUISTADOR

BY

JOHN EOGHAN KELLY

PRINCETON

PRINCETON UNIVERSITY PRESS

1932

PRINTED AT THE PRINCETON UNIVERSITY PRESS
PRINCETON, NEW JERSEY, U.S.A.

TO JACK

PREFACE

THE life of Pedro de Alvarado falls into two clearly defined parts. Until the year 1523 it is a record of preparation, of high courage and reckless daring as the chief lieutenant of Hernan Cortes. Thereafter Alvarado emerges as a conqueror in his own right. During the remainder of his life he was a Captain General, extending the empire of Charles V and adding vivid dashes of colour to the panorama of the discovery and conquest of Latin America, on equal footing with his colleagues ruling the other newly subjugated nations.

The first part of his story is necessarily that of Hernan Cortes and the conquest of Mexico, in which Alvarado played a leading rôle. It has not been given herein in as great detail as in the accounts of Prescott and Bernal Diaz del Castillo, but an attempt has been made to present the campaign at sufficient length to depict the obstacles overcome by the Spaniards and the actions of the subject of this volume.

With the departure of Alvarado from Mexico in December 1523, the second phase is reached. While compiling this part of the record, the author has had access to material in manuscript form, especially in Central America, unknown to earlier writers. In the course of seven journeys to Guatemala in the past decade, the author was afforded the opportunity to study the life of the Conqueror on the scene of his exploits.

From every point of view, Pedro de Alvarado holds high rank among the Conquistadores, possessing Alexander-like vision and boundless ambition. Cortes and Pizarro overcame greater empires and found ruin, disappointment and, in the case of Pizarro, murder, their reward from an ungrateful sovereign. Jimenez de Quesada, conqueror of Colombia, Vasco Nuñez de Balboa, who first sighted the Pacific, and Hernando de Soto rank first among the Conquistadores for nobility of character. Alvarado stands much closer to Jimenez de Quesada, who, dying of leprosy, willed *funds for the perpetual supply of jars of water to travellers athirst on the mountain trail to Bogota, than to Pedro Arias Davila, Governor of Panama, in shameful isolation at the foot of the scale. The cruel traits of his nature, measured from a modern viewpoint, were offset by his generous nature and gift of leadership. Principal associate of Cortes, conqueror of the Indian kingdoms of Guatemala and El Salvador, the restless Alvarado plunged into the inferno of the expedition to Ecuador and was en route to further discoveries in the East Indies when a characteristically generous action cost him his life in a desert valley of Jalisco. Overbold, impetuous to the point of rashness in his earlier years, Alvarado possessed the quality of personal magnetism that won and held the allegiance of his turbulent followers and the awe and respect of his Indian adversaries.*

No complete biography of Alvarado has heretofore been published in any language, to the best of the present writer's knowledge. Even in Guatemala only fragmentary references to his career appear in the works of the contemporary historians of the Conquest.

ACKNOWLEDGEMENTS

THE author is indebted to Colonel Felix Castellanos B., Ingeniero Fernando Cruz and Don Victor Miguel Diaz of Guatemala for suggestions and data; to His Excellency Doctor Fernando Iglesias, Minister of the Republic of Costa Rica to Guatemala, for permission to reproduce the Jenkins portrait of Pedro de Alvarado; and to Hubert J. Hannon and James Finucane for their patience in transcribing the manuscript.

J. E. K.

New York, May 1931.

FORM OF PROPER NAMES

THE names of the principal Indian characters and towns have been rendered in a great variety of forms by the original chroniclers of the Conquest and their successors. The outstanding example of this diversity is that of the Aztec Emperor, Moctezuma. Cortes in his letters to the Emperor Charles V spells the name Mutezcuma and Muctezuma and is followed by Lorenzana and Folsom while de Solis writes Motezuma. Prescott and Bancroft prefer Montezuma although it is doubtful if there is sufficient authority for their use of the letter "n." Bernal Diaz del Castillo uses Motecuhzoma, Bayard Morris Monteczuma, and still different variations are to be found in other works. In the present volume I have used the spelling Moctezuma, a simplified form of Cortes' version and favoured by modern Mexican opinion.

In general, names and places and characters in Mexico have been rendered as written by Cortes and Diaz del Castillo; names of places and persons in Central America follow the forms used by the Guatemalan historian, Don Jose Milla.

CONTENTS

LIST OF ILLUSTRATIONS

PART ONE

THE LIEUTENANT OF HERNAN CORTES

1485-1523

THE CURTAIN RISES

DURING the life span of Pedro de Alvarado, 1485-1541, the world emerged from the mists of the unknown. Before the dazzled vision of the Caucasian nations, timidly expanding their heritage of Europe, West Asia and North Africa, a new continent was disclosed. The imagination of mankind awoke from the long sleep of the Middle Ages and men of all races rushed to explore and seize the treasures revealed by the voyages of Columbus and Vasco da Gama.

Spain, the discoverer, played the dominant rôle in the conquest of the Western World. During the century succeeding the discovery, hardly a portion of the vast continent stretching from Alaska to Tierra del Fuego escaped the impress of the Latin heel. The densest jungles of tropical America, to all appearances untouched by man, reveal to the chagrined modern explorer the mouldering walls erected by his Spanish predecessor four centuries ago. After the spectacular conquerors of empire, Cortes, Pizarro, Alvarado, Almagro and Jimenez de Quesada, a host of fearless captains, De Soto, Coronado, Nuñez de Balboa, Nuñez Cabeza de Vaca, Cabrilla and their fellows wrote the name of Spain large across the continent. The resulting empire was so vast that Spain was unprepared to comprehend it. Never in the history of the world had so huge a territory been conquered by one people, in so short a lapse of time and in face of such overwhelming odds.

When Pedro de Alvarado was born, in 1485, the Spanish nation was but painfully finding itself. The marriage of Ferdinand to Isabella the Catholic, in 1479, had united the kingdoms of Aragon and Castile. It was not until 1492 that the Moor was conquered at Granada and continental Spain united. The release of so many ambitious spirits from warfare at home and under Gonzalo de Cordoba in Italy, coinciding with the discovery by Columbus, provided the nucleus of the conquerors, who swept in resistless tides to

the Americas and to the East, until at the close of the reign of
Phillip II, in 1598, the mountain principalities of Castile and
Aragon had become masters of nearly one-fourth of the earth.

Church and State quarrelled over their respective rights in the
new found lands, over the bodies and souls of the Indians, over the
treasures found. Stay-at-home courtier and cleric joined forces,
however, to defraud the actual conqueror of his hard-won gains.
The great majority of the leaders of the Conquest died in poverty,
many in prison, some were murdered. The treasures flowed to
Spain, to the strong boxes of the Crown, of the Council of the
Indies, of the Church. The conquistador who defrayed the heavy
expenses of his expedition, often at a loss, saw the government of
the newly won lands given to some pampered favourite of the
Crown who proceeded to open an investigation into the conqueror's
acts as a prelude to depriving the victim of honours, fortune and
often life.

Pedro de Alvarado was born in the little town of Badajoz, of
the Province of Estremadura, where Hernan Cortes was born in
the same year. His father, Don Diego de Alvarado, an impoverished minor noble, had distinguished himself in the campaign in
Italy, winning the title of Commendador of Lobon, of the Order
of Santiago. Little is known of the childhood of Alvarado, other
than that he received the usual rudimentary education of children
of good family in the fifteenth century. In 1510, in company with
his brothers, Jorge, Gonzalo, Gomez and Juan, he joined an expedition to the West Indies, settling in Santo Domingo, then the capital
of the Spanish Americas and headquarters of the Admiral of the
Ocean Sea. For eight years he made an indifferent success of a
plantation allotted to him, preferring to pass his time in the court
of Don Luis Columbus, nephew and successor of the discoverer.

While in Santo Domingo there occurred an incident, trifling in
itself, which was seized upon by the enemies of Alvarado at his
trial in Mexico in 1529. Alvarado had in his possession an old
velvet cloak of his father's, on which there had been sewn a red
cross, insignia of the Order of Santiago. Although the cross had
been removed, the impression was clearly visible. At first Alvarado
wore the cloak in such manner as to hide the mark, but the Admiral
having noticed it, he boldly stated that he himself was the owner of

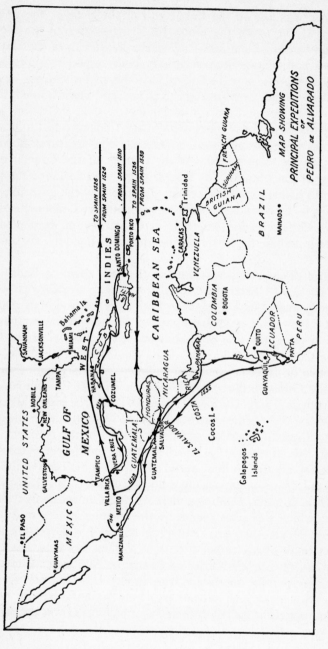

Map by the Author

MAP SHOWING
PRINCIPAL EXPEDITIONS
of
PEDRO de ALVARADO

the order and thereafter used the title in referring to himself and in signing letters. The chronicler, Remesal, employs the incident as evidence of Alvarado's overmastering ambition and will to power.

Pedro de Alvarado was about thirty-three when opportunity presented itself, in Juan de Grijalva's expedition to Yucatan and Mexico. He was slenderly but strongly built, somewhat about middle height, with a pleasing countenance and well cut features. His hair and beard were of a striking reddish brown shade, distinguishing him from his darker companions in the eyes of the Indians and bringing him the Tlascalan nickname of "Tonatiuh" (the sun).[1] A good horseman, accounted a brave soldier, generous and frank in speech, Alvarado was popular with the men of his age in the new colonies and wielded much influence over the more adventurous spirits. He was fond of display in dress. The Spaniards of the new colonies, living in the most primitive conditions in their bare forts and plantation blockhouses, had brought with them their love for the silks and velvets of Spain. Bancroft[2] describes the costume of a Spanish nobleman of this period as consisting of silk garbardine, with puffed and slashed sleeves, tight at the wrist; a velvet or chamois skin doublet, silk hose and slashed silken trousers, long, bell-topped leather boots, a soft, low-crowned, wide-brimmed beaver hat ornamented with an ostrich feather and a cape or cloak laced and faced with gold or silver embroidery, worn hanging from one shoulder. In battle a metal helmet and body armour of plate or chain mail replaced the hat and cloak.

By the opening of the year 1517, Spain had discovered and conquered the West Indies, had traced the shore of the mainland from Venezuela to Panama and north to the inlands of Roatan in the Gulf of Honduras and, passing the Gulf of Mexico unheeded, from Florida to the Carolinas. Only to the west of Cuba the mystery remained unsolved. The authorities in the West Indies needed new discoveries desperately. The lands heretofore conquered had been lacking in the anticipated riches. The fourth voyage of Columbus and the explorations of Pinzon along the coast of Central America were disappointments. This new mainland was no India and just as evidently barred the passage to the East. Columbus and Pinzon found Indians who told of great cities, shining with gold and jade, lying far to the north and west. The Arawak inhabitants of Jamaica and Cuba confirmed these rumours. Diego Velasquez, Governor of Cuba, whose Spanish subjects grumbled openly at the slight return from their mines and plantations, resolved to determine the truth of these rumours. If they proved correct, additional power and wealth were his; if they were shown false or the expedition were lost, he was temporarily or permanently rid of the most troublesome and restless of his colonists.

Velasquez had been sent by Diego Columbus in 1511 with three hundred men to conquer Cuba. The Indian inhabitants offered little resistance and settlements were soon established at Santiago, the capital Mantanzas, Trinidad, Habana,[3] San Salvador and others. Having accomplished his conquest, Velasquez repudiated his contract with and his allegiance to the Admiral and obtained from the Crown, always eager to foment dissensions among its governors in order to weaken them, the coveted authority to rule as direct representative of Spain. We shall see that as Velasquez served Diego Columbus, so was he served by those he sent to conquer lands which held riches beyond the imagination of the most grasping conquistador. Indeed this disloyalty among the conquistadores was only matched by the disloyalty of Spain, civil and clerical, to the soldiers fighting her battles in the Americas. From the outset, Spain cheated and robbed every discoverer of his share of the spoils. Solemn covenants were entered into with Columbus, and religiously adhered to,—until wealth and new colonies were a reality. Thereupon Spain sent Bobadilla to imprison the Admiral and flouted the contract. For the next two centuries the descendants of Columbus appeared continuously before the tribunals to obtain even a portion of the lands and authority promised the Grand Admiral on the faith of His Most Catholic Majesty.

Velasquez was about forty-five years of age in 1517, a nobleman, veteran of the wars against the Moors and well educated. Of fine appearance, he was vacillating in policy, envious and ambitious in temperament. He preferred to make his conquests by proxy whenever possible, remaining safely in Santiago until the fighting was over. He did not scruple to intrigue against the commanders sent on expeditions for his account and to plot their murder when he felt they might set up independently as he had done.

New groups of colonists came to Cuba at frequent intervals from Spain and Santo Domingo. In 1516 there appeared about one hundred veterans of the settlement at Panama. In Panama they had found war and gold and starvation; in Cuba there was food, peace and work but little gold. Restless and idle, they shortly became a worry to the not over-courageous Governor.

Therefore, Diego Velasquez grasped eagerly at the opportunity when Francisco Hernandez de Cordoba, a prosperous planter resident in the town of Santo Espiritu, proposed a voyage to the unknown West, taking with him the majority of the newcomers from Panama. On February 8, 1517, Hernandez de Cordoba set sail from Santiago de Cuba in three vessels, the largest of sixty tons burden. A contract was drawn up, whereby Velasquez contributed one of the vessels, a small bark of thirty tons, and was to have a share of the profits. Hernandez de Cordoba obtained the right to explore and take possession of all newly discovered lands in the name of Spain and as lieutenant of Velasquez. The wily Governor withheld the right to make settlements; if the new lands were worth while he intended to have them for himself, meantime he was well pleased that Hernandez de Cordoba and his followers made the effort at their own risk and expense. There were in all one hundred and ten soldiers, a priest, a pilot and the representative of the Royal Treasury, for the Crown, that took no risk and contributed no share of the expense, claimed one-fifth of all spoil and treasure. Bernal Diaz del Castillo, the eyewitness chronicler of the Conquest, was a member of this expedition.

After a stormy voyage of twenty-one days they reached the mainland of Yucatan at Cape Catoche and found Indians living in towns of stone houses so large that the pilot stated Seville itself could not have presented a better appearance. Invited ashore by the natives, Hernandez de Cordoba fell into an ambush and lost two men. Here two Indians were captured that afterward played an important part as interpreters in this and succeeding expeditions. Turning about and following the coast westwardly for fifteen days, the Spaniards landed at Campeche to take on fresh water, of which they were in dire need. While so engaged a party of Indians wearing elaborately figured cotton mantles and feather headdresses approached them and by signs invited them to enter the nearby town.

The Indians pointed in the direction of the east and repeated the word "Castilan" several times, to the mystification of the explorers. It is not known that any Spanish vessel had landed in Mexico previously but this and other indications that the white man was not entirely unknown prior to 1517 have provided fascinating enigmas for the historian. Moctezuma possessed, before the arrival of the first recorded Spaniards, a Toledo sword which his nobles vainly endeavoured to break. Spaniards exploring the vicinity of Acapulco, on the Pacific coast of Mexico, were met by a procession of Indians, dressed as priests, with shaven heads and carrying a banner of the Cross.[4]

The landing party was horrified to find the walls of the stone temples dominating the town drenched with the blood of recent human sacrifice. As large squadrons of Indian warriors approached in battle array, the Spaniards retreated to their ships and continued westward. Arriving at the mouth of the river Champoton, shaken by a severe storm, they landed again for water, near a large town. Menacing crowds surrounded them, whereupon Hernandez landed almost his entire force to protect the precious water. Matters remained unchanged during the night, the Spaniards keeping constant watch. At daybreak they were attacked by hordes of warriors, two hundred for every Spaniard, says Diaz del Castillo. Fifty-seven of the invaders were killed, five died of their wounds and two were carried off by the Indians. Only one man escaped unwounded. Hernandez divided his remaining force between the two larger ships, stripped the bark of its stores and cordage and burned it. Suffering agonies of thirst, for all of their water casks had been lost at Champoton, the survivors set sail for Cuba, where the leader died of his wounds.

The tales of the expeditionaires and most especially the gold and jade ornaments seized at Punta Catoche spurred Velasquez to new efforts. Counting as negligible the losses and sufferings of Hernandez de Cordoba and his followers, the Governor set about organizing a new army to conquer the lands emerging so temptingly beyond the western sea. Four vessels were prepared, including the two brought back by Hernandez de Cordoba. The young men and dissatisfied planters rushed to enlist. Juan de Grijalva, only twenty-eight years of age, nephew of the Governor, gentle, brave and handsome, too honest and confiding for his own good, was chosen commander of the fleet. Two hundred and forty soldiers were divided among four captains, Grijalva, Pedro de Alvarado, Francisco de Montejo and Alonso de Avila, each of whom commanded a vessel. Alvarado had been temporarily in Santiago de Cuba when the expedition was projected and through his wealth and reputation for leadership had easily persuaded Velasquez to name him master of one of the ships. Velasquez contributed the ships, each captain provided provisions and equipment for his men. Grijalva was bound by the same covenant to explore and trade but not to make settlements. At this time the Cardinal Jimenez ruled as Regent of Spain instead of the mad Joanna. He had replaced the military governors of the Indies by a trio of Jeronimite Fathers, who promptly granted the royal licence to the expedition, sent Francisco de Peñalosa to collect the King's Fifth of all treasure, Juan Diaz as Chaplain and Diego de Godoy as Notary. The Spaniards were most punctilious as explorers, each important act, taking possession of new lands, settlement of towns, division of spoils, being solemnly recorded on the spot by notarial document. The fleet sailed from Santiago April 8, 1518, and reached the Island of Cozumel, south of Punta Catoche, on May 4, being carried off its course by the strong current that runs along the coast. Grijalva landed and found towns of stone houses and paved streets deserted save by two old Indians unable to flee. While they were talking with them by means of the interpreters captured on the previous voyage, an Indian woman approached who spoke to them in the language of the West Indian natives, known to Bernal Diaz del Castillo and many other soldiers. Being unable to induce the islanders to return, Grijalva took the woman, the only survivor of a castaway party of Jamaican Indians, whose companions had been sacrificed to the idols, on board as an additional interpreter and the fleet put about, doubled Cape Catoche and on May 25 arrived off Champoton. Here, at the scene of Hernandez de Cordoba's disastrous defeat, the Spaniards landed with caution, but impelled by their need of water, and found the triumphant Indians awaiting them. The Christians wore heavy quilted armor reaching to the knees, copied from the native warriors, in addition to their metal helmets and breastplates. The natives showered the approaching small boats with a rain of arrows and spears tipped with knife-edged obsidian, running into the water in their eagerness. Seven Spaniards were killed, sixty wounded, Grijalva three times, before the Indians retreated under the superior swordplay of the Europeans. Grijalva pressed forward to the town which the inhabitants had deserted, buried two hundred enemy dead and after three days spent in fruitless attempts to induce the Indians to return in peace, withdrew to his ships and continued the voyage. On the thirtieth of May the Laguna de Terminos was discovered and partially mapped by the Spaniards. Early maps show Yucatan as an island, cut off from the mainland by a strait emerging to the southward at the Golfo Dulce in Guatemala and to the north in this terminal lagoon. The explorers profited by this stop to hunt deer and game which were abundant in the bay islands. A hunting dog, pet of the commander, took so active a part in the chase that she could not be found when the ships weighed anchor and was left behind. A year later, when Cortes stopped at the islands he was welcomed by the dog, fat and healthy, which had escaped the alligators and myriad other predatory enemies.

The fleet next arrived off the mouth of the Tabasco or Grijalva river where shoal water at the bar prevented the two larger ships from entering. The entire expedition, save those indispensable to the care of the larger vessels, crowded into the small ships and ascended the river to within a mile of the city. Both the town and the chief thereof bore the name Tabasco. In the distance the Indians could be seen hastily chopping down trees, erecting stockades and preparing for combat. Grijalva halted his ships and disembarked on a low sandy point where a clump of palm trees grew. Fifty canoes filled with warriors approached and through the interpreters, Julianillo and Melchorejo, Grijalva signified his peaceful intentions, reinforcing his words with gifts of mirrors and blue and green beads. As the mineral jadeite was sacred to the Maya and Nahua peoples, these green beads were of priceless worth in the eyes of the recipients, even as gold in the eyes of the Spaniards. De las Casas has indicted the Spanish explorers because they traded beads for gold, and his example has been eagerly followed by some who from their easy chairs undertake to weigh the characters and motives of these sculptors of empire. There is no such thing as absolute value. The handful of green glass beads for which the Indian traded a moderate fortune in coarse gold, was entirely unique in the Aztec Empire and worth a thousand slaves to the possessor. Gold on the other hand was to be had by any native chief by relatively little effort and therefore the Indian thought he was driving a very good bargain, and from his point of view, he was undoubtedly correct.

Grijalva explained that he was the vassal of the Great Emperor beyond the Eastern seas, asked his auditors to acknowledge Charles V as overlord and coming to matters of more immediate importance, asked for poultry and fruit in exchange for the gifts. The Indian spokesman replied that they already had a chief of their own, with whom they were well satisfied, promised to bring food and to barter with the Spaniards and in withdrawing to consult his fellow chiefs, warned the strangers that if they came to make war, that twenty-four thousand warriors were assembled in the vicinity, stouter men than those of the tribes at Champoton. The following day Tabasco came in state, attended by thirty subordinate chiefs and preceded by priests chanting and swinging braziers of live coals and incense. They brought a large amount of food, roast fowls, fish, fruit and cakes made of corn and a number of hollow golden ornaments in the shape of animals and three necklaces of golden beads. Though the value of the gold did not exceed two or three hundred dollars, the spirits of the Spaniards rose exultantly at this first evidence of hoped-for treasure. Tabasco also brought a chief's ceremonial dress, of quilted cotton finely worked with golden ornaments and feather work, according to Diaz del Castillo,[5] and a golden mask in token of friendship. Grijalva, touched by the act, presented Tabasco with a velvet cap and coat and shoes, all of crimson, to the manifest delight of the Indian. The chiefs made plain that they had no more gold to give, but since their guests wished this metal, there was much to be found in the country of Colua (Mexico), pointing in the direction of the setting sun. Grijalva distributed beads among the chiefs, thanked them for their hospitality and as a storm was coming up, the Europeans returned to their ships lest they be cast upon the lee shore. So ended one of the few bloodless contacts between Spaniard and Mexican.

Continuing along the coast, the Spaniards observed Indians

carrying great shields of tortoise shell which glistened like gold and passing the mouths of numerous rivers without entering, saw in the distance the snow-capped mountains of Mexico. Alvarado's ship was a better sailer than the remainder of the fleet, and drawing ahead of his companions, he impulsively entered the mouth of the Rio Papaloapan, now Rio Alvarado, and sailed upstream some distance, where he bartered for fish. Grijalva, who had waited at the bar, severely reprimanded Alvarado for his action, since if an accident had occurred to the vessel, the fleet would have been powerless to aid. This eager, bold, incautious Alvarado is the Alvarado of Mexico City. The eagerness and courage remained undimmed throughout his life, but the example of Cortes and bitter experience are evident in the more deliberate, astute Alvarado, the conqueror of Guatemala.

Three days later they sighted another river, on the shore of which were many Indians, holding lances on which were long white cloth banners, waving as in signal or invitation. Here on the banks of the Rio de Banderas (banners) or Jamapa, the Spaniards were entering the territory of the Aztec Empire. Moctezuma having advices in his capital of the arrival of the two expeditions of bearded strangers, their appearance carefully painted on sheets of henequen (sisal) cloth, had ordered his governor to welcome the newcomers and endeavour to learn their plans. Six days were spent here in complete friendliness, conversing in signs, for the language was no longer known to the interpreters. Food and gold worked in various forms to the value of fifteen thousand dollars[6] were received in exchange for a variety of gifts. The weather threatening, the Spaniards embarked, taking with them an Indian, who became Christian, baptized Francisco, to act as interpreter.

On the eighteenth of June the fleet dropped anchor opposite a large island from which smoke was rising. Two boatloads of soldiers landed but found no living thing. In the foreground there arose two well built masonry temples, with steeply rising steps. Ascending these the soldiers of Spain were horrified to find the bodies of five boys sacrificed during the preceding night. Their hearts had been torn out, the bodies opened and the limbs cut off. The walls of the temples were daubed with blood and human heads fixed on poles.[7]

Sickened by this travesty on religion, the Spaniards abandoned the island, which they named Isla de Sacrificios, and proceeded to the mainland, where they traded for gold with the inhabitants. Shortly afterward they landed on another island, San Juan de Ulua, possessing ample supplies of potable water. Here they took stock of their equipment and as their remaining provisions were mouldy and worm-eaten, thirteen soldiers had died of their wounds and they were unceasingly tortured by swarms of mosquitoes and sand flies, they resolved to inform Diego Velasquez of their discoveries and plight and ask further orders. The new interpreter told them that the human sacrifices were ordered by the Lord of Mexico beyond the mountains, to which all these territories were tributary. This seemed an additional weighty reason for refitting and securing reinforcements before venturing further into the country of this bloodthirsty people and, accordingly, Grijalva despatched Pedro de Alvarado with the treasure in the best ship to inform Velasquez, while the remainder of the expedition continued northward along the Gulf Coast.

The fleet reached the vicinity of Tampico where a serious battle with the Indians, who attempted to seize one of the vessels anchored in a river, and the impossibility of passing a headland owing to a strong current, induced Grijalva to return to Cuba. Retracing his course, touching at several points to take on water and to trade, Grijalva refused the entreaties of his men to settle on the new lands. About four thousand dollars in gold ornaments and six hundred copper axes which the Spaniards thought were debased gold were secured on the return voyage. On this occasion the orange was introduced into Mexico by Bernal Diaz del Castillo, who planted seeds at Tonala, where the fleet halted to repair a leaky vessel.

Juan de Grijalva arrived in Santiago de Cuba about November 1, 1518, to find that the gold and reports of Alvarado had set Cuba aflame with excitement and ambition for new conquest. To Grijalva was due the credit. He had scrupulously kept his agreement with the Governor, he had displayed leadership, courage and prudence, had discovered a great stretch of territory peopled by warlike tribes possessing gold, of which he had brought twenty thousand dollars' worth; he returned to meet slights and disdain. Velasquez wished to eliminate a possible rival, the more so as most of the soldiers desired to sail again under Grijalva, and he gave eager ear to the complaints of Alvarado, Montejo and Avila, who, sensing Velasquez' attitude, were quick to advance their own causes at the expense of their whilom commander.

Velasquez applied to Santo Domingo for permission to fit out another expedition, which was promptly granted. He also sent Benito Martinez to Spain to gain the ear and favour of Fonseca, Bishop of Burgos, the all-powerful Secretary of the Council of the Indies, with such good success that the Bishop, the evil genius of the Conquest, confirmed Velasquez in his possession of all discoveries of Hernandez de Cordoba and Grijalva and authorized him to govern all new lands discovered by his expeditions. Secure in his authority, Velasquez set about the enlisting of a third and more formidable expedition. Ten vessels, including the four of Grijalva's fleet, were prepared. As usual, Velasquez bore the minor share of the expense. The adventurers were volunteers who as far as possible provided their own arms and supplies. Seven of the vessels and over twenty thousand dollars in supplies, arms, horses and trade goods were supplied by the commander of the fleet; Velasquez furnished only three vessels and these under charter, while he sold the produce of his farms to the volunteers at high prices. Soldiers and captains clamoured for places; only the commander remained to be named. Velasquez desired a leader who could perform prodigies in the field while remaining absolutely subservient to the Governor. After weighing the claims of many candidates, urged by Andres de Duero, secretary to the Governor, and Amador de Lares, the Royal Auditor, who had entered into a secret contract with their nominee, Velasquez selected the Mayor of the Town of Santiago Baracoa, Hernan Cortes, as Captain General.

FOOTNOTES FOR CHAPTER ONE

[1] "First, there was the fiery and impetuous Pedro de Alvarado, a hero of the Achilles or Sir Lancelot school, strong and symmetrical as a goddess-born; haughty, choleric, sometimes staunch and generous, passionate in his loves and hates, with the usual mixture of license, loyalty, and zeal for the Church. He had not eyes to see, from where he stood in the warfare of his day, at once the decline of the fiercer barbarism and the dawn of a truer and gentler heroism.

Already we have discovered flashes of temper and tendencies to treachery that display his character by too sulphurous a flame; but we shall find in him much to admire as a conquistador and governor." Bancroft, *Annals of Early Mexico,* p. 73.

[2] Bancroft, *History of the Pacific States.*

[3] The original site of Habana was on the south shore of the island of Cuba.

[4] "The people of Tuito, on the west coast of Mexico, held that before the Conquest a vessel was lost there, from which there landed more than forty persons, dressed like Spaniards, and whom the natives received kindly, but finally slew because they insisted on the worship of the Cross. A box thrown up by the waves, and containing peculiar clothing, gold rings, and sword which no one could break, was said to have been in Montezuma's possession." Bancroft, *Annals of Early Mexico,* p. 100.

"When Francisco Cortes entered the town, shortly after the fall of Mexico, he was met by a body of Indians with their hair tonsured like priests, and with crosses in their hands, headed by the chief in flowing white gown and scapulary. This they explained had been the practice of the shipwrecked crew, who had held up the cross as a recourse from all danger." Frejes, *Historia de la Conquista,* pp. 63-4.

[5] "In great state, unarmed, and without sign of fear, Tabasco next day visited Grijalva on board his vessel. He had already sent roasted fish, fowl, maize bread, and fruit, and now he brought gold and feather-work. Out of a chest borne by his attendants was taken a suit of armor, of wood overlaid with gold, which Tabasco placed upon Grijalva, and on his head a golden helmet, giving him likewise masks and breast plates of gold and mosaic, and targets, collars, bracelets, and beads, all of beaten gold, three thousand pesos in value." Bancroft, *Annals of Early Mexico,* p. 24.

[6] As nearly as can be calculated in present-day values.

[7] In commenting on this incident, Bancroft, *Annals of Early Mexico,* p. 26, gives evidence of the anti-Spanish bias which mars his otherwise valuable works by its constant appearance.

II

HERNAN CORTES

ERNAN CORTES had been in the Indies for fifteen years when appointed to the command of the Mexican expedition. Son of good but impoverished family, Cortes was a sickly youth and little inclined to study. In 1504, a distant relative, Ovando, having been named Governor of the Indies, Cortes came to Santo Domingo where he remained for seven years. In 1511 he passed over to Cuba with Diego Velasquez and assisted in the pacification of the island. He broke with the Governor over the affections of his future wife, escaped from prison and took sanctuary in a church. Lured from safety by strategy, Cortes was captured and sentenced to hang, the sentence, however, being commuted to banishment to Santo Domingo. Watching his chance the first night at sea, he slipped off his shackles, dropped into the tender astern and pulled back to Cuba. The boat upset in a cross current when several miles from shore and only his great determination and good fortune brought Cortes safely through the shark-infested waters in the darkness. Reaching land, he again took refuge in a church until an opportunity presented itself to make peace on honourable terms with the Governor. Shortly thereafter he rendered important services in an Indian uprising and was named Alcalde (Mayor) of Santiago Baracoa. Some authorities state that Velasquez and Cortes married sisters; certain it is that Velasquez was godfather to a child of his lieutenant. But while Velasquez apparently forgot his one-time death sentence and resentment against Cortes, the time was to come when the latter repaid him full measure in his own coin.

Hernan Cortes, as soldier, landowner and official, was popular among his fellow Spaniards. Generous and amiable, the determination to succeed against all obstacles, nurtured when he was one of few poor pupils among patronizing richer schoolmates, showed itself increasingly with the passage of time. Though they were of

the same age, at this time Cortes was a far more finished character
and leader than Alvarado. Possessing all of the latter's bravery,
Cortes was statesman as well as soldier. He was capable of desperate forays, but they were carefully planned in advance. The conquest of Mexico was due as much to Cortes' diplomacy at Tlascala
and Tuzcuco as to the valour of the Spanish arms. Physically, he
was of middle height, broad shouldered and sturdily made, with
a high square forehead, dark complexion and eyes, sharply cut
prominent nose, and full beard. Ambitious, cool, intelligent, such
was the heretofore undistinguished son of Spain destined to rank
among the great captains of all time.[1] Alexander, Genghis Khan,
Napoleon, commanded great masses of veteran soldiery; Hernan
Cortes led six hundred and fifteen undisciplined adventurers to the
conquest of an empire outranking in man-power any European
nation of the sixteenth century.

No sooner had Velasquez appointed Cortes to the chief command
than he began to repent his action, for there were not lacking
malicious tongues to whisper that the leader would renounce his
allegiance to the Governor as soon as the fleet set sail. Too timor-
ous to remove Cortes, he sent a number of his partisans, headed by
Diego de Ordaz, to join the expedition and to watch for and prevent
plots against the authority of Velasquez. Cortes, advised of the
campaign, showed himself very politic and flattering to the Governor and was assiduously aided by the latter's secretary and the
Auditor, whose hopes of profit from the expedition depended on
the continuance of their nominee in command.

The commission to Hernan Cortes was dated October 23, 1518,
but the expedition did not sail from Santiago de Cuba until the
morning of November 18. Velasquez' fears and suspicions had
risen to such a pitch that an open rupture could no longer be
averted. Having placed all available supplies and three hundred
seventy-five men aboard the ten ships, Cortes presented himself
before the Governor late at night on the seventeenth and announced
his imminent departure. Velasquez raged inwardly but dared not
give orders to seize the Captain General. Indeed it is doubtful if
Velasquez possessed sufficient men to carry out such an order
against the followers of Cortes. After early Mass the next morning
the fleet sailed, Cortes and the Governor making polite speeches to

each other at parting. Touching at the town of Trinidad, he was joined by over a hundred volunteers, many of them veterans of the Grijalva expedition. Among the newcomers were the five Alvarado brothers, Sandoval, Avila, Velasquez de Leon, Puertocarrero and others who were to distinguish themselves in the conquest. Puertocarrero having no horse nor the funds to purchase one, Cortes bought him a spirited animal with three gold knots from his velvet cloak. Two small vessels laden with provisions were also acquired, on credit, for the commander possessed no more funds, and their owners and crews joined the fleet. While at Trinidad, messengers arrived from Velasquez with orders to Francisco Verdugo, Mayor of Trinidad and brother-in-law of the Governor, to seize the fleet and depose Cortes. Verdugo, however, secretly sympathized with the latter and in addition had no force at his command. A further stop was made at the town of La Habana, then located on the south shore of the island, where more recruits were received, the fleet reviewed and captains appointed. Among the latter was Pedro de Alvarado who was given command of the *San Sebastian,* the same vessel he had commanded under Juan de Grijalva. Velasquez wrote to Pedro Barba, officer in charge at La Habana, ordering him to arrest Cortes, but in vain. The very messenger who brought the letter deserted the Governor and took service under the Captain General.

On February 10, 1519, the fleet of eleven vessels finally set sail for the island of Cozumel off the coast of Yucatan. The largest vessel was of one hundred tons displacement, three were of seventy and eighty tons and the rest smaller, some of them not being decked over. No modern sailor would venture to navigate the stormy waters of the Mexican Gulf in such unmanageable cockle-shells. Five hundred and eight soldiers, one hundred and nine sailors, two priests and about two hundred Cuban and Negro servants composed the party. Thirteen soldiers only had firearms, thirty-two crossbows, while the remainder were armed with swords and spears. The artillery consisted of fourteen small guns, difficult to transport and handle and of short range. Sixteen horses were perhaps the most valuable equipment of the army for their presence decided many a battle in favour of the out-numbered invaders. Bernal Diaz del Castillo, writing his memoirs of the Conquest

after thirty years, gives a list of these hardy animals, with owner-
ship, description, characteristics and even names, evidence of
the impression made on him.

The soldiers were divided among eleven captains, Alvarado,
Montejo and Avila, who had held equal rank in the fleet of Juan de
Grijalva, Diego de Ordaz, the spy of Velasquez, Escobar, Sandoval, Juan de Escalante, de Morla, Puertocarrero, Juan Velasquez
de Leon, relative of the Governor of Cuba, whose flame of life was
to be snuffed out in the headlong horror of the Noche Triste, and
Cristobal de Olid, accounted brave even among these valiant men,
who came safely through every battle of the Conquest to perish at
the hands of assassins whose lives he had spared in the lonely
wastes of Honduras. Among all the company none outranked
Alvarado save only the Captain General himself and none stood
higher in the leader's affections. Under Alvarado's direct command
were seventy soldiers, including Diaz del Castillo.

Alvarado arrived at Cozumel two days before the remainder of
the fleet which was delayed to permit of urgent repairs to de
Morla's vessel. He landed in full panoply of war, whereupon the
Indians fled to the mainland. The Spaniards seized poultry, a few
trifles in the temple and captured two old Indians and an Indian
woman. Cortes, apprized of the action upon landing, flew into a
rage, reprimanded Alvarado severely for frightening the Indians,
with whom he wished to treat, flogged seven sailors for theft, put
the pilot in chains for outsailing the fleet and returned the spoils
to their rightful owners. Thus early in the voyage did Cortes make
it plain that there was but one master and that he would be obeyed.

While in Cozumel Cortes was informed that bearded men were
captives of the Indians on the mainland. Diego de Ordaz was
despatched with a light vessel to patrol the coast and a messenger
was sent to the chief of a neighbouring tribe, said to hold the
Spaniards, bearing a letter to the prisoners. After a week's fruitless search, Ordaz rejoined the fleet which set sail for Cape
Catoche and the Mexican Gulf. Hardly started, however, a leak
developed in Juan de Escalante's ship, which carried all the foodstuffs, forcing the fleet to return to Cozumel. This delay had an
important effect on the success of the expedition, for Jeronimo de
Aguilar, a priest who had been for the past eight years a slave of

DON PEDRO DE ALVARADO
The Portrait in the City Hall of the Municipality of Guatemala.

the Indians, approached and falling on his knees, in broken Spanish gave thanks to God for his delivery. To Aguilar Cortes owed much of his knowledge of Indian character, customs and languages and the former also was of much value as an interpreter. Aguilar had been a member of a ship commanded by Valdivia that had sailed from Panama for Santo Domingo in 1511, numbering fifteen men and two women.[2] Wrecked by a storm off the coast of Yucatan, nine men and the women reached shore, only to fall into the hands of the inhabitants. Placed in cages, they were fed well and fattened until one day Valdivia and four companions were sacrificed to the idols and their bodies eaten by the worshipers. The remaining captives managed to escape and make their way to a neighbouring chieftain, who worked them as slaves, but spared their lives. At the arrival of Cortes, only Aguilar and a sailor, Gonzalo Guerrero, were alive. The latter refused to leave, having married an Indian woman and risen to a position of some prominence in the tribe. It was he, indeed, that instigated the ambush and attack upon Hernandez de Cordoba two years before.

On March 4, 1519, the fleet sailed again and, after a stormy voyage during which Grijalva's dog was rescued, reached the domains of Tabasco on the twelfth. Here the Spaniards found the Indians, whom Grijalva had left in peace, showing a most hostile spirit. No less than twelve thousand warriors crowded the banks of the river. This change was due to the taunts of the men of Champoton, that they had driven off and killed the invaders, while Tabasco had meekly bartered with them. Through the interpreter, Aguilar, Cortes asked for water and food. The Indians pointed to the river for the former, said they would bring what food they could on the morrow but that if the white men did not leave immediately thereafter they would be killed. Seeing there was no help for it, Cortes prepared for battle and early the next morning Alonso de Avila landed with one hundred men and took a circuitous path to the rear of the town. The small boats of the fleet were loaded with soldiers and prior to landing, Cortes made a further appeal for peace. A hail of arrows answered him and a horde of warriors rushed to dispute the passage. Firearms cleared a path momentarily and the discipline of the Spaniards forced the Indians to retreat to their town, which was protected by a stout log stockade.

As Cortes made a breach in the wall, Avila's men scaled the rear palisade and the defenders broke and fled incontinently to the forest. Secure in his control of the town, Cortes took formal possession of the land in the name of the Emperor, it being noted that the name of Diego Velasquez was conspicuous by its absence. The worthy Governor was receiving payment in his own coin. The next day, however, the Indians evened the score, as Alvarado and Francisco de Lugo, each in command of one hundred men and sent to scour the surrounding country for food, were confronted by great masses of warriors and forced to retire to the town, losing two men killed. The Indian interpreter, Melchorejo, deserted to his fellow countrymen during the night, leaving his European clothing hanging on a tree in derisive farewell to his captors.

Meantime, Tabasco had aroused the province and a great host of Indians—Bernal Diaz del Castillo says five squadrons of eight thousand men each[3]—were assembled at the nearby town of Centla to exterminate the invaders. Cortes landed all his force, horses and guns, and on the twenty-fifth of March the two armies met. The Indian warriors, painted and wearing thick quilted cotton armour, jeered at the little band of Spaniards, whose bodies they confidently expected to devour before the setting of the sun. The field of battle was a great cornfield, boggy in places and intersected with drainage ditches, imperilling the movements of the heavily laden foot soldiers and cavalry. The tropical sun blazed on the steel armour of the invaders, who gasped in a temperature of nearly one hundred degrees Fahrenheit.

Cortes formed the thirteen best horsemen, including Alvarado, into a troop, of which he took personal command and executed a wide circuit to the rear of the enemy, while the infantry marched directly toward the centre of the Indian array. The natives swarmed about their antagonists, nearly overpowering them by weight of numbers, but receiving a sharp object lesson from the Spanish blades, drew off in a circle about the invaders the better to shoot their arrows and javelins. When the firearms spoke the Indians threw dust and leaves into the air and shouted in chorus, as if to hide the effect of the shots, or perhaps to counteract them by other noise and haze. The Spaniards formed a square and remained in position for they could not charge the enemy without being taken in the flank and rear. Just as heat and exhaustion were about to win the battle for the natives, Cortes and his followers, who had been delayed crossing a swamp, arrived at full gallop and fell upon the Indians so intent on the battle before them that they did not perceive the horsemen until the first ranks were trampled under the flying hoofs. The natives thought horse and man one animal and before these apparitions in shining metal towering above them, their morale broke and they fled, pursued in all directions by the horsemen. Eight hundred Indians lay dead under the eyes of the weary victors. Two Spaniards were killed and sixty wounded in this first major combat in New Spain.

Tabasco, thoroughly frightened, sued for peace, and forty chiefs came in his name bearing gifts. Cortes contented himself with commanding the Indians to acknowledge the sovereignty of the Emperor Charles V and embrace the Christian religion, to all of which they agreed. Altars were erected and on the following day, Palm Sunday, Mass was celebrated, which Aguilar translated to the assembled Indians; Tabasco sent Cortes a gift of twenty Indian girls as slaves, accompanying a young woman of high station among the natives. This girl, who became a Christian and was baptized with the name of Doña Marina, played one of the principal rôles in the drama of the Conquest. Cortes gave her to Puertocarrero, but after the latter returned to Spain and the wife of the Conqueror had died, she bore him a son, Don Martin Cortes. She rendered invaluable aid to the Spaniards and also succeeded in saving many an Aztec tribe and town from the fury of the invader.[4] The very name of Malinche, which the Mexicans bestowed upon Cortes, was a corruption of Marina, for the Aztec tongue balked at the letter "r."

On the following morning the Spaniards embarked and passing the Rio de Banderas without stopping, arrived off San Juan de Ulua on the fifth day.

When the heel of Cortes pressed the strand of San Juan de Ulua the curtain rose on the mighty drama of the Conquest of Mexico. The civilizations of America and Europe, in the persons of their most advanced representatives, came to a test of strength for the first time. Confronting the might of the Aztec Empire stood a group of six hundred Spanish soldiers. The reader is already

familiar with their equipment, their sixteen horses, the few un-
wieldy pieces of primitive artillery, the thirteen muskets. The
invaders had no conception of the task before them, no medicines,
no maps. Over two years of constant warfare were to elapse before
Mexico City fell before them. Difficult as their position was, it
became more precarious still. Dissension and open rebellion broke
out in the army, their communications with Cuba and Spain were
severed with the destruction of the fleet and, at the most critical
moment, they were assailed from the rear by another and superior
Spanish army sent by Diego Velasquez with orders to kill or capture Cortes and his followers. The genius of the Captain General
rose superior to all obstacles and by August 1521 Hernan Cortes,
leader of the forlorn hope, was undisputed master of New Spain.

Efforts have been made, by Robertson and others, to detract
from the achievements of Hernan Cortes by alleging for the Spaniards an overwhelming superiority in arms and equipment. Robertson, who described the massive pyramid temples and palaces of the
Mexican Empire as palm-thatched mud huts, claims that the
Indians fled in terror before the horses, armour and firearms of the
invader. If this was ever true, it was only at the outset and was a
passing phase. Cortes in his letters to the Emperor, speaking of the
investment of Mexico City by the Spanish forces in May 1521,
records that the Indian soldiers threw themselves against the horsemen and gunners of the European army in such masses that the
Spaniards were not able to manœuvre or to fire their pieces. The
fact is that the native forces took the aggressive in almost every
combat, coming out to meet the Christians in front of their cities
and fortifications, and pursuing them on their retreats with the
utmost eagerness and disregard for personal safety. The Aztec
warriors confided in the charms and prayers of their priests as did
their opponents in the power and protection of the Cross and Saint
James. Cowardice was never a characteristic of the Indian. Robertson and his fellow traducers are, however, completely refuted
when, on their flight from Mexico City after the Noche Triste, the
decimated Spanish army met the flower of the Mexican nation on
the field of Otumba. Their power gone, the few guns worse than
useless, only seven horses remaining alive, the four hundred Spaniards who had escaped the rout were making their painful way to

the coast and safety. Every man bore wounds, some had lost their arms, there had been no food save cactus pears and roots for two days. In this state, straggling over the pass into the parched plain of Otumba, the starving, thirsty band of adventurers saw barring their way an Aztec army of over thirty thousand warriors, stretching away to the left and right toward the horizon, the plumed banners waving joyously in anticipation of victory. Here was no superior foreign army slaughtering naked savages. This was man to man, sword to sword, thirty thousand picked, fresh warriors matched against the four hundred drooping Spaniards. All day the battle raged. At sunset, ten thousand Aztecs, including their Prince, lay dead scattered in heaps, ranks and singly far and wide over the plain. The survivors had vanished over the horizon. The only living beings in sight were the exhausted Spaniards, binding up their fresh wounds and offering fervent thanks to God.

"The Battle of Otumba, one of the decisive combats of all history, demonstrated conclusively that it was the Spaniards themselves, not their superior equipment, that conquered the Aztec Empire. Only men of extraordinary physical strength and courage could have escaped annihilation through sheer weight of numbers."[5]

The Aztec Empire was at the height of its power and glory in 1519. Founded by a wandering tribe in 1325, it had grown swiftly through good fortune and the friendship of the neaiby States of Tuzcuco and Tlalcopan, until at the landing of Cortes the Mexican Emperor had reduced his allies to subject monarchs and his sway extended over an area twice the size of New England.[6] To the northward the boundary of the Empire was indefinite, somewhere along the line from Tuxpam to Queretaro, while to the southward the Aztec realms reached unbroken to the borders of Guatemala and included the area of the present Mexican State of Chiapas. A colony was maintained in Nicaragua and trade routes established as far south as Colombia. The Quiche nation of Guatemala, although friendly to the Aztecs, was independent, as was Tabasco in the State that bears his name and the Tarascan tribes inhabiting the State of Michoacan. War was waged constantly to extend the frontiers of the Empire and to supply material for the human sacrifices demanded by the Aztec religion. Prisoners of war were invariably reserved for the temple sacrifice.

From the eighteenth to the twenty-first degrees North Latitude on the Atlantic seaboard and from the fourteenth to the nineteenth parallels on the Pacific, lacking only Tabasco and Michoacan, the rule of the Mexicans was supreme—with one fatal exception. The Achilles heel was the tiny republic of Tlascala, entirely surrounded by Aztec territory. Were it not for the sanctuary afforded by this territory and the valiant cooperation of the Tlascalan warriors, it is doubtful if even Cortes could have overcome Moctezuma. After the Conquest one of the Spanish chieftains expressed his surprise that Tlascala had been permitted to remain unconquered, as the Aztecs undoubtedly were able to subjugate it at any time. His Mexican companion replied cynically that Tlascala had been permitted to retain its freedom that wars might be waged against it from time to time, whenever prisoners of war were required for sacrifice.

The confusing mixture of brutality and scientific attainment exhibited by the Aztec Empire may be traced to its history. The Aztecs were a barbarous northern race that conquered and fell heir to the remnants of the Toltec and Maya civilizations. From these latter the Aztecs drew their knowledge of astronomy and medicine, in which they surpassed European nations at the time of the Conquest. Yet the Aztecs do not appear to have advanced beyond the intellectual level of their predecessors, and, indeed, seem to have lost ground in important particulars. Human sacrifice was not apparently a feature of the early Maya empires. The Aztecs took over the benevolent religion of the Mayan Kukulkan or Quetzalcoatl, transformed it to suit their natures and joined it to the rites in honour of Huitzilopotchli, the God of War, on whose altars more than one hundred thousand persons perished annually. At the coronation of Moctezuma it is said that seventy-two thousand prisoners were executed in ceremonies lasting over a month's time.[7]

The Aztecs were skilled workers in precious metals, in cotton, feathers and other materials. They had a remarkably advanced judiciary system, with judges of the supreme tribunal independent of the monarch. Prescott estimates their political evolution about equal to that of Britain under Alfred, or in the early stages of the feudal system. The emperor was elected, and must be a warrior or a priest. In practice he was usually one of the four members of his predecessor's Council of State. The Empire was divided among the great nobles, each of whom resided in the capital or left members of his family as hostages in the Emperor's power. Beneath the jurisdiction of the feudal chiefs who governed the provinces, were lesser lords and knights, who were commoners that had distinguished themselves in battle. The official chronicler of the Conquest[8] states that the Emperor and the nobles had dominion over three million vassals, using the term to denote males, slave or free, capable of military service. This would be equivalent to a total population of fifteen million, about equal to that of the present-day population of the Republic of Mexico.

An elaborate system of trails and roads, sometimes constructed with much engineering skill, formed a network throughout the Empire and enabled the capital to keep in close touch with all parts. So rapid was this communication that fish were served on Moctezuma's table that had been swimming in the Gulf of Mexico, two hundred miles away, twenty-four hours before.[9] Stations were built along the trails at distances of about three leagues and relays of runners carried strips of sisal fibre cloth, bleached and painted with description of persons and events. Thus Moctezuma and his court were informed of the appearance and actions of Juan de Grijalva and his companions, while the Spanish fleet was still at anchor in the Rio de Banderas.

In 1519 Moctezuma II, nephew of the previous Emperor, had occupied the Serpent Throne for seventeen years. Physically valiant, rendered a moral coward by his superstitious nature, relying for success upon craft when force failed, torn between his conflicting impulses, he was about to match wits with a forthright spirit to whom vacillation and hesitation were unknown qualities. Moctezuma possessed unlimited power, semi-divine prestige, a record as a conqueror who had extended the Aztec Empire far beyond all previous limits. He could call to battle armies greater than those at the command of any European monarch of his time, his will was law in the Aztec heaven as well as on earth. Opposed to this colossus stood the pathetic figure of the Spanish captain on the distant shores of the Mexican Gulf, cut off from his race, disowned by his superior, comparatively without force, base or hope of success. Under the gorgeous feathered headdress of the Emperor ruled the demon of doubt, while the brain under the steel casque of Spain knew only one master, the determination to scale the heights of Anahuac. All was staked on this one throw, with a careful cold attention to detail. Determination conquered might, the leader of another forlorn hope joined the ranks of the immortals.

The third of four nephews of the bloody Ahuitzotl, who died without legitimate issue, Moctezuma had cunningly brought about his election as Emperor, in place of his eldest brother, Cuitlahuatzin. Trained for war in common with all Aztec nobles, Moctezuma had early gained a reputation as a daring and successful soldier. As soon as this fame was securely won, he abandoned the profession of arms and entered the priesthood, that on the day of election he might be sure of support from the warrior nobles and the hierarchy. Disguising his haughty nature and licentious proclivities, he busied himself at humble tasks in the presence of the high priests. He chose to have himself called "The Sad, the Severe." As he had foreseen, on the death of Ahuitzotl, he secured a majority of votes of those entitled by Aztec law to choose the successor and was proclaimed Emperor. So well were his plans laid that his elder brothers contented themselves with a little innocuous grumbling and accepted the lesser posts offered them by the new monarch.

Now that the power was firmly in his hands, Moctezuma threw off the mask of humility and democracy, dismissed those generals of inferior birth who had won their posts through merit under his predecessor and ground the nation and the vassal States under ever increasing tax levies. Roast children were served as delicacies[10] to favoured guests at his banquets and the domains of the Empire were searched far and wide to provide new inmates for his harem.

Yet with all this, Moctezuma was a man of education and considerable talent. He laboured incessantly for the improvement of his capital and empire, building avenues and highways, cities and temples. He was an astronomer of note and liberally endowed scientists and artists. But his exactions had made him unpopular with his people, who murmured at every opportunity. Alarmed, the Emperor sought to stamp out resistance by granting greater power to the nobles and taking from the freeborn Aztec citizen rights he had enjoyed since the foundation of the State. The clergy ardently abetted Moctezuma's plans and the empire rapidly changed from a loosely bound, democratic league of cities to a rigid military and religious autocracy, ruthlessly exploiting a cowed citizenry, bowed before the smoking temples of Huitzilopotchli and Quetzalcoatl.

Constant repetition has given semblance of fact to the alleged extreme cruelty of the Spanish conquerors toward the Indian inhabitants of America. Viewed in the light of history, the Spanish treatment of the vanquished was not extraordinarily severe. The great bulk of the inhabitants of Latin America today is largely of Indian blood and in almost every republic there are large tribes living freely in the customs of their ancestors. Great numbers of Indians apart from warriors killed in battle against the invaders, were slaughtered, particularly among the Arawak tribes of the West Indies, or died under forced labor. Yet as early as 1546[11] Indian slavery had been prohibited in the colonies by Royal Decree. Only in the United States and particularly in that portion of the country settled by other nations than Spain has the aborigine been practically exterminated. Public opinion of the sixteenth century was indifferent to the fate of the infidel. Succeeding generations that were to witness the burning of witches and Negroes in North America, the English atrocities in Ireland and the bath of blood that accompanied the Reformation cannot sit in judgement on the morals of the Conquest. Nor were the cruelties all on one side. The ghastly Aztec religion required from eighty thousand to two hundred thousand human victims annually with accompanying cannibalistic rites and the unfortunate Spanish soldiers who fell into the hands of the Emperors were subjected to nameless tortures before their hearts were torn from the living bodies for the delectation of the Aztec gods.

FOOTNOTES FOR CHAPTER TWO

[1] "If any would place Cortes, his genius, and his exploits, below those of the world's greatest generals, because he warred on enemies weaker than their enemies, we have only to consider the means at his command, how much less was his force than theirs. What could the Scipios or the Caesars have done with

half a thousand men; or Washington or Wellington, with five hundred against five hundred thousand? Napoleon's tactics were always to have at hand more forces than the enemy. In this the Corsican displayed his astuteness. But a keener astuteness was required by Cortes to conquer thousands with hundreds and tens. Perhaps Moltke, who, with a stronger force, could wage successful war on France, perhaps he and a handful of his veterans, could land on the deadly shores of the Mexican Gulf, and with Montezuma there, and all the interior as dark to them as Erebus, by strategy and force of arms possess themselves of the country. I doubt it exceedingly." Bancroft, *Annals of Early Mexico*, p. 153.

[2] Bancroft, *History of the Pacific States*, p. 350, states twenty men and mentions no women.

[3] The Indian armies were formed in Xiquipilli, of five thousand men each, composed of archers, javelin throwers and soldiers armed with sword and lance.

[4] "Before telling about the great Montezuma and his famous City of Mexico and the Mexicans, I wish to give some account of Doña Marina, who from her childhood had been the mistress and Cacica of towns and vassals. It happened in this way:

"Her father and mother were chiefs and Caciques of a town called Paynala, which had other towns subject to it, and stood about eight leagues from the town of Coatzacoalcos. Her father died while she was still a little child, and her mother married another Cacique, a young man, and bore him a son. It seems that the father and mother had a great affection for this son and it was agreed between them that he should succeed to their honours when their days were done. So that there should be no impediment to this, they gave the little girl, Doña Marina, to some Indians from Xicalango, and this they did by night so as to escape observation, and they then spread the report that she had died, and as it happened at this time that a child of one of their Indian slaves died they gave out that it was their daughter and the heiress who was dead.

"The Indians of Xicalango gave the child to the people of Tabasco and the Tabasco people gave her to Cortes. I, myself, knew her mother, and the old woman's son and her half-brother, when he was already grown up and ruled the town jointly with his mother, for the second husband of the old lady was dead. When they became Christians, the old lady was called Marta and the son Lazaro. I knew all this very well because in the year 1523 after the Conquest of Mexico and the other provinces, when Cristobal de Olid revolted in Honduras, and Cortes was on his way there, he passed through Coatzacoatcos and I and the greater number of the settlers of that town accompanied him on that expedition as I shall relate in the proper time and place. As Doña Marina proved herself such an excellent woman and good interpreter throughout the wars in New Spain, Tlascala and Mexico (as I shall show later on) Cortes always took her with him, and during that expedition she was married to a gentleman named Juan Jaramillo at the town of Orizaba.

"Doña Marina was a person of the greatest importance and was obeyed without question by the Indians throughout New Spain."

Diaz del Castillo, *Discovery and Conquest of Mexico*, p. 115.

[5] Prescott, *History of the Conquest of Mexico*, p. 396.

[6] "The Mexicans with whom our history is principally concerned, came, also, as we have seen, from the remote regions of the north,—the populous hive of

nations in the New World, as it had been in the Old. They arrived on the borders of Anahuac, towards the beginning of the thirteenth century, some time after the occupation of the land by the kindred races. For a long time they did not establish themselves in any permanent residence; but continued shifting their quarters to different parts of the Mexican valley, enduring all the casualties and hardships of a migratory life. On one occasion, they were enslaved by a more powerful tribe; but their ferocity soon made them formidable to their masters. After a series of wanderings and adventures, which need not shrink from comparison with the most extravagant legends of the heroic ages of antiquity, they at length halted on the southwestern borders of the principal lake, in the year 1325." Prescott, *History of the Conquest of Mexico,* Vol. I, pp. 15-16.

"The forlorn condition of the new settlers was made still worse by domestic feuds. A part of the citizens seceded from the main body and formed a separate community on the neighbouring marshes. Thus divided, it was long before they could aspire to the acquisition of territory on the mainland. They gradually increased, however, in numbers, and strengthened themselves yet more by various improvements in their polity and military discipline, while they established a reputation for courage as well as cruelty in war, which made their name terrible throughout the valley. In the early part of the fifteenth century, nearly a hundred years from the foundation of the country, an event took place which created an entire revolution in the circumstances, and, to some extent, in the character of the Aztecs. This was the subversion of the Tuzcucan monarchy by the Tepanecs, already noticed. When the oppressive conduct of the victors had at length aroused a spirit of resistance, its prince, Nezahualcoyotl, succeeded, after incredible perils and escapes, in mustering such a force, as with the aid of the Mexicans, placed him on a level with his enemies. In two successive battles, these were defeated with great slaughter, their chief slain and their territory, by one of those sudden reverses which characterize the wars of petty States, passed into the hands of the conquerors. It was awarded to Mexico in return for its important service.

"Then was formed that remarkable league, which, indeed, has no parallel in history. It was agreed between the States of Mexico, Tuzcuco, and the neighbouring little kingdom of Tlacopan, that they should mutually support each other in their wars, offensive and defensive, and that, in the distribution of the spoil, one-fifth should be assigned to Tlacopan, and the remainder be divided, in what proportion is uncertain, between the other powers. The Tuzcucan writers claim an equal share for their nation with the Aztecs. But this does not seem to be warranted by the immense increase of territory subsequently appropriated by the latter. And we may account for any advantage conceded to them by the treaty, on the supposition, that, however inferior they may have been originally, they were, at the time of making it, in a more prosperous condition than their allies, broken and dispirited by long oppression. What is more extraordinary than the treaty itself, however, is the fidelity with which it was maintained. During a century of uninterrupted warfare that ensued, no instance occurred where the parties quarrelled over the division of the spoil, which so often makes shipwreck of similar confederacies among civilized States.

"The allies for some time found sufficient occupation for their arms in their own valley; but they soon overleaped its rocky ramparts, and by the middle of the fifteenth century, under the first Montezuma, had spread down the sides of the tableland to the borders of the Gulf of Mexico. Tenochtitlan, the Aztec capital, gave evidence of the public prosperity. Its frail tenements were supplanted by solid structures of stone and lime. Its population rapidly increased. Its old feuds were healed. The citizens who had seceded were again brought under a common government with the main body, and the quarter they occupied was permanently connected with the parent city; the dimensions of which, covering the same ground, were much larger than those of the modern capital of Mexico.

"Fortunately, the throne was filled by a succession of able princes, who knew how to profit by their enlarged resources and by the martial enthusiasm of the nation. Year after year saw them return loaded with the spoils of conquered cities, and with throngs of devoted captives, to their capital. No State was able long to resist the accumulated strength of the confederates. At the beginning of the sixteenth century, just before the arrival of the Spaniards, the Aztec dominion reached across the continent, from the Atlantic to the Pacific; and under the bold and bloody Ahuitzotl, its arms had been carried far over the limits already noticed as defining its permanent territory, into the farthest corners of Guatemala [Prescott is in error here. The Aztec Empire never included Guatemala.—J.E.K.] and Nicaragua. This extent of empire, however limited in comparison with that of many other States, is truly wonderful, considering it as the acquisition of a people whose whole population and resources had so recently been comprised within the walls of their own petty city; and considering, moreover, that the conquered territory was thickly settled by various races, bred to arms like the Mexicans, and little inferior to them in social organization. The history of the Aztecs suggests some strong points of resemblance to that of the ancient Romans, not only in their military successes, but in the policy which led to them." Prescott, *History of the Conquest of Mexico*, Vol. I, pp. 17-21.

[7] Torquemada, *Historia de la Inquisicion,* states 72,344.

"On great occasions, as the coronation of a king, or the consecration of a temple, the number becomes still more appalling. At the dedication of the great temple of Huitzilopotchli, in 1486, the prisoners who for some years had been reserved for the purpose, were drawn from all quarters to the capital. They were ranged in files, forming a procession nearly two miles long. The ceremony consumed several days, and seventy thousand captives are said to have perished at the shrine of this terrible deity!" Prescott, *History of the Conquest of Mexico,* Vol. I, p. 80.

[8] Herrera, *Historia General.*

[9] Prescott, *History of the Conquest of Mexico,* Vol. I, p. 42.

[10] Diaz del Castillo, *Discovery and Conquest of Mexico;* de Solis, *Historia de la Conquista de Mejico.*

[11] Milla, *Historia de la America Central.*

III

THE CONQUEST IMPENDS

O
N HOLY THURSDAY, 1519, the fleet of Cortes came
to anchor off the sandy shore of San Juan de Ulua, the
site of the present city of Vera Cruz. Met by a friendly
message from the Aztec Governor, Teuhtlile, the entire
force landed on the following day, placing the artillery to protect
the camp. On Easter Sunday the Aztec chieftain was present at
High Mass and tasted the strange wines and foods of the newcomers with expressions of delight. He did not as kindly receive a
request for an interview with Moctezuma, but softened the snub
by borrowing the helmet of a soldier to exhibit to the Emperor,
saying that their God Quetzalcoatl had worn a similar one which
hung in a shrine in Mexico.

The legend and identity of Quetzalcoatl, inextricable mixture
of fact and fiction, which played so great a part in the history of
the Maya and Aztec peoples and contributed directly to the down-
fall of the Mexican Empire, can only be briefly touched upon here.
Quetzalcoatl, the Kukulcan of the Mayas, the "Fair God" of General Lew Wallace, was represented as having arrived on the shores
of the Gulf in the distant past, found the inhabitants devoid of
knowledge and arts, and established the Golden Age. After a reign
of forty years, during which he taught his subjects their knowledge
of astronomy, weaving and engineering and decreed the establishment of a bloodless religion, he departed over the seas to the East,
stating that he would some day return. The belief in the restoration
of the Golden Age, coupled with signs and portents recorded by
Aztec historians, readily induced Moctezuma to believe that Quetzalcoatl was come again in the person of the commander of the
blond, bearded men in the "floating houses." Bancroft, losing no
opportunity to sneer at the conquerors, remarks that if Cortes had
informed Teuhtlile that he was Quetzalcoatl, he could have ridden
in peaceful triumph to Mexico City and received the throne from

a welcoming Moctezuma. He conveniently overlooks the fact that Cortes could not have known of the legend at the time of this interview.

Quetzalcoatl was represented in the Aztec codices and on the statues at Chichen Itza[1] as a tall, bearded man and native tradition made him blond and blue-eyed. He has been identified by some writers as the Apostle Thomas and by others as a Viking, pointing to the incident of the helmet. Still others have endeavoured to claim him as Saint Brendan, who left Ireland in A.D. 542 and returned after a lengthy absence with tales of a tropical world and flourishing nations far beyond the rim of the earth.

Moctezuma received the news and gifts of Cortes with mixed feelings and summoned his Council of State to answer the request for an audience. The helmet, compared with that in the War God's temple, the beards and blond complexions of the newcomers, their ability to tame giant deer (horses) and control the lightning and thunder, all bespoke the return of the Fair God. Self-interest, pride, the imminent loss of his throne and fear of the unknown argued for resistance. Moctezuma was oppressed in spirit by the dire visions of the temple soothsayers. Men mounted upon strange animals had been seen in mortal combat in the clouds by all Mexico City not long before and as the Emperor gazed upon the painted representation of Cortes' horses, he felt that the end of his reign was near. He finally decided to send further and richer presents and beg the strangers to depart. He could hardly have chosen a more disastrous answer. If the invaders were Quetzalcoatl and his suite, such treatment would anger them and lead to the destruction of the Empire; if the newcomers were mortals, they would be rendered more avaricious by this display of wealth.

Two great disks, which Diaz del Castillo states were large as cartwheels, of solid gold and silver respectively, chased with designs representing the sun, animals and agriculture, headed an interminable list of golden ornaments worked in the shape of dogs, tigers, monkeys and ducks, ten golden collars, a lance, a bow and its arrows and two magistrate's maces, all in pure gold, bundles of headdresses and cloaks of exquisite featherwork, thirty loads of cotton mantles and other articles. The borrowed helmet was returned heaped with gold dust, to the value of three thousand dollars, while the great golden disk was appraised at four times that sum. These presents sealed the fate of the Aztec Empire. Here was the gold the Spaniards had sought in the Indies; henceforth the Mexicans would never shake off the hold of the conqueror. The envoy depicted the interest of Moctezuma in the presents and account of Cortes, but blandly stated that the Emperor could not make the long journey to the coast, while there was no need for Cortes to tire himself, for were there not ambassadors available? Not to be rebuffed, the Captain General replied that grateful as he was for the gifts, he could not face his sovereign if he had not seen Moctezuma. He gave the Mexican some further articles of Spanish and Italian textiles and carvings and begged him to carry the message to his Emperor. Quintalbor returned an evasive answer and took his leave.

The site of the camp was unhealthy and during the delays incident to the negotiations thirty Spaniards died of fever while the Aztec attitude became unfriendly and the food supply dwindled. The camp was finally moved thirty miles to the north where a rocky bluff and a river offered a haven to the fleet and a forest and firm ground provided a townsite and building material. Dissension arose, fed by rumours circulated by the partisans of Velasquez, who wished to return to Cuba and lay plans for a new expedition —without Cortes. The Captain General could not return without incurring prison and perhaps death for ignoring Velasquez in his proclamations and flouting his orders not to settle. He had come to the breaking-point with the Mexicans and further contact could be maintained only by force. It was a moment for desperate decisions and Cortes rose to it. Taking counsel with his intimates, Alvarado, Cristobal de Olid, Puertocarrero and Francisco de Lugo, he determined to resign his commission. The expeditionaries were bound by no rules and if they chose to settle and elected him their leader, his responsibility to Velasquez was ended. He cleverly circumvented a demand for instant return by issuing an order for such a move, so worded as to appear that the legion was losing a fortune by abandoning Mexico. Instantly almost the entire force clamoured to remain. Incited by Alvarado and Puertocarrero, they decided to form a settlement and establish civil government, Alvarado becoming Alderman and Captain of the Port. Before this soi-disant authority Cortes surrendered his powers from the Cuban Governor and was invested, in the name of Their Most Catholic Majesties, with the posts of Commander-in-Chief and Chief Justice.

While Alvarado scoured the surrounding country for food, Cortes accepted an invitation to visit the city of Cempoala, capital of the Totonac nation, distant three days' march. The Totonacs, recently conquered by the Aztecs, were anxious to gain the cooperation of these powerful strangers in throwing off the yoke. Cortes agreed and instructed his new allies to send tidings to all other subject nations of the coast, to refuse further tribute to Moctezuma. Five Aztec nobles, arriving at the psychological moment, were seized and delivered to the Spaniard, who sent two of them secretly to Mexico as evidence of his pacific intentions, retaining the others to witness his ascendancy over their rebellious vassals. The Totonacs, deeply impressed, yielded readily to the demand that they forsake their religion of human sacrifice for that of the Cross.

As he was about to depart for the unknown interior, Cortes received word that Velasquez had been confirmed by Charles V as Governor of all lands bordering on the Mexican Gulf. He immediately despatched Puertocarrero and Francisco de Montejo to Spain, reinforcing their arguments with the greater portion of the treasure, specimens of native handicraft and four Indian slaves, liberated from the sacrifice pens of Cempoala. Letters signed by the leader, the municipal officials and the expedition as a whole, setting forth the richness of the new lands and the claims of the discoverers, pleaded for a separation from the authority of Velasquez. When the messengers arrived in Spain in October, they were cast into prison and the treasure and letters confiscated. It is a curious commentary on the state of Spain in the sixteenth century that messengers to the most powerful temporal monarch of the time might be seized on his very doorstep by a Bishop of the Roman Catholic Church and held in prison while he filled the imperial ear with distorted versions and slanders. Fonseca converted to his own use part of the treasure and withheld the letters until a peremptory demand from Charles V made him give them up. He was, nevertheless, able to delay the case for two years.

The Velasquez faction made one final attempt to overthrow Cortes' authority, planning to seize the fleet and depart for Cuba, leaving their comrades helpless. The plot was discovered on the eve of its execution and after imprisoning the ringleaders, two of whom were sentenced to death, Cortes set out in haste for Cempoala to take counsel with Alvarado. Bitter thoughts filled the mind of the Conqueror on this early morning ride and from these thoughts sprang a resolution matchless in audacity. He could not go forward to Mexico with half of his followers disgruntled and anxious to return to Cuba. He must unify them, imbue them with his spirit, infuse in them that determination that comes to men fighting with their backs to the wall. He would destroy the fleet. The ships gone, the Velasquez party would have no opportunity to desert. Neither would Cortes have a means of escape from Mexico, but he wanted none. He was determined to sit on the throne of the Moctezumas or die in the attempt. He would return to Spain the acknowledged conqueror of the Empire or he would remain forever buried beneath Mexican soil.

Duly instructed, the captains of the five largest ships, partisans of Cortes, announced publicly that their vessels were no longer seaworthy. The ropes, sails, ironwork and other useful parts were brought ashore and the vessels sunk by holes drilled in the hulls. Secure now against desertion Cortes revived the drooping spirits of the soldiers by painting the glory and fortune awaiting them in Moctezuma's realm, to such an extent that they finally acquiesced to his suggestion that as all the army could not embark in the one vessel remaining, that it be sunk too. Cortes stood on the shore of the Mexican Gulf, penniless, for his fortune was invested in the fleet, the desperate leader of an unruly handful of adventurers, staking the lives of all on his one card, his unshakable determination to conquer.

Their spirits rebounding from the shock of the loss of the ships, the partisans of Velasquez and Cortes alike clamoured to be led against Mexico. Sixty of the older and infirm adventurers were left to garrison the port, their commander, Escalante, receiving orders to prevent any landing by Velasquez. On August 16, 1519, the army set out for Mexico after an alarm of ships off the coast that turned out to be, not Velasquez, but a notary of Francisco de

Garay, Governor of Jamaica, sent to warn Cortes against "trespassing" on the territories of the Panuco granted to his master. There is something of the ludicrous in this red tape and partition of a nation between two Spanish captains, neither of whom knew anything about the country he professed to own, except a short portion of the coast line. Garay continued his ineffectual forays until 1523, when Alvarado expelled and captured him. Straight toward the might of the Serpent Throne, well symbolized by the towering ranges before them, marched the Spanish legion. Fifteen horsemen, four hundred twenty foot and seven small pieces of artillery were followed by thirteen hundred Totonac warriors and a thousand slaves carrying baggage. Forty Totonac chiefs accompanied the column as guides, counsellors and perhaps principally as hostages for the loyalty of their warriors. Save for continued storms of rain and later hail, the march was without incident until on August 24 the army reached the Aztec city of Xocotlan, situated beyond the Bishop's Pass at an altitude of seven thousand feet. Here the Spaniards were well within Moctezuma's territory. If the Emperor desired the audacious strangers to penetrate far into his realm, so far that they would never emerge, his strategy was unfolding according to plan. On the way to Xocotlan they had passed two Aztec fortresses, situated on almost impregnable sites overlooking the tortuous passes through the Cortillera. The garrisons had made no unfriendly move; indeed they had offered provisions and guides. But now that the passes were behind the Spaniards, the trap sprung. The Aztec demeanour began to change.

The army filed through the streets of the well built city, with its thirteen temples set on pyramids towering over all. Beside the temples, set in a public square, was a tower built of human skulls. Bernal Diaz del Castillo[2] reports that he counted over one hundred thousand. In an adjoining place was a huge heap of thigh bones and the rafters of the palace where the Spanish captains were lodged were festooned with whitened skulls, relics of sacrifices. Olintetl, Lord of Xocotlan, explained to Cortes that he, chief over thirty thousand vassals, was a nobody in the eyes of the Emperor, thirty of whose chiefs could each place one hundred thousand warriors in the field. Little food was given the army here and with obvious ill will, though the Cempoalan allies exerted themselves to tell of the wonders done and possessed by the white men. Olintetl, however, made no openly hostile move and on August 28 the army left Xocotlan.

Before Cortes lay the Republic of Tlascala, the Mexican Switzerland of Tell and Winkleried, surrounded by Aztec enemies, warlike and vigilant as the price of existence. The Spanish leader counted upon a friendly reception from this nation of one hundred fifty thousand families and sent four Totonac chiefs to ask welcome and sanctuary. Stressing the prodigies performed by the invaders, their defiance of Moctezuma, the liberation of the Totonacs from the Aztec yoke, their horses, cannon, dogs and armour, their bloodless faith, the chiefs from Cempoala besought their kinsmen of Tlascala to welcome these strangers and speed them on the way to try conclusions with the hated Mexicans. The council deliberated, hearing arguments curiously like those of modern diplomats. One chief recalled the signs and prophecies foretelling the coming of these strangers and counselled welcome. A second feared they might be allies of Moctezuma striving to gain entry into the heart of Tlascala in this guise. A third counsellor, the Machiavelli of his nation, suggested a compromise plan. Let them determine without expense to Tlascala if these strangers were gods or not. On the frontier dwelt the half savage tribe of Otomi. The Spaniards on crossing the wall would be attacked by the tribesmen, led by the chief general of Tlascala's armies. If the Whites were defeated, Tlascala would claim the credit; if they conquered, the nation could still meet the Spaniards in peace and throw the blame for the battle on the Otomis. So it was agreed.

Receiving no reply and distrusting an Aztec invitation to follow a highway leading directly to Cholula, whose garrison had prepared an ambuscade, Cortes determined to visit Tlascala immediately and passing the boundary wall, nine feet high and twenty wide with one narrow but unguarded entrance, found himself attacked by three thousand Otomis, who pretended flight and led him toward an ambush. At nightfall the enemy withdrew and Tlascalan ambassadors appeared pretending surprise and sorrow at the occurrence and promising a friendly reception on the morrow. It came in the guise of forty thousand Tlascalan warriors, commanded by their chief general, Xicotencatl, son of one of the chiefs of State. The Spaniards held tenaciously to a small hill while the cavalry charged with loose rein, lances levelled at the heads of their opponents, opening lanes through the dense masses. One horse was killed and the body carried off by the Tlascalans who sent parts thereof throughout the nation as proof that this feared beast was mortal. The horseshoes and head were offered to the Gods in the great temple of Tlascala in a plea for victory.

After two days spent in skirmishing and searching nearby villages for food, of which the invaders stood in great need, Xicotencatl approached the Spanish position on September 5 with his greatest force, fifty thousand Tlascalan and Otomi warriors. From the hillock on which the Spanish army halted, the native array could be seen stretching across the entire width of the valley before them, the sunlight glinting on countless spear and dart tips of obsidian, the light breeze stirring the plumes of the headdresses and the banners of the divisions of the State, crowned over all by the great banner of the Tlascalan nation, bearing the insignia of a golden eagle with extended wings.[3]

The Indian warriors wore a garment of tightly quilted cotton, two inches in thickness, covering the body and thighs. So strongly made were these tunics that they would turn the blow of a native sword, of tough wood edged with obsidian, sharp as broken glass, though the metal blades of the conquerors, directed by practised arms, found the quilting an indifferent protection. The Tlascalans carried shields of leather or quilted cotton on a wooden frame. For offence they were armed with spears or maces, bows and arrows, slings, darts and throwing sticks or hul-ches, and two-edged, two-handed swords, tipped with copper and having jagged pieces of obsidian set in the sides at intervals.

The Tlascalan general had re-formed his men and attacked in mobile columns, copying his opponent's tactics, with such success that at one moment the Spaniards were swept from their positions and mixed hopelessly with the native warriors. Only the super-human efforts of the cavalry and the artillery which opened point-blank on friend and foe alike, cleared a space wherein the scattered steel-clad invaders might reunite. But for a dispute between Xicotencatl and another chief, resulting in the withdrawal of half the native army, the invasion might have ended this day on the sacrificial stone. All of the horses and most of the soldiers had been wounded, several had been killed and the Totonacs, displaying great courage, had suffered severely.

A night attack, urged by a soothsayer's pledge that the Children of the Sun were helpless without the protection of its rays, proved a complete failure and left a ridge of Tlascalan dead about the Spanish camp, including the unlucky augur, slain by the chagrined Xicotencatl. Spies sent to burn the camp were detected and sent back to Tlascala with their thumbs cut off and a message that the Children of the Sun were ready for enemies by day or night. This was too much, the Indian army refused to be led against men who could read their very thoughts; the moderate party removed the General and made peace with Cortes, a peace, be it said to Tlascala's honour, that was never broken.

The repeated victories of the little Spanish force over the legions of Tlascala, which the Aztecs had attempted in vain, made a deep impression upon Mexico. Moctezuma was now ready to acknowledge Charles V and pay any tribute of gold, cotton, feathers and jewels that Cortes might fix, upon the sole condition that the Spaniards not enter Mexico City. Several of the chiefs proposed indeed that the strangers be invited to the city, trapped and slaughtered, to the greater glory of Huitzilopotchli, Aztec God of War. Moctezuma would adopt both suggestions. He would buy off the invaders if possible. If they refused, he would trap and massacre them in another city of his realm, that his capital might be unstained by their impious tread. Five nobles of the Mexican court stood respectfully before the Spanish captain, reeling in his seat from fever. Gone was the overbearing demeanour of the tribute collectors. They were ready to concede anything, promise anything to keep these fearsome men in iron from the sacred lake of Mexico. Cortes dissembled his intentions, expressed his thanks for the message and the rich presents, and replied that he would answer Moctezuma from Tlascala in a short time. Two hundred bearers advanced with sixty thousand dollars' worth of gold dust, cotton mantles and armour, featherwork and other evidences of Aztec handicraft.

For the first time since landing on the shores of New Spain, Cortes could draw a free breath. He had scrambled up the first steep slope of the heights of power and glory. He had overthrown in battle the great warrior race of Tlascala and henceforth they were to be his allies. At sunset on September 23, 1519, Cortes entered the city in triumph, his troops crowned with flowers thrown by women lining the flat roofs, the streets echoing with the exultant songs and cheers of the populace. For if Moctezuma was playing politics, the Tlascalans were not far behind. Having proven conclusively in their own persons that the Spaniard was irresistible, what was more natural than that they should seek to employ this terrible weapon against their pitiless enemy, Mexico? So if they approached the Christians with smiling faces and hands filled with gifts, it was not that they had forgotten their dead scarcely cold. Nor, with the exception of Xicotencatl, did they meditate treachery. Here were the instruments of the Gods for the destruction of Moctezuma, and Tlascala was filled with overflowing, exultant happiness at the approach of the longed-for hour. The Spaniards were entertained at a great banquet, served in the palace of Xicotencatl the Elder, father of the Tlascalan general and at this time chief of the Council of State. Cortes showed great respect to the old warrior, bent and nearly blind, and the friendship thus founded endured until the death of the Tlascalan.

The visitors were overwhelmed with attentions, culminating in a proposal that Cortes and his captains marry daughters of the Tlascalan nobles. Cortes declined for himself, stating that he was married in Cuba, although this union did not prevent his attachment to Doña Marina, but agreed to permit his captains to take Tlascalan princesses in marriage, provided that the nation would abandon its bloody religion and embrace Christianity. Xicotencatl replied that they were convinced of the power of the White Man's God, and would accept and worship him, but that they could not summarily eject the ancient deities, lest the people rise in revolt. Cortes insisted and would have resorted to force, as at Cempoala, but Father Olmedo and Alvarado, more politic than his chief for once, persuaded the Captain General to accept the concessions offered and let time work its way with the idols. The Cross was installed in the Great Temple and the cages filled with prisoners awaiting death on the sacrificial stone were destroyed. The liberated eagerly entered the service of the Spaniards and fervently embraced the Faith that literally had saved them.

This obstacle surmounted, the Princesses were baptized and Teculihuatzin, renamed Doña Luisa, was married to Pedro de Alvarado. This captain had excited the admiration of the Tlascalans by his martial bearing and blond colouring. They named him "Tonatiuh" (the sun), and by this name he was known throughout the Americas. From this marriage there was born Doña Leonor, beloved daughter of Alvarado, his faithful companion in camp and court, and the Conqueror's only link to posterity through her marriage with Don Francisco de la Cueva, nephew of the Duke of Alburquerque. Alvarado appears to have been happy with his Indian bride and not until after her death and when the need for powerful connections arose did he seek her Spanish successor.

Successive embassies from Moctezuma stood before Cortes, striving to destroy the Tlascalan alliance and to bring the Spaniards to Cholula. Ten great plates of solid gold, hundreds of embroidered mantles and featherwork reinforced the invitation. The Captain General was deep in negotiations. The Tlascalans were for joining the Spaniards with all their forces and taking Mexico by storm, but Cortes wished to exhaust all peaceful means of entry first. He spoke of a treaty and peace between Mexico and Tlascala. The Council listened with polite, incredulous smiles. Who could live in peace, trustfully, with the Great Serpent?

The storm clouds gathered. Another envoy arrived from Moctezuma and with honeyed words besought the Captain General to leave this rude village, fit only for its barbarian inhabitants but not for the favourites of the Sun God. Let them come to the holy city of Cholula, where his master, the Emperor, had arranged a fitting welcome for them. The Tlascalans made haste to point out what sort of reception was in store. Knowing Moctezuma, they read his plans. The temples and courts would be filled with Aztec warriors ready to spring upon the unsuspecting Spaniards when they should be feasting. Their spies had reported the arrival of strong Aztec reinforcements. They urged him to take the road that led through Calpulalpan and avoid Cholula, but Cortes sent the Tlascalan chief, Patlahuatzin, to Cholula to announce his arrival and acceptance of Moctezuma's invitation. Whether emboldened by the presence of the Aztec garrison, or infuriated at the sight of this hereditary enemy, Cholula stepped for a moment out of the rôle assigned to it by the crafty Emperor. Violating the immunity due ambassadors, the Cholultecs flayed the skin from the face and arms of Patlahuatzin, and cut off his hands, leaving them dangling by strips of skin. They sent their victim back to Tlascala with the insolent message that thus would they treat the Children of the Sun God should they set foot in Cholula. Determination to visit the city turned to a cold rage when Cortes beheld the dying Tlascalan. Fully convinced of the Emperor's intended treachery, he set forth, aware of the unfavourable fighting conditions he would encounter, confident of the valour of his handful of soldiers and prepared to take a terrible revenge at the first sign of hostility.

Cholula, thirty miles south of Tlascala, was the religious capital and one of the chief commercial centres of Mexico. The walled city boasted four hundred temples, that of Quetzalcoatl, twice the size of the Pyramid of Cheops, rising one hundred and eighty feet above the paved streets. The inhabitants, more than two hundred thousand in number, although of Tlascalan stock, were crafty rather than brave and in submitting to Aztec domination, had earned the lasting enmity of their kinsmen. With ill-concealed eagerness they watched the approach of the Spanish column, accompanied by the five thousand Tlascalans Cortes had selected from the multitude clamouring for an opportunity to settle accounts with the murderers of Patlahuatzin. What a sacrifice to the tutelary deities would arise from the clustering temples when the fair-haired strangers walked into the trap!

The city fathers were at the gate to meet Cortes and escorted their unwelcome visitors to the quarters assigned to them. The Spaniard acceded readily to a request that the Tlascalans encamp without the wall, to the manifest astonishment of the chiefs. Surely the White Man was doomed by the Gods that they had separated him from his allies! No flowers greeted the Spaniards here, but bursts of savage martial music and dense, curious crowds, silent before the spectacle of men in mail, the strange beasts, the rumbling cannon. The invaders came on briskly, watching for ambuscades, in close ranks. Cortes and Sandoval with ten horsemen and half the foot-soldiers led the column. The Totonac allies and the baggage followed, protected by the remaining Spaniards. Last of all, in the post of danger, haughty yet vigilant, erect upon his charger, rode Alvarado. Staring from the housetops, the priests with matted hair clotted with fresh blood from their pierced ears, pointed out the foreign chiefs as objects of the morrow's sacrifice.

The victim had walked into the trap and accordingly the Cholultecs made ready for his capture. On the morning of their fourth day in the city, a Tlascalan came in to inform Cortes that ten children had been sacrificed at dawn in the temples to ensure victory and that the oracles had promised a great success. Several nearby streets had been blocked by stone walls and pits dug, set with sharp-pointed sticks and covered with mats, as traps for the cavalry. Great piles of stone had been carried during the night to the flat roofs of houses surrounding the quarter occupied by the strangers. The town for blocks about was deserted and long files of women and children were leaving the city gates. Even more positive evidence was brought by Doña Marina, whose many services in the nick of time well merit her title of "Good Angel of the Conquest." Her beauty and evident wealth had impressed the wife of a Cholultec chief who approached with many mysterious gestures to say that if Marina would come to her house and marry her son, her life would be spared. Pretending to agree, Marina learned full details and making some excuse, hurried to warn Cortes. Captured by a patrol, a woman confirmed Marina's information. Two priests brought in a few moments later related the same tale. So sure were the Cholultecs of their easy victory that ropes and cages had been prepared to hold the Spaniards until the moment of sacrifice.

The captains were summoned to learn the situation. The more cautious were for an immediate return to Tlascala but the majority elected to meet the enemy on his own ground. Cortes then sent for the chiefs and the Aztec ambassadors. When the Cholultecs appeared he reproached them for their attitude and declared his intention of leaving for Mexico at dawn. He demanded food for the journey and two thousand carriers. The Cholultecs readily agreed to bring both in the morning and left the audience in high spirits. As they passed through the courtyard gate, a Tlascalan interpreter heard the Cholultec overlord cry exultantly to his neighbour: "What need have these Whites of food, when they are so soon to be cooked and eaten?"

The Spaniards occupied a vast courtyard, formed on three sides by the buildings housing the troops and on the fourth by a high wall. Three gates led from the streets to the open space. There was no sleep in the Spanish camp that night. Sending word to the Tlascalan allies to force the city gates at the noise of the first shots, Cortes posted his cannon, some to sweep the courtyard, others behind the gates to command the streets. Horses were saddled and the walls manned with archers. The soldiers armed with sword and lance and the Totonac warriors were posted in groups about the open space.

True to Indian tradition, the enemy made no movement during the hours of darkness, but scarcely had the false dawn grayed the East than an immense crowd, led by the chiefs and priests, appeared at the gates. The leaders and the carriers, who were warriors disguised as slaves and carrying arms, were admitted after which the gates closed in the face of the populace. The antagonists were face to face. The Cholultecs had come determined to kill and eat their unwelcome guests, the latter prepared to teach an unforgettable lesson to treachery. Outside the crowd howled and danced in joy, frantic priests swung their censers of copal incense, the sun arose in majesty untrammelled by clouds. A further favourable omen, Huitzilopotchli would work his will with the strangers. The impassive Spanish soldiers on the walls leaned on their weapons and scanned the crowd. Huitzilopotchli was about to be served, indeed, but in a manner new to the dread God of War.

Calling apart forty of the principal chiefs, and in the presence of the Mexican envoys, Cortes addressed them in tones devoid of all semblance of friendship. He stated that he had visited their city at the express wish of the Emperor and at their own request, that they had not only failed to supply food but had plotted the basest treachery, nothing less than the murder of those whose lives were sacred by the laws of hospitality. When one of the chiefs would have denied the charge, Cortes recounted the warlike preparations, the sacrifice of the children, the pits in the streets and dramatically pointing to the disguised warriors in the courtyard, he denounced the chiefs as traitors. Superstition combining with guilty conscience, the Cholultecs blurted out the truth, but begged forgiveness, casting all of the blame on Moctezuma, by whose orders they said the massacre had been planned. The Aztec ambassadors, whom the crafty Cortes had retained within earshot, indignantly if insincerely denied the accusations. Cortes pretended to believe them, for it suited his purpose to avoid any open break with the Emperor —yet. Turning again to the Cholultecs, whose boastful arrogance of the moment had turned to acute discomfiture before the bearded man who could read their very thoughts, he told them sharply that their excuse only increased their guilt and he would be avenged on them on behalf of Moctezuma as well.

The two priests who had contributed important information the previous day were now led to a place of safety, as were several nobles who had opposed the plot and the few real carriers within the gates. It is characteristic of the Captain General that in this moment, the lives of all of his command in the balance, he took time to rescue the innocent from the impending holocaust.

Cortes raised his hand in signal. A crossbowman on the housetop shot the Cholultec chief through the head. Instantly the cannon in the corners of the courtyard roared, a rain of arrows and balls assailed the confused mass of warriors, who had never experienced firearms before. The Spanish footmen and the Totonacs hurled themselves upon the enemy within the gates. There was no escape. Those who tried to scale the walls faced the archers, those who would force the gates met the implacable Spanish lances. Within the hour none remained alive.

At the first uproar within the courtyard the crowd outside shouted in triumph, but the noise of the cannon and the despairing cries of their fellows swiftly disabused them. In an instant they attacked the Spanish quarter on all sides. The troopers on the walls kept the Indians in check until the courtyard battle was over, then the gates swung back and the cannon belched forth, cutting bloody swaths through the closely packed enemy. While the gunners recharged their pieces, the horsemen emerged at full gallop, trampling and cutting their way through the now terror-stricken natives. The Cholultecs fought bravely but they were confronted by men, weapons and tactics beyond their experience and comprehension. As they strove to rally, the Tlascalans, who had overcome the guard at the city gates, fell upon their rear, thirsting for the settling of old scores.

The inhabitants fled for protection to the temples, which were taken by the allies in rapid succession. The last resistance was offered by a strong group headed by priests who barricaded themselves in the wooden temple atop the great pyramid of Quetzalcoatl and shot burning arrows at the Spaniards toiling up the almost perpendicular staircase. The Europeans sent the flaming shafts back, setting fire to the temple, the defenders perishing in the flames or leaping to their death from the heights.

For six hours the battle raged and two days thereafter the victorious Tlascalans were still looting the city. Over five thousand Cholultecs had been killed and many houses destroyed. By strict orders of Cortes, women and children were safe from molestation and more remarkable still, in a day when every nation in the world recognized slavery as an accepted social institution, he forced the Tlascalans to set free twenty thousand Cholultecs whom they had seized and destined for bondage. The conquerors set to work to bury the dead and assist the wounded. The streets were cleaned and dangerous ruins removed. At the solicitation of the remaining Cholultec chiefs, Cortes, in accordance with Indian law, selected the brother of the late head chief as overlord of the city. Finding this irresistible white god allowed no sacrifices of prisoners nor violation of women, the people came forth from their houses and moved about their occupations. As they had hated and despised the strangers before, now they were prepared to obey and venerate them. Even in his proselyting zeal, the Spanish Captain acted with discretion. The débris on the pyramid of Quetzalcoatl was removed and a Cross erected, to be replaced later by the graceful church of La Virgen de los Remedios. Other emblems of Christianity were placed about the city, objects of respect if not adoration by the natives, but the idols were undisturbed though deprived of their daily fare of human hearts. As Father Olmedo reasoned, the Cholultecs had just witnessed the failure of their Gods; it were better to leave Huitzilopotchli to the vengeance of his own people. This brave priest, who took his place in the forefront of battle, laboured as energetically to lighten the burden of the vanquished.

More tolerant and more intelligent than de las Casas, Olmedo rather than the Bishop of Chiapa was the true "Apostle to the Indies."

Moctezuma took counsel with his gods, five thousand victims dying on the sacrificial altars in propitiation. Another Mexican ambassador stood before the Captain General, bearing gifts, life-size turkeys of solid gold and fifteen hundred embroidered mantles. Always the same request not to visit Mexico; ever the same reply that the servant of the King of Kings beyond the waters of the sunrise dare not disobey his orders to bear a message personally to Moctezuma. Each gift of gold only whetted the Spanish appetite for treasure and increased Cortes' determination to set foot in the city, cost what it might. On the Noche Triste, the Conqueror was to review his ambition with a heavy heart. After two weeks' time, during which Cortes received offers of allegiance from several nations beyond the Aztec frontiers and took regretful leave of the Totonacs, retiring laden with honours and spoils, to protect Cempoala from the Aztec governor of Nuatla, who had broken the truce, the army took the road to Mexico, winding upward through maguey plantations, beneath the shadow of the great volcanoes, through the snows of the pass.

From a turn in the route the shivering troops and freezing allies saw before their eager eyes the valley of Mexico shining in the sun, its myriad streams, lakes and towns interspersed with fields and woodlands. In the distance lay the great lake of Tuzcuco or Mexico, with the capital city overflowing the island on its breast and connected by causeways to suburbs on the mainland. The very multitude of towns and the great extent of the capital gave pause to the most impetuous Spaniard. This little army of four hundred men stood on the edge of a great bowl-shaped depression peopled by over two million Aztecs and their confederates. What chance had they to overthrow so populous an empire? Had they foreseen the incredible audacity with which the feat was to be accomplished, of the odds presently to be matched against them, perhaps only the leader himself and his most valiant captains would have been driven onward by ambition. Some of the troops grumbled and openly wished themselves safe in Cuba but the will of the majority called them forward and the heroic band marched resolutely down the winding road into the heart of Aztecdom.

Moctezuma wavered again. He sent supplies to the invaders encamped at Quauhtechcatl, while an army of twenty thousand men lurked in the nearby forest fearing to attack. A noble greatly resembling him impersonated the Emperor and greeted the Spaniards but the trick was detected by a Tlascalan who had seen Moctezuma. The envoy pledged an annual tribute payable on the seacoast in any amount Cortes might fix, and in addition offered at once, if the army would forthwith retrace its steps, four loads of gold to Cortes and one for each other Spaniard, an amount which Bancroft estimates at over five million dollars. The Captain General rejected the offer, thinking with superb confidence that if Moctezuma could offer so much, there would be more to seize when he was master of Mexico.

Reaching Ayotzinco on the shores of Lake Tuzcuco without further hostile demonstrations, Cortes was met by Cacama, King of Tuzcuco and nephew of the Emperor. Before the glory of this suite, previous embassies paled. The King, a handsome Indian of some twenty-five years, reclined in a litter of carved wood, plated with gold and jade, covered with a canopy of the finest cotton, intricately woven, from which waved the sacred quetzal feathers, that only a king might use. Cacama at first sought to dissuade Cortes from entering the city, but finding the Spaniard inflexible, changed his tactics and proffered the hospitality of the Emperor. He withdrew in state, leaving the army much impressed. If this was the subordinate, Moctezuma must be a great personage indeed. Passing along the smiling shores of the lake, Cortes was lodged in the palace of the Lord of Iztapalapan, Cuitlahuatzin, brother of Moctezuma, an edifice, the Conqueror wrote Charles V, equal of any in Spain. Yet Cortes may well have been restless amongst his luxurious surroundings, for across the waves of the salt lake, towers and temples gilded by the afternoon sun, lay his long sought goal, Mexico.

_____

FOOTNOTES FOR CHAPTER THREE

[1] Willard, *The City of the Sacred Well.*

[2] Torquemada, *Historia de la Inquisicion,* p. 417.

[3] Diaz del Castillo, *Historia Verdadera de la Nueva España,* p. 45, estimates this army at fifty thousand men.

IV

ENTRY INTO MEXICO

WHERE in 1325 the wandering ancestors of the Aztecs had beheld the eagle, the serpent in his talons, perched on the cactus and, seeing in this a favourable omen, built their huts, now stretched the greatest city of the New World. Founded on an island in the salt lake of Tuzcuco, the area of the capital city had been greatly extended by filling in the shallows and by the erection of entire wards of the capital on piles over the waters. Still other considerable portions of the population lived in their canoes or on the floating island gardens. The city was connected to the mainland by three massive stone causeways, miles in length and paved with granite blocks, wide enough for ten horsemen to ride abreast. Wooden bridges covered gaps in the highways, designed for defence of the city and to control the waters of the lake. Midway on the causeways were erected fortresses of cut stone blocks with battlements extending on either side into deep water and pierced by an archway closed by a wooden gate.

The Aztecs, masters of the art of irrigation, conveyed streams of potable water in stone aqueducts from the mainland to supply the inhabitants of Mexico. In the city proper, canals alternated with the principal paved avenues, permitting canoes laden with foodstuffs and merchandise to reach all districts.

The area of the Aztec city was not surpassed by its Spanish successor until the present century, comprising sixty thousand houses sheltering close to half a million persons. The homes of the poor were built of adobe whitewashed and thatched with reeds, while the palace of the nobles and the homes of wealthier citizens were made of stone blocks, carefully fitted together, polished or painted in bright colours. The flat roofs were crowned with parapets, sometimes with towers, converting every house into a fortress. Many of the homes stood upon terraces raised above the level of the island surface reached from the streets by broad flights of stairs and connected to the canal system by a rear entrance. In every ward arose the pyramid temples, exalting the Gods high above the

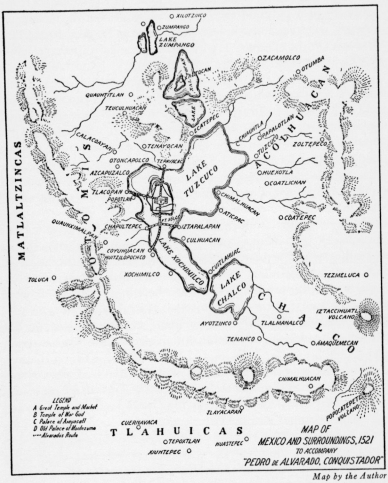

Map by the Author

abodes of men. Though Quetzalcoatl was the venerable dean of Aztec deities, his temple was surpassed in size and prominence by that of Huitzilopotchli. The God of War could and often did grant conquest and slaves to his devotees, Quetzalcoatl could only offer the lesser rewards of peace. It is not unnatural therefore that the warlike Aztecs respected Quetzalcoatl but adored Huitzilopotchli. His temple stood in the centre of the city, at the junction of the four avenues running to the cardinal points of the compass. It was composed of a pyramid faced with cut stone, with a rectangular base 375 feet long and 300 feet wide and rose 86 feet through five terraces. On the summit, 325 by 250 feet, stood the altars, whose thirst was assuaged each dawn with blood.

At daybreak on the eighth of November, 1519, Cortes led his army of less than four hundred Spanish veterans and seven thousand Indian allies forth from Iztapalapan and over the causeway of Xoloc, named from the fortress astride it. In the van rode the Captain General followed by those of his captains still fortunate enough to possess a horse. Of the sixteen animals landed at Villa Rica, two had been left with Escalante at the port and four killed en route to Mexico. The Aztecs crowded to the sides of the causeway or stared from canoes at the strange beasts, whose iron-shod hoofs drew sparks from the flagstones. Behind the cavalry came the Spanish foot-soldiers, marching in close order, their weapons in readiness and armour flashing in the sun, then the baggage, then the Tlascalan allies. A furious murmur arose from the watching crowd at this presumption of their hereditary enemies. A word should be said for the valour of the Tlascalan warriors in thus boldly entering Mexico. Man for man, weapon for weapon, the Tlascalan was but slightly more formidable than the Aztec warrior, and should hostilities break out, he could not hope to return alive. Yet so great was their confidence in these palefaced allies whose prowess they had tested in the field, that the Tlascalan contingents averted their eyes from the threatening mobs and calmly followed the Spanish banner into the city.

At Xoloc the expedition was greeted by Moctezuma in person. The Emperor of the Mexicans was fifty-one years of age, having ascended the throne when thirty-four. He was of medium height, slender, darkly copper coloured, with a thin deeply lined face and large eyes. His black straight hair was worn rather long, as was the fashion among Aztec nobles, and a sparse beard covered his cheeks and chin. Sandals with soles of solid gold bound by leather thongs worked in gold protected his feet. On his head floated a plume of the sacred quetzal feather, while his costume, covered with jewels, was the customary ceremonial square cloak and girdle of his nation.

He presented Cortes with a bouquet in welcome, to which the Spanish leader made answer by placing about the imperial neck a string of crystal beads. Moctezuma then withdrew, ordering his brother to escort the army to the quarters assigned to them. This proved to be the palace of Axayacatl, deceased father of the Emperor. The palace consisted of a large number of one-story buildings, strongly built of stone, surmounted by a central tower, and facing the great temple. So large was the structure that the entire army, including the Tlascalan allies, was housed therein. Cortes was much pleased with the defensive possibilities of the quarters and posting sentinels, announced that any infraction of his orders would result in instant death of the offender. Now that at last he was fully within the parlour of the spider, the fly was doubly vigilant.

Later in the day Moctezuma called upon his guests in their quarters, delivering an address which well illustrated the mixed traits of his character. In the same breath that he acknowledged the newcomers as descendants of Quetzalcoatl and professed allegiance to Charles V, he stated that while his subjects might consider the Spaniards supernatural, he knew them for men, the horses for large deer, while the tale of the caged lightning was pure invention. As the Mexican left the palace the Spanish army was drawn up on parade. The cannon roared in salute that the Aztec might be convinced of the dreadful reality of the caged lightning.

Several days were spent in visiting the principal markets where over one hundred thousand persons gathered daily to traffic in all the products of the realm. Climbing the one hundred and twenty-five steps that led unbroken from the base of the pyramid of Tlatelulco, Cortes found Moctezuma awaiting him surrounded by a brilliant suite framed by the ghastly implements of human sacrifice, including a cage for holding the victims, blood drenched altars and a great snakeskin drum whose sinister reverberations were the last sounds heard by the prisoners of the temple. The images glittered with gold and precious stones. Before each idol, between them and the sacrificial stone, stood an altar on which burned an eternal fire.

The largest figure was that of Huitzilopotchli with very broad face and monstrous eyes, distorted into a caricature of rage. In his hands were a bow and a bunch of golden arrows indicating the victories which he brought to his people. The body was clothed by the folds of a great snake made of pearls, copper and gold and about his neck was a chain of beads and hearts of gold, silver and some blue stone. On the altar before him were five human hearts still warm and palpitating. The walls of the chapel were black with clotted blood and the odour sickened the Spaniards. Before the altar lay a large block of jasper on which the victims were stretched, shaped so as to raise the breast enabling the priest to tear out the heart more readily.

Rendered indiscreet by his indignation, Cortes reproached the Aztec for permitting so ghastly a travesty on religion whereupon Moctezuma, himself enraged, declared that the visitors had insulted his Gods and the Spaniards withdrew in stiff silence. The Emperor permitted the construction of a Christian chapel within the palace of Axayacatl. While under construction a Spanish carpenter, seeking the best site for the altar, discovered signs of a doorway recently closed. By orders of Cortes who feared that this might prove a secret entrance for Moctezuma's legions, the wall was opened and a treasure chamber filled with gold, silver and semi-precious stones was discovered. This was the treasure of Moctezuma's predecessor, left intact upon his death, as by Aztec law it had become the property of the Gods.

The break with Moctezuma did not heal and his subjects taking their cue from the monarch's demeanour adopted an insolent attitude toward the Spaniards, jostling them in the streets and intercepting the food supply. The local Aztec Governor attacked Escalante at Villa Rica, killing the commander and six more Spaniards. Confident of his power, Moctezuma was about to throw off the mask. Calling Alvarado, Sandoval and fourteen other Spaniards into conference, Cortes revealed his plan to seize the Emperor and hold him as hostage for the good behaviour of his subjects. He could not retreat. If he escaped the Indians he had still to deal with Velasquez and Fonseca. The only solution required almost incredible audacity, the capture of the demigod in his very palace.

Cortes spent a sleepless night pacing his apartment planning the details of the coup. Early on the following morning, having arranged an interview with the Emperor, he set out for the royal palace accompanied by Alvarado, Sandoval, Velasquez de Leon, Lugo, Avila, Diaz del Castillo and the interpreters, Doña Marina and Aguilar. All were in full armour and followed by twenty-five Spanish soldiers in groups of two and three who unostentatiously made their way into the audience chamber. The remainder of the army and the Tlascalan allies were drawn up in their quarters ready for instant action.

Moctezuma was uneasy in his mind at the forthcoming interview but did not dare refuse. Brushing aside an offer of women of royal rank as brides for himself and his captains, Cortes bluntly accused Moctezuma of responsibility for the attack upon Escalante. The Emperor denied the charge and sent messengers to order the Governor's instant appearance in Mexico. Convinced now that he held the mental ascendency over the Emperor, Cortes stated that until the guilty had been punished in order to convince the Spaniards of his innocence, it would be well if Moctezuma would come and reside in their palace. The Aztec monarch bridled, he was not one to take orders, he would not go. Cortes was undertaking to persuade him with fair words when Velasquez de Leon broke in in a thundering voice declaring for no more delay, that the Emperor should be taken prisoner or killed, the lives of the invaders hung in the balance and that he for one wanted an immediate decision. In the meantime the twenty-five Spanish soldiers had crowded close to the negotiators. Terrified by the threatening glances of the mail-clad strangers, the Emperor inquired of Marina what Velasquez had said. The diplomatic Princess softened the statement as much as she could and begged Moctezuma to consent, declaring that he would be treated with the honour due his rank and that further refusal might endanger his life as he well knew these men would stop at nothing. Had the Emperor but raised his hand, although conceivably he might have lost his life in the first instant, the Spaniards would have been torn limb from limb by the thousands of warriors comprising the Emperor's bodyguard. But in this crisis, as heretofore, he lacked moral courage. He raised his hand indeed, but to summon his litter. Closely escorted by the

Spanish soldiers, scarcely daring to believe in their success, Moctezuma left his palace. He never returned.

The Emperor was installed in the apartment adjoining that of
Cortes and permitted to retain the forms of his power. Cortes
treated him with real or feigned respect, bowing low on entering
the Emperor's apartment and never seating himself until requested
to do so by Moctezuma. He severely punished a number of Spaniards of the guard who were discourteous to the Mexican and in
other ways made the weak monarch absolutely dependent on him.
The captive was closely guarded, twenty Spanish soldiers being
present in his apartment at every hour of the night and day.

The Aztec Governor Quauhpopoca, obedient to the summons of
his Emperor, arrived surrounded by his suite and with the demeanour of a conquering hero proceeded directly to prostrate
himself before Moctezuma. What was his surprise to find his lord
gazing at him with a stern face and accusing him of attacking the
Spaniards without orders. His explanations were cut short and
he and his captains turned over to Cortes for punishment. The
confused Governor was tried before the astute Captain General
and the Spaniard soon forced a confession that the attack was by
direct orders of the Emperor himself. While the inquisition was
under way, Cortes made a surprise raid on the arsenals surrounding the great pyramid of the War God and seized the weapons
therein which were carried back to the Spanish fortress. As an
object lesson to the Mexican nobles, Quauhpopoca and his followers were ordered burned alive, the pyre formed of the captured
weapons. As the moment for the execution approached, the Spanish army and the Tlascalan allies mounted the walls of the palace
to guard against an attempt at rescue, but the populace was quiet
believing the order Moctezuma's. Cortes approached the Emperor
who was seated on a balcony overlooking the courtyard and in
a severe tone told him the prisoners had confessed that their
actions were directed by him and said that, as the Emperor had
decreed death for any of his followers attacking the Spaniards,
he himself was not exempt. However, so great was his love for
the Mexican that the sentence on the monarch himself would not
be carried out although he must be made to feel some part of the
punishment. Cortes turned on his heel and a Spanish soldier

snapped iron shackles about the sacred ankles of the Son of the Serpent God.

Moctezuma was momentarily speechless with rage and shock while his courtiers clinched their fists impotently at the sacrilege. Broken-hearted, the captive Emperor watched the deaths of his faithful vassals, trembling lest the morrow might find him in the midst of the flames. He felt he would never escape from these merciless White invaders, nor did he. The execution over, Cortes reentered Moctezuma's chamber and with real or affected tears in his eyes removed the shackles stating that he loved the Mexican like a brother and that he was now free to return to his own palace. The monarch declined for two very sound reasons. A Spanish page who had acquired a considerable knowledge of the Aztec tongue and who had been lent to Moctezuma, had informed him, doubtless by Cortes' instructions, that although the latter desired the Emperor to return to his palace and freedom the Spanish captains and soldiers would in no wise permit it and, further, many of Moctezuma's friends and relatives, outraged by his weakness, would have attempted his life had he shown himself then outside the palace walls.[1]

The moral effect of Moctezuma's imprisonment and the execution of Quauhpopoca was so great that small parties of Spaniards wandered unharmed throughout the Aztec Empire, searching for gold, making record of natural resources, communications and population of the provinces explored. This truce could not last, but Cortes made good use of it, and when the storm burst again he possessed accurate knowledge of the resources of Moctezuma's realm as well as its weaknesses. The messengers penetrated beyond the Aztec border into domains of nations hostile to Mexico, where they were well received and assistance offered to the Spanish leader.

The exploring parties returned with highly favourable reports of the country. A young soldier named Pizarro had penetrated into the country of Chinantecs, an independent nation hostile to the Aztecs, residing in the southern part of the present State of Puebla. The inhabitants invited the Spaniards to enter but refused to permit the Mexican escort to cross the border. Pizarro washed the streams for gold, collecting several hundred pesos worth, mostly

in large grains, and finding the inhabitants so friendly and the
province rich in resources, left four of his party behind to establish an agricultural colony and to search for more gold. Plantations
were also established in the neighbouring Aztec colony, Alminal-
tepec, where within two months' time four large houses and a res-
ervoir had been constructed, a great tract of land brought under
cultivation and twenty thousand pesos spent in improvements.[2]

While the Aztec nobles and the subject kings conspired for the
overthrow of their sovereign and the expulsion of the White foreigners, Cortes and the Emperor diverted themselves in many
ways, although the vigilance of the Captain General was never
relaxed and his carefully formed plans were further elaborated
as each day brought new information of the incredible riches of
the Aztec Empire. Moctezuma was very fond of a game called
Totoloque, something similar to pitching pennies, wherein the
player won or lost as small tokens of gold fell in squares marked
on the playing ground. Cortes played with the captive daily. On
one occasion when Pedro de Alvarado was scorekeeper for the
Captain General and a nephew of the Emperor for the latter, the
Mexican noted that Alvarado always marked one more point than
the Spaniard made, laughingly remarking that he did not approve
the fair-haired Captain as scorekeeper, as he was too ardent a
partisan of his commander. Cortes' winnings were distributed
among the native attendants of Moctezuma; the Emperor's among
the soldiers of the guard.

Many of the nobles and tributary kings would not countenance
Moctezuma's apparent subservience to the Whites and planned his
overthrow. His nephew Cacama, the ringleader, could count upon
the support of allies leading one hundred thousand warriors and
resolved to seize the opportunity to seat himself on the Serpent
Throne. His programme included the death of both Moctezuma and
Cortes. A disgruntled conspirator informed the Emperor who took
counsel with the Captain General. Cacama refused an invitation
to court, tantamount to a declaration of war, and Cortes prepared
to lead an army against him, but the wily uncle subsidized a number
of Cacama's courtiers who seized the rebellious youth at an isolated villa where the final plans of the revolt were being formulated. The captive was hurried to Mexico where his sovereign

passed him on to Cortes. The Captain General might well have been justified in executing so dangerous an antagonist—had the tables been turned he would have died on a Tuzcucan altar—but contented himself with imprisoning the fiery young King and naming his younger brother Cuicuitza to succeed him, an example of moderation that made a deep impression upon Indian minds.

The conspiracy overthrown, Cortes pressed Moctezuma for a formal declaration of allegiance to Charles V. The Emperor summoned his vassals and within ten days' time, a multitude of Aztec warriors, standing before the throne and dismayed to see their demigod in tears, unanimously agreed to accept Charles as overlord and to pay an annual tribute. Parties of collectors accompanied by one or more Spaniards visited the cities of the Empire and returned with great heaps of treasure. At Alvarado's trial he was accused of pouring burning pitch upon the body of Cacama to force the Tuzcucan king to deliver more gold, obviously an error as the monarch had been a captive for several weeks before the collection. After twenty days the collectors returned and, in the presence of his court, Moctezuma ordered all of their harvest as well as the treasure of Axayacatl spread before the Europeans. Never had Spanish eyes beheld such wealth. Prescott[3] values the collection at $6,300,000, although a third of this is probably closer to the correct figure.[4] A large part of the metal was in grains as washed from the streams, some had been melted into bars, but the greater portion was in the form of birds and animals of all kinds. In addition there was a great heap of wonderfully worked ornaments of jade (chalchiuites) esteemed by the Aztecs far above gold. The grains, bars, and heavier ornaments were cast into ingots stamped with the Spanish royal arms, while the finer pieces were saved for exhibition in Spain.

Shortly after this, while the troops were engaged in gambling away their shares, Moctezuma offered Cortes one of his daughters in marriage. The Captain General demurred on the ground that his religion did not permit of a second wife, but out of courtesy to the Emperor he would accept and maintain the lady in the state to which her rank entitled her, provided she became a Christian![5] The Mexican agreed and Cortes, pressing his advantage, demanded that human sacrifices cease, Aztec idols be banished from the capital, and that his host renounce Huitzilopotchli for Christ. Alvarado, who was present at the interview, was so determined that Moctezuma become a convert that the latter temporized, agreed to baptism if given time, and set aside one of the chapels on the Great Pyramid for Christian services. The priesthood rebelled and in their turn demanded the removal of the Cross, extermination of the invaders and the restoration of the treasure. Troubled, Moctezuma sent for Cortes who arrived accompanied by Alvarado, Olid and the interpreters to hear the monarch implore him for his own safety to leave Mexico immediately. Told there were no ships for the return to Spain, the Emperor ordered artisans to Villa Rica to construct the necessary vessels. So convinced were the Spaniards of their imminent danger that they slept fully clothed, weapons within easy reach, horses saddled and bridled all day long.

The spring of 1520 was a period of great drought in Mexico, ruining the crops and causing much distress among the poor. A few days after the Cross had been erected on the temple of the War God a group of peasants appeared before the Captain of the Guard, humbly bearing in their hands withered corn stalks and asking the blond strangers to intercede with their Deity lest the people die of thirst and hunger, for, they said, Huitzilopotchli and Teztecepuca had been driven away by the stranger's God and could not hear their prayers. Cortes received them kindly and on the following day the Spanish army in festal array marched to the great temple through dense crowds at once wondering and hostile, to pray for rain. The column proceeded under a blazing sun but, as Mass was being said, dark clouds appeared behind Mount Tepcaquilla and a storm burst, so heavy that the streets of the city were flooded. Before this evidence of the power of the white man's God, the Aztec population cringed in awe. This stroke of fortune gave Cortes a few days' much needed respite, for danger appeared suddenly from another quarter. The ice was growing thinner daily under the feet of this prince of adventurers.

Francisco de Montejo, envoy of Cortes and custodian of the gold designed to propitiate Charles V, loved his home. He disobeyed instructions from the Captain General and stopped in Cuba to visit his plantations, giving Velasquez a clue to Cortes' intentions. Montejo and Puertocarrero were met at San Lucar, Spain, by warrants of Fonseca seizing the ships and cargo. Making their way to Tordesillas with funds supplied by Cortes' father, they presented their case to the young King, but the monarch, engrossed with the illusory grandeur of the Holy Roman Empire, found no time to decide the matter, although he had recently conferred upon Velasquez the title of "Adelantado" with largely increased powers.[6]

Secure in his new authority the Governor of Cuba prepared an expedition to punish Cortes, conferring the command upon his favourite, Panfilo de Narvaez, tall, red-bearded, brave, arrogant and impatient of counsel. All Cuba rushed to enlist, fired by tales of shiploads of gold en route to Spain. The largest expedition ever assembled in the New World, nineteen ships with one thousand four hundred soldiers, twenty cannon, eighty horsemen, ninety crossbowmen, and seventy musketeers,[7,8] gathered at Santiago in March 1520, to crush Cortes who mustered less than half their number with greatly depleted powder and stores. Over the protest of the Audiencia of Santo Domingo, which claimed judicial jurisdiction over all Spanish colonies in the West Indies and sent its representative aboard the flagship, Narvaez founded a new settlement at Vera Cruz on the site of Cortes' first landing. Narvaez amazed the Totonac and Aztec chieftains gathered to greet him by loud assertions that he had come to punish Cortes, a welcome intelligence that speedily reached Moctezuma's ears.

Moctezuma exhibited to the Captain General sisal sheets with painted representations of the ships and army of Narvaez, informing his auditor that there was no longer a reason for not leaving Mexico. The Aztec Emperor, fully informed of the hostile intentions of the newcomers, apparently believed that Cortes would be easily overthrown by his countrymen who thereafter would leave Mexican soil. He therefore urged him to meet Narvaez and learn his mission. The Cuban expedition meantime had advanced to the town of Cempoala, breathing threats against Cortes and outraging the Totonacs by looting and the ill treatment of the native women.

Cortes was now faced with perhaps his greatest dilemma. If he remained in Mexico City, Narvaez would undoubtedly attack him and, as the newcomer proclaimed himself the liberator of Moctezuma, the Aztec Empire would join him. The result would be the extermination of Cortes and his followers and also probably that of the army of Diego Velasquez, as the Mexicans would fall upon them when they were disorganized in the moment of victory. If he took the field against the Cubans it would mean either abandoning Mexico and the Emperor, the great prize for which he had come so far and endured so many hardships, or he must divide his force, leaving a small garrison in the capital to hold the position by prestige rather than by arms, while he himself marched against Cempoala. This would dangerously weaken his forces and expose him to defeat by both Narvaez and Moctezuma. Yet weighing all his chances this seemed the only possible solution. Calling on the Emperor, accompanied by Pedro de Alvarado and Doña Marina, he found the Mexican ruler in a thoughtful mood. The Emperor opened the conversation by stating that Cortes had seemed very distraught of late, had reduced the number of his visits to his Imperial captive and that he had learned from the page Orteguilla that the Captain General intended to fight the newcomers. He was very anxious that no misfortune befall his friend, and that as he had received information that the newcomers were five times as numerous as the Spanish garrison of the capital, that they were Christians and vassals of the same King, said Mass and set up Crosses as did the followers of Cortes, and stated that the Captain General and his people were fugitives from justice whom they had come to capture and kill, the Emperor could not understand and was worried for their safety. Doña Marina gave Cortes to understand that the anxiety shown by Moctezuma was pure pretence and that he was delighted with this apparent check of the Captain General, that he would make common cause with Narvaez immediately the latter took the aggressive. Cortes replied craftily that Charles V, being a great sovereign, had under his rule men of many races, that the newcomers were Christians, but just as in the Aztec domains, there were savage peoples such as the Otomis, so in the realms of Charles V there lived barbarians known as Biscayans. These were bad people, untruthful, who had come to Mexico with an evil purpose but that he, Cortes, proposed to march against and punish them for disturbing the peace and would bring them prisoners to the Emperor. He asked Moctezuma to consider his dear friend Pedro de Alvarado captain in his absence, begged him not to permit the natives to disturb the peace and offered on his return to join with him in a campaign to extend vastly the borders of the Aztec Empire. Moctezuma pretended to be worried, embraced him repeatedly and promised faithfully to keep the peace until his return. We shall see the worth of the Mexican Emperor's word.

Cortes had sent orders to Juan Velasquez de Leon to return from the coast to meet him at Cholula. The wounded, the older soldiers and those suspected of sympathy for the Governor of Cuba, to a total of eighty, were left in Mexico City under command of Pedro de Alvarado, to whom was entrusted the safety of the city and the Emperor.[9] With this handful of men Alvarado was to hold in check the entire Aztec Empire, while his chief went forth to settle accounts with Narvaez. None of this was lost on Moctezuma nor the Aztec nobles who confidently expected his defeat at the hands of the more powerful expedition. As the troops of the Captain General in light order crossed the causeway leading to the mainland, Alvarado and his tiny garrison were already marked for the sacrificial stone.

The Tlascalan Republic, requested to send five thousand warriors to aid the Captain General, replied that against Indians he could count upon their last man but against Spaniards they had proven themselves helpless and sent a large amount of food instead. Calling all able-bodied soldiers from Villa Rica, Cortes found himself before his rival's position with less than three hundred Spaniards, five horses, fourteen archers and musketeers. Crossing the Rio de Canoas with difficulty, as it was in flood, the army slept that night without fires on the banks of a small stream in the jungle about three miles from Cempoala. Narvaez had compelled the Totonac chiefs to send scouts into the forest to watch for Cortes' arrival and on the following morning when the veterans of Mexico were busy with preparations for attack, an Indian appeared at his quarters to say the enemy was at hand. Narvaez formed his entire army in cornfields between Cempoala and the position of Cortes. Somewhat dismayed by this change of fortune the Captain General remained in camp that day while the army of Narvaez stood miserably in a pouring rain. By evening, as no enemy had appeared, the morale of the soldiers was so low and their complaints so menacing that he withdrew to the town, leaving forty horsemen to patrol the fields. The Totonac chiefs, alarmed lest Cortes take vengeance for harbouring his enemies, protested at this lack of preparation, stating that when Narvaez least expected it Cortes would be upon him and kill him.[10] The Cuban laughed disdainfully and proceeded to his headquarters. Salvatierra supported him saying: "What, my Lord, do you take Cortes to be so valiant as to dare with the three cats which he commands to come to this camp merely because this fat Indian says so? He has merely made this fuss and pretence of coming so that Your Excellency may grant him good terms."[11]

Narvaez' position was very strong. The city was patrolled by guards, eighteen cannon protected the headquarters, a stone temple on top of the principal pyramid where Father Olmedo had erected the Cross the year before, cavalry encamped in the surrounding square and crossbowmen occupied the steps. The Cuban leader reviewed his men, offering a reward of two thousand pesos for the head of Cortes or Sandoval, and retired to slumber well pleased with his efforts, believing himself as safe as in Spain. Meantime Cortes harangued his followers, arousing their wrath to fever pitch, pledging three thousand pesos to the captor of Narvaez, and divided the little column between Christobal de Olid and Sandoval, the latter aided by Jorge and Gonzalo de Alvarado. Twenty men remained as the personal command of the Captain General. Doña Marina was left in charge of the Indian carriers, horses and baggage as the army set forth for the final assault. The storm was still raging at midnight on May 20, 1520, when Cortes entered the principal square of Cempoala. Dimly arising before them was the temple occupied by the lieutenant of Velasquez, bristling with artillery and crossbows. Narvaez' guns had opportunity to fire once, bringing down three enemy troopers before the long Chinantec lances drove away the gunners. Sandoval at the head of his men rushed up the steps of the great temple fighting in so frenzied a fashion that the crossbowmen stationed on the heights could not withstand them. Narvaez was wounded in the eye and withdrew into the strongly built stone headquarters which resisted assault until Martin Lopez set fire to the palm-thatched roof. A cry arose that the commander was dead, whereupon the Cubans hastened to surrender. In the midnight engagement Cortes lost six men killed, Narvaez twelve and many wounded. The captured commander, in chains but still maintaining his superior manner, was brought to the victor. The Cuban Captain spoke first: "You have great reason, Señor Cortes, to thank fortune for having given you the victory so easily and to place me thus in your power." "I have much to be thankful for," he replied, "but as for my victory over you I consider it as the least of my achievements since my arrival in this country."[12] The wounded prisoners were sent under strong guard to Vera Cruz which promptly went over to the winners.

Cortes' victory not only gave him immensely valuable reinforcements of men and material, but it completely ruined Diego Velasquez' pretension to the government of Mexico. The failure of Narvaez eliminated the support of the Council of the Indies and while Velasquez intrigued against Cortes in Spain he attempted no further use of force. After resting, the Captain General's first thought was to make use of this additional strength to consolidate his position in Mexico City where events were moving to a crisis, the high priests furnishing the straw of provocation and the impetuous Alvarado the flame.

FOOTNOTES FOR CHAPTER FOUR

[1] "By rendering Moctezuma contemptible in his own eyes and those of his subjects, Cortes deprived him of the support of his people and forced him to lean on the arm of the stranger. It was a politic proceeding—to which few men could have been equal, who had a touch of humanity in their natures." Prescott, *History of the Conquest of Mexico,* Book II, p. 177.

[2] Folsom, *Despatches of Cortes to Charles V*, p. 99.

[3] Prescott, *History of the Conquest of Mexico,* Vol. II, p. 203.

[4] The present-day values of Spanish coins of the early sixteenth century are not readily available. The author has consulted standard authorities on European coinage of this period to find that they differ greatly among themselves.

Between 1497 and 1556 a number of royal edicts changed the weight, size and gold content of the Spanish coins and the terms employed by Cortes and Diaz in speaking of their finds were not always those used in contemporary banking records in Spain. Subercaseaux (see Bibliography) states that by the decree of Charles V of 1537 the gold peso or castellano was equal to 556 maravedis and contained 4.6 gr. of gold of a .937 fineness. Fifty pesos equalled one gold mark. However, there was also a peso worth 450 maravedis and in addition a silver peso whose content was equivalent to 2.5 gr. of gold.

Sentenach (see Bibliography) states that in the reign of Charles V the gold escudo or crown was equivalent to 350 maravedis. Lonchay, who has made an exhaustive study of the coinage of Europe in the sixteenth and seventeenth centuries, states that the Spanish crown in 1537 contained 3.1 gr. of gold and sixty-eight make one gold mark of 230 grains. He agrees with Sentenach that the crown was worth 350 maravedis. Originally the maravedi was 1/72 of the Roman pound and was a gold coin, but under Alfonso X of Spain, was cast in silver and thereafter depreciated rapidly.

By the close of the reign of Ferdinand and Isabella, 1497, the maravedi as a coin had disappeared from circulation but was still used in computations much as the English farthing is today. Lonchay states that the castellano or peso was also known as the dobla which the pirates translated "doubloon." Fifty pesos made a gold mark that contained 4.6 gr. of gold of 9.89 fineness. Ferdinand and Isabella struck a ducat equal to the Florentine coin of the same name, also called "excelente," equal to 375 maravedis, and 65 1/3 were equal in value to one gold mark.

Charles V minted a new coin called the "escudo" or crown of the value of 350 maravedis of which 68 made one mark. Lonchay states that a coin of two escudos was called a doubloon. There was also a gold piece of four doubloons weighing one ounce.

Summarizing the above information, in the year 1537 when the value ratio of gold to silver was 10.58/1 the ducat was worth 375 maravedis, the escudo 350, and the real 34. The ducat of 1537 would have a value in present-day U.S. currency of $1.51, the escudo or crown $1.41, the real 13.7 cents, and the maravedi 4/100 of one cent. We have, therefore, three different coins, the castellano, ducat, and crown, closely approximating each other in value. This overlapping of functions was due to the imitation of Italian currency on one hand and the desire of Charles V to have his own coinage system on the other. Strictly speaking there was no such coin as a "peso." The Spaniards in the New World were short of minted coins and therefore they spoke of gold to the weight (peso) of so many castellanos or ducats and from this use the word "peso" was afterwards given to the coins struck by the royal mints in the New World.

In calculating the values of the treasure mentioned by Cortes and his followers, the author had taken the peso at 4.6 gr. and as an interchangeable term with that of ducat, as apparently these words were loosely used by the Conquerors.

It is interesting to note that during the period 1497-1642, although Spain was the only European nation maintaining the gold standard, that silver was fixed while gold fluctuated. This pegging of the price of silver coupled with the enormous shipments received from the New World after the Conquest caused a gold inflation so that the gold crown which was worth 350 maravedis in 1537 had risen to 400 in 1566.

Prescott, *History of the Conquest of Mexico*, Vol. II, p. 204, gives the gold peso a value of $11.67 in present U.S. currency, stating that he takes into account the depreciation of silver, and that in the time of Cortes silver was worth four times its price when Prescott wrote (1850). He then multiplies this result by three, stating that the gold peso was worth three times the silver peso. We have seen above, however, that the gold peso was not quite twice the value of the silver peso and further there is no reason for believing that Cortes' calculations were in silver rather than in gold.

[5] This daughter of Moctezuma who had been baptized Doña Juana, perished in the Spanish retreat from Mexico City.

[6] Which may be translated "foremost." Cortes and Alvarado later were awarded this title. De las Casas remarks bitterly that the Conquerors well deserved this honour as they were foremost in robbing the Indians.

[7] Prescott, *History of the Conquest of Mexico,* Vol. II, p. 226, says eighteen ships, nine hundred Spaniards and one thousand Indians.

Diaz del Castillo, *Discovery and Conquest of Mexico,* p. 349.

[8] Diaz del Castillo, *op. cit.,* p. 363.

[9] Prescott, *History of the Conquest of Mexico,* Vol. II, p. 240, says one hundred and forty soldiers remained with Alvarado, but as Cortes required the greater part of his army, if he was to confront Narvaez, he could not have done so with only seventy men which Prescott says accompanied the Captain General.

[10] Diaz del Castillo, *Conquête de la Nouvelle-Espagne,* p. 121.

[11] Diaz del Castillo, *Discovery and Conquest of Mexico,* p. 384.

[12] Diaz del Castillo, *Conquête de la Nouvelle-Espagne,* Chap. CXXII.

V

CHAOS

ON THE following morning while Alvarado in Mexico was looking on the bright face of danger, Narvaez and Salvatierra were sent as prisoners to Villa Rica together with the more seriously wounded. Command of the port and fleet, garrisoned by one hundred men, was confided to Rodrigo Rangel, as Sandoval was required for more important duties. Velasquez de Leon with one hundred and fifty men, many of them from the expedition of Narvaez, was selected to subdue the Panuco, claimed but not settled by Francisco de Garay, Governor of Jamaica, two small vessels being allotted to him that supplies, food, seeds and domestic animals might be brought to the new settlement from Santo Domingo. The sails, anchors, artillery, ironwork and ropes of the remainder of the fleet were brought for safekeeping to Cempoala.

Cortes offered the soldiers of Narvaez the alternative of enlisting in his forces and seeking wealth in Mexico or proceeding to Santo Domingo. Dazzled by the gold of his veterans, all elected to remain, whereupon he distributed among them a large amount of treasure brought from Mexico for the purpose much to the discontent of his own soldiers who protested against this favour to their late enemies. Cortes, however, reasoned with the protestants, particularly Father Olmedo and Captain Alonso de Avila, pointing out that it was necessary to cement the allegiance of the newcomers. For the same reason their arms and horses were returned although force was required in some cases to make the victors surrender the coveted weapons. Another expedition of one hundred and twenty under command of Diego de Ordaz had been organized to resume Cortes' favourite project of the colonization of Guazacoalco,[1] [2] when two Tlascalan messengers, nearly exhausted from their hurried trip, arrived in the camp with information which caused him to cancel orders for the expeditions and to depart forthwith for Mexico with his entire force, excepting only the garrison at Villa Rica.

On leaving Mexico City Cortes had instructed Pedro de Alvarado to keep a close watch upon Moctezuma and while paying him the respect due his rank not to let him escape even though it were necessary to kill him in the act. He was to respect the customs of the Mexican people but not to permit human sacrifice nor the progress of intrigues aimed at the destruction of the Spanish position. To prevent the escape of Moctezuma and the uprising of the Aztecs, Alvarado possessed eighty Spaniards, a few small bronze cannon, a limited amount of powder and limitless courage, perhaps more courage than prudence. In saying farewell to Moctezuma Cortes earnestly requested him to remain on good terms with his lieutenant and warned the Emperor that any disturbance would have him as its first victim. The Aztec promised glibly, made great show of his grief at the departing of his friend, Cortes, and resumed his plotting.[3]

This was Alvarado's first important independent command, and the tall blond Spaniard, his habitual gaiety overlaid by the sombre mask of the great responsibility reposed upon him, scarcely slept, so filled was the air with rumours of Aztec intentions. Prince Tecocaltzin, who commanded the two thousand Tlascalan warriors attached to the Spanish expedition, discovered an undermined wall which would fall inward upon pressure exerted by Aztecs massed in the adjoining streets and expose the great courtyard of the palace of Axayacatl to the Mexican attack. Many of the Spanish soldiers possessed Mexican mistresses, given them by Moctezuma, living in the palace, and these, swayed by their emotions, disclosed particulars of the conspiracy learned from their relatives in the city. The Tlascalan and Totonac servants of the Spaniards, seeking food in the great market, were roughly handled, and the Christians themselves, heretofore treated with superficial courtesy, were jostled by angry crowds on their brief appearances in the streets.

The fifth month in the Aztec year, Toxcatl, was sacred to the God Tezcatliopoca,[4] identified with the planting and harvesting festivals which were occasions for the sacrifice of many prisoners, including one who had represented the God during the preceding year and who now must die that his blood should symbolically fertilize the Aztec cornfields. This ceremony was very similar to that practised in the Stone Age[5] in Europe.

Moctezuma asked permission of Alvarado to hold the usual ceremony on the great pyramid. The Captain consented on condition that the Cross not be disturbed and human sacrifice abolished. To be sure his orders were obeyed, he proposed to be present at the "raising" of Tezcatliopoca when an image of the God, made of dough and ornamented with human bones, would be venerated and the human proxy sacrificed. Upon inspection of the pyramid several days before the ceremony Alvarado found fresh human hearts lying on the altars and released slaves, imprisoned in interior rooms awaiting sacrifice. A number of the minor priests were seized from whom the White Captain learned that an immense quantity of arms had been made and stored in the interior of the temple and in the surrounding buildings. There could only be one use for such weapons and Alvarado, outnumbered a thousand to one, was no man to wait for the enemy to strike first. The prisoners further informed him that at the completion of the ceremony the Cross would be hurled down the steps of the pyramid, a signal for a general uprising and massacre of the Spaniards.

Mexico City was thronged with pilgrims, one hundred thousand in number, come to venerate the God. These were among the most fanatically religious of the Aztecs, and Moctezuma and his advisers saw in them instruments of their purpose. Their sense of outrage when for the first time and without prior notice they beheld the Cross and its tall blond guardians on the platform of the temple, sacred to Aztec divinities, would provide the force. If by another miracle the little handful of Spaniards could overcome the horde of enraged warriors, which even the fearful Moctezuma did not believe possible, the Emperor could cast all blame upon the rustic visitors. The Mexican was thus prepared, as he thought, for all eventualities. A secret meeting of the nobles was held at which speakers informed the gathering that, contrary to expectations and hopes, the dreaded Cortes had overthrown and incorporated into his own army the large force sent against him to liberate their Emperor and that they must strike at once and exterminate Alvarado and his followers before the Captain General returned.

In the courtyard surrounding the great temple, long slender poles were erected on which the Spaniards were to be impaled in the short interval between their capture and the sacrifice, and large pots with all other ingredients already prepared were collected for cooking the bodies of the Whites. Alvarado having informed Moctezuma of his intention to be present at the ceremony, the Emperor promptly advised his fellow conspirators who took counsel among themselves as to the best way to accomplish their purpose by dividing the Spanish force and for that purpose invited the Captain to attend the dance in honour of the God just prior to the ceremony on the temple. The ceremony would thus be crowned with success as Alvarado and his followers, captured only a few moments before, might be sacrificed that same day. Surely Tezcatliopoca would send bountiful harvests this year. The dance was to be held in the great courtyard lying between the temple and the Spanish quarters.

At noon on May 18, 1520, six hundred young Aztec nobles of the highest rank and chosen for their skill at arms as well as in the dance, in gorgeous festival costumes, glittering with gold and crowned with plumes of sacred quetzal feathers, entered the courtyard. A horde carrying arms packed the surrounding streets, and the corners of the courtyard were lined with servants of the nobles bearing the chiefs' weapons. Another great crowd of nobles had gone to call on Moctezuma and despite the protest of the Tlascalan chief, Alvarado admitted them. The Spanish Captain divided his small force into two equal groups and, leaving one to guard the palace and the Emperor, set out at the head of the remaining Spaniards, pushing his way through despite murmurs of the angry crowd. The arrival of the forty Christians was the signal for a great warlike shout from the throats of the Aztec nobles. Learning nothing from Cholula, the Indian spider had the Spanish fly in his power again and proposed to devour him in short order. But Alvarado struck first. Scarcely had a procession of priests and dancing girls with masked and painted faces, carrying jars of Indian corn and cornstalks, given way to warriors, grinning with jubilation and anticipation of the proximate feast around the proxy of the God Texcatliopoca, than at Alvarado's signal his forty soldiers fell upon the crowd. The Indians ran for their weapons and a bloody, furious combat followed, but the superstitious fears of the natives and the superior equipment and swordsmanship of the invaders quickly gave Alvarado the victory. No quarter was asked nor given. Nobles, priests and servants were cut down, the blood ran in rivulets, and in less than two hours' time the flower of Aztec nobility had been exterminated by the swords of the Spaniards. If Alvarado had delayed one hour, he and his men would have been the victims. By this blow, the Aztecs were deprived of aggressive leadership. Had these nobles remained alive to direct their warriors, the task of the Conquerors, tremendous as it was to be, would have been impossible of fulfilment.[6] A thousand warriors of the Tlascalan escort had fought their way to the courtyard during the battle and effectually prevented the entry of the Aztec warriors in the adjoining streets who were attempting to climb the walls. As a reward for this opportune intervention Alvarado gave the Tlascalans the jewels and gold in the costumes of the slain. The short march back to the palace was fought step by step, the commander and a number of his men being severely wounded and forty of the Tlascalans killed.

At a preconcerted signal the nobles visiting Moctezuma had attacked the palace guards who killed over fifty before the remainder took refuge in the private courtyard of the Emperor. To the surprise of all, including Moctezuma who trembled in the presence of the angry Captain, sure that he was now at last to meet punishment for his conspiracy, Alvarado contented himself with imprisoning the surviving nobles in the quarters already occupied by Cacama. A great crowd of warriors besieged the palace of Axayacatl, shaking the walls with the fury of their onslaught and crying for the blood of the Spaniards and of Moctezuma. This attack lasted continuously for over a week during which the besieged suffered greatly from lack of food and sleep, the extent of the palace being such that the Tlascalans and White soldiers were hard put to defend the great expanse of wall. Being short of water a well was dug in a small courtyard although the Lake of Mexico, barely three feet below the level of the ground, was salt and little relief could have been expected. To the amazement of the soldiers, a large fresh water spring was discovered which was declared a miracle and an omen of success. The principal attack of the Aztecs

was against a great wall, the same that had previously been undermined. The gate therein was defended by a bronze cannon. Numerous attacks had been beaten off and in the crucial moment, when
an overwhelming horde of warriors attacked in such number that
standing on each other's shoulders they were swarming up the
wall, damp powder failed to ignite and the cannon was useless.
In desperation the Spaniards made a sortie, killing many of the
enemy, but were nearly overwhelmed and their swordplay hampered by the closely packed mob. Two White soldiers were captured alive and carried off for sacrifice. As they were being forced
away from the gate which was their salvation, the smouldering
powder took fire and the cannon loaded with a charge of broken
stones exploded, clearing a space about the gate and killing thirty
Indians among them two of the principal surviving chiefs. The
Christians saw therein another miracle. At nightfall, in accordance with Indian custom, the attack slackened, but the garrison
dared not relax its vigilance. The bridge on the causeways had
been destroyed to prevent the return of Cortes. During the night,
great crowds of women surrounded the palace shrieking curses
and taunts at the Spaniards and their Tlascalan allies and especially
at the members of their harems, shouting that they would be sacrificed and eaten and that if the Gods did not themselves strike the
invaders dead with their supernatural powers, the inhabitants
would, if need be, tear the fortress to bits, stone by stone, to seize
those inside.

On the third day Alvarado requested Moctezuma to use his
influence for the cessation of the attacks. Seven Spaniards and
many Tlascalans had been killed, nearly all of the survivors including the commander wounded, and the defenders were thoroughly
exhausted. The Emperor could not refuse openly and sent secret
instructions to the warriors to moderate their attacks but sit down
grimly to starve the Spaniards out. The gates were closed and no
one except the messengers of Moctezuma himself could leave the
fortress.

Meantime, filled with apprehension, Cortes was hurrying along
the rough trails from Cempoala, not even pausing during the heat
of midday, so that several soldiers suffered from sunstroke. The
Tlascalans received him with acclaim and would have lent their

entire army to his service, but the Captain General contented himself with two thousand picked warriors. The Tlascalans, aware of the situation of Moctezuma and the dissension between the Emperor and Cacama, were very anxious to take advantage of the opportunity to destroy their sanguinary enemies. In addition to the new allies, Cortes commanded one thousand Spaniards, foot-soldiers and horsemen.[7] The artillery of Narvaez had been left behind as the heavy pieces would have delayed the march. Leaving Tlascala, the army took a short route to Tuzcuco, passing to the north of Cholula, descending into the Valley of Mexico. They found the residents of the small towns, heretofore welcoming, sullen but passive. In Tuzcuco the demeanour was still more strongly marked—there was no reception committee and the streets were deserted. Even Cuicuitza who owed his throne to Cortes shunned the column. Cortes' veterans who had boasted to their new comrades of their popularity in the Empire were morti-fied at this changed attitude while their leader was frankly wor-ried. On their way along the lake shore to the Iztapalapan, they were met by Indian messengers in a canoe bringing a letter from Alvarado advising of the events of the siege and expressing con-fidence that the arrival of Cortes would restore peace. Moctezuma also sent word to the Captain General, probably prompted by his bad conscience, disclaiming in advance any part in the attack upon the Spaniards.

On St. John's Day, June 24, 1520, the army entered Mexico City. As in Tuzcuco the streets were deserted and only scouts of the Aztec army were to be seen in the streets, slipping away like shadows around distant corners. An unnatural silence brooded over the capital. In fear lest Alvarado and his men had fallen victims to the Aztecs, Cortes ordered the bugles blown; the brazen notes echoed and reechoed from the silent houses and empty streets and were answered a moment later by the roar of Alvarado's artillery. This greatly heartened the army which pushed on with rapid steps to the palace of Axayacatl where the despairing gar-rison received them with shouts of joy. Cortes, exhausted mentally and physically, was in a bad temper and both Alvarado and Mocte-zuma felt the weight of his displeasure. He ordered the Aztec, in a brusque manner, calling him a dog, to open the markets forth-

with and to see that the Spaniards and their allies were supplied
with food. Moctezuma replied that without the presence of a member of the imperial family, all of whom were now prisoners, the
populace would not obey. Cortes, without stopping to consult with
his captains, released Cuitlahuatzin, brother of Moctezuma and
Lord of Iztapalapan. This was an error as the released prisoner
was a bitter enemy of everything Spanish and in addition an heir
to the Mexican throne and Chief General of the Aztec armies. He
immediately sent messengers to the armies of the outlying cities,
bidding them to come to Mexico to make war on the foreigners.
He followed Cortes to the extent of imitating the Chinantec pikes,
broke down bridges on the causeways and dug pits in the streets
to impede the manœuvres of the cavalry. To strengthen his defence, Cortes sent Antonio del Rio, a horseman, to Villa Rica with
orders to forward all the artillery and stores. Less than half an
hour after he had left the palace, del Rio came back at full gallop,
his helmet gone and bleeding from spear and arrow wounds. At
the entrance to the causeway he had been stopped by a great horde
of Mexican warriors and, finding it impossible to cut his way
through, had returned to the palace. From every side street, groups
of Indians emerged to attack him and once almost dragged him
from his saddle. While Cortes was listening to this a deep murmur
arose appearing to come from all points of the city and sentinels
on the wall called down that every street leading to the palace was
thronged with Indian warriors brandishing spears and slings.
While he made hurried preparations for defence, Cortez sent
Diego de Ordaz with four hundred soldiers, including cavalry
and crossbowmen, to clear the principal avenue leading to the great
market and if possible to arrange a truce with the Indian leaders.
The great crowd of warriors fell upon Ordaz before his column
was free of the palace, killing eight soldiers and wounding all of
the remainder, the commander himself receiving three dangerous
cuts. Forty-six Spaniards were so badly wounded in this initial
encounter as to be unavailable for service for some days.

The attacking force numbered more than fifty thousand warriors while Cortes commanded less than fifteen hundred Spanish
soldiers and four thousand valiant Tlascalan allies. Courageous as
the Tlascalans were, they could not with their lack of armour and

primitive weapons account for more than an equal number of their Indian enemies so that the Spaniards were outnumbered at least twenty-five to one. In addition to this their food supply was cut off and their position dominated by Indian slingers and archers on nearby high buildings. As the natives attempted to scale the walls on all sides simultaneously the few small cannon spoke. The Mexican troops, fresh from the provinces, had never encountered these instruments of war, and many of the city's citizens who had seen them at salute believed the bronze cylinders to be censers of the service of the Fair God.

The charges of stones and iron scraps tore great holes in the ranks of the Indian warriors and, provided with this momentary respite, Cortes sallied from the main gate with two hundred troops including eight horsemen, and six hundred Tlascalan allies to cut his way to the Iztapalapan causeway. So great was the rush of warriors, augmented at each cross street and by the great throngs on the roof immune from the Spanish lances, that after losing twenty-three Spaniards and many allies, Cortes sought the shelter of the palace. The general attack continued in full fury throughout the day, the Indians shooting burning brands which set fire to the Tlascalan camp and to several compartments of the palace, nearly choking the defenders with their stifling smoke. The Spaniards returned the compliment, blazing arrows igniting nearby houses, but failed to daunt the attackers so great was their number. The Aztecs huddled in the shelter of the wall where the muzzles of the cannon could not be depressed to reach them. They burrowed beneath the wall hoping to remove the foundations and cause its collapse so that a special detail of the defenders was told off to watch for this activity. At dark the Indians drew off, according to their custom. The besieged spent a busy night tending the wounded, repairing the breaches in the wall and preparing for the morrow's battle.

Defensive fighting was never to the liking of Cortes and on the morrow he proposed to recapture the initiative. Perhaps he had some hope that the day's attack, even on so tremendous a scale, was merely a riot, spontaneous and ephemeral. But the first rays of dawn showed the Indian army, stronger and refreshed, crowding every street—a few steps from the palace walls.

A volley from the cannon initiated the battle, staggering the assailants momentarily, while Cortes with all of his cavalry, the major part of his foot-soldiers and half the Tlascalan allies rushed out to do battle in the open. The impetus of the charge carried the Indians before it for several hundred yards where they rallied behind a wooden blockade thrown up across the street during the night. Meantime, great companies of warriors took the column in the rear and on the flanks while other hordes lined nearby roofs casting large stones on the soldiers so effectually that horsemen were knocked from their saddles. The army crossed a canal on a foot-bridge which broke as the Tlascalan allies were passing, drowning many of them. Exasperated at the attack from the roofs, Cortes ordered fire set to the adjoining houses. The thatch-roofed stone buildings burned briskly, the walls caving in, burying hundreds of enemies in the ruins, but the Aztecs could lose two hundred warriors with less damage than the Spaniards could suffer the loss of a single trooper. Cortes sent for three light guns whose discharge cleared the street of the blockade. So great was the mass of Indians that they fought in relays, giving their troops an opportunity to regain their strength. There was no rest for the exhausted Europeans. Cortes led his men back and forth through the principal streets, slaughtering his opponents who were so packed together that they could not escape the Spanish thrusts until the streets ran with blood and the horses stumbled on the slippery stones. Many Spaniards and Tlascalans were killed, however, when at sunset Cortes withdrew to the palace having gained a Pyrrhic victory, as during the day the Indians had been reinforced by great hordes from the surrounding country. The attack on the palace, continued throughout the day, failed, thanks to the superhuman efforts of its handful of defenders, the dull booms of the cannon cheering the column fighting in the streets.

The courage of the Indians was especially noteworthy on this day.[8] Warriors hurled themselves at the horses, locking their arms about the knees of the beasts, striving to upset them, and many were crushed beneath the iron hoofs.[9] The nights were made hideous with the yells and shrieks of the women, and unexpected showers of missiles gave the garrison little rest.

On the third day, Cortes, two of whose fingers had been crushed

by a blow from a spear late on the evening before, sent word to
Moctezuma asking him to quiet his subjects. The Emperor refused to receive the message, having brooded over Cortes' angry
arrival from Cempoala, and replied that he could no longer help
the Spaniards, their fate was sealed and none of them would leave
the city alive. Yet in his usual vacillating manner, he appears to
have secretly ordered the Cross removed from the temple of Huitzilopotchli and brought to his quarters that it might suffer no
indignity from the enraged priests. Father Olmedo and Cristobal
de Olid returned to reason with him and with soothing words
persuaded him to make the effort. The Mexican answered that his
people now had a new leader and that his efforts would be in vain
but he would do what he could. As the group of chieftains was at
this moment close to the palace, Moctezuma arrayed himself in his
imperial robes studded with jewels and with a great diadem, much
resembling the Pontifical Tiara, on his head. Preceded by the
golden wand, symbol of his sovereignty, and surrounded by nobles
of his suite, he appeared on the battlements in full view of the
Indian army. Close beside him stood Spaniards ready to protect
the monarch with their shields. Instantly the tumult ceased and
many of the warriors prostrated themselves in the street before
the person of their sovereign. The chiefs approached, but in a hostile mood. Their personal ambitions were aroused and they had
no intention of permitting the captive to reign as Emperor. Cuitlahuatzin spoke first, tongue in his cheek, lamenting the misfortune
of the monarch and his family and then feeling sure of himself
stated that the war must be continued; he had vowed to the Gods
not to relax his efforts until the last Spaniard had been killed or
sacrificed and that Moctezuma must agree with them. Moctezuma
replied in a gentle voice that he appreciated the motives of the insurrection but that it was mistaken and ill-timed, that the Whites
had done him no harm and that if the Aztec troops would retire,
Cortes had given his word to leave Mexico. Quauhtemotzin sensing
the opportunity to become the popular idol shrieked a curse at his
sovereign while Cacama standing behind the Emperor raised his
hand indicating contempt for Moctezuma. From Cuitlahuatzin's
bodyguard came a shower of stones and arrows, Quauhtemotzin
setting the example with the first stone. Before the Spanish

guards, who had relaxed their vigilance at the apparent obedience of the people, could interpose their shields, three stones struck the Emperor in the forehead, arm and leg. So great was the force of Quauhtemotzin's missile that he expired within a few moments.[10] In the Aztec heaven Moctezuma II would justify his conduct to Huitzilopotchli.

The fall of the Emperor, cut down by his own vassals, caused a momentary revulsion of feeling and fright. With a great cry the warriors rushed away from the fatal spot in all directions.

Cortes and the soldiers who had come in close touch with the Emperor bore him genuine friendship, for despite his weak and treacherous nature, Moctezuma possessed many attractive qualities. They regretted that he had not become a Christian that they might enjoy his society in the next world. After the first shock of his death had passed, Cortes sent a priest and an Aztec chief to advise Cuitlahuatzin of the demise of Moctezuma and asking for a parley during which he would deliver the body of the late Emperor. The envoys were charged to tell the Mexican leader that they had witnessed the death of the Emperor, how grieved the Spaniards were at his passing, and that Cortes wished him buried with full honours due his rank.[11] He gave notice that the young cousin of Moctezuma, also a prisoner in the palace, would be proclaimed King in accordance with Aztec custom, as Cuitlahuatzin was not eligible, and that he would negotiate a treaty of peace by which the Spaniards would leave Mexico peaceably and unharmed. If the Aztecs would not permit them to depart in peace now, he, Cortes, who had heretofore spared Mexico out of love for Moctezuma, would destroy the city and its inhabitants, taking vengeance equally for the death of his friend, Moctezuma, and for the rebellion against Charles V to whom they had but recently sworn allegiance. To convince them that the Emperor really was dead, he subsequently sent the body, borne by six native chiefs and escorted by the priests whom Alvarado had taken prisoners in the great temple, to Cuitlahuatzin, trusting that conscience might cause the Mexicans, repenting of their act, to permit the friend of Moctezuma to leave in peace. Instead of a peaceful answer the Aztecs attacked within the hour in great force, breaking down a portion of the wall through which they poured. Recovering from the surprise the

Spaniards exterminated the invaders and closed their breach while a defiant message from the Aztec commander painted on sisal cloth and thrown over the wall was interpreted by Indian prisoners to read that Cuitlahuatzin and his associates would be revenged on the Spaniards for the death of their Emperor. They would never make peace until the last Spaniard was dead; the making of a King and his burial concerned the Aztecs themselves and needed no intervention of foreigners, and their new King was no simpleton to be deceived by the word of the Whites.

The death of the Emperor made the Spanish position untenable. Without the protection exerted by the sacred person of Moctezuma, it was only a question of time and a short time at that before the Spaniards would be so reduced in numbers by their daily casualties that the Aztecs would swarm unmolested over the palace walls. The Captain General determined, therefore, to cut his way out of the city, an almost impossible task. On the first of July, 1520, Cortes stood at the crossroads of his career. Before him opened the abyss of his greatest defeat out of which broken in body, prestige and force, he was to snatch an overwhelming victory. With frantic thanksgiving the Aztecs saw the hated invaders, defeated and exhausted, passing over the rim of the tableland of Mexico leaving many comrades to endure nameless tortures at the hands of the native priests. They were to behold with stupefaction and superstitious terror the figure of the implacable Spanish Captain again on the shore of their lake before the first snows of winter swept out of the north. There is no doubt that Cortes' very determination and his ability to mould circumstances to his needs contributed greatly to the Indian belief that he was, in some respects at least, more than man.

On the night after the unsuccessful parley Cortes took the Aztecs off guard and burned three hundred houses east of the palace that they might no longer serve as cover for Indian archers. The great pyramid of the War God, which overlooked the palace of Axayacatl, caused the Spaniards much concern as their position was raked continually with arrows and stones. On the morning following the fire, Cortes, Alvarado, Olid and Sandoval with five hundred Spaniards and three thousand Tlascalan allies, emerged suddenly from the fortress and drove toward the Tlacopan causeway. To cope with the warriors on the roofs, Cortes had constructed three two-story towers of wood with projecting aprons beneath which Indian servants carried the structure. The towers were provided with slits for the use of the crossbowmen and musketeers stationed inside and with doors permitting the defenders to step out on the flat roofs when desired. At first the towers struck terror to the Aztecs who believed themselves faced with living creatures, but when one of them was set afire by blazing arrows, the terror passed and they were so savagely attacked that the bearers could make little progress. Cortes fought his way almost to the causeway where a raised bridge prevented the passage of the horses. Here the army halted and after a furious fight of several hours during which the neighbouring houses and their defenders were destroyed, he abandoned the attempt and retired to the palace. Five Spaniards and over one hundred Tlascalans were killed and two hundred Whites wounded.

When the Captain General set out for the Tlacopan causeway, he had sent one hundred Spaniards and five hundred Tlascalans to capture the great temple. The top of this structure, three hundred feet square at the base and eighty in height was reached by a winding path which made five circuits of the pyramid before reaching the top. The huge pile was composed of a series of stone terraces each receding six feet from the one beneath. The stairs from terrace to terrace on the path leading to the platform on the top were placed on the extreme corners and the whole pyramid so arranged that religious processions winding up to the altar of sacrifice could be viewed by the entire city and, not less important, enemies seeking to climb the structure would be subject to attack by the warriors posted on the heights. On the summit was a great square platform without balustrade or retaining wall, its edges falling sheer into space. On this platform were built two three-story temples, each of fifty feet in height, dedicated respectively to Huitzilopotchli and Tezcatliopoca.[12] The lower stories of these chapels where the altars of the Gods were placed were strongly built of stone while the upper floors were of wood, brightly painted and crowned with golden ornaments. The platform and the upper reaches of the pathway were garrisoned by five hundred of the most renowned Aztec warriors, well supplied with food and water and armed in addition to lances, swords, slings and bows and arrows with a quantity of stones, boulders and logs to hurl down the slopes. Four thousand more protected the base of the pyramid and the surrounding courtyards. So strong did Cortes consider this position that, in his letters to the Emperor,[13] he states twenty men could have held it against a thousand.

As the column was retiring disconsolately from the causeway, Cortes received word that Escobar, commanding the attack on the pyramid, was at the point of defeat. Three times the Spaniards had forced their way through the surrounding warriors and up the steep pathway only to be repelled by the frenzied defence of the Indians above them. Many Christians suffered injuries falling from the terraces as great stones and logs swept them off their feet. Cortes immediately led his men to the assistance of Escobar. A brisk battle took place in the courtyards at the foot of the pyramid where the horses slipped on the slippery stones, wet with the night's rain, and were sent back to the palace. The dense mass of Indians in the courtyard proved an advantage to Cortes as only the front ranks were able to make use of their weapons. Tying his shield to his left arm, as the injury to his fingers prevented him from grasping the crossbar, he rushed up the pathway closely followed by Pedro de Alvarado, Sandoval, Olid, Ordaz and other captains and soldiers to a number not exceeding three hundred while the remainder, together with Escobar's contingent and the Tlascalan allies, engaged in desperate combat with the warriors in the courtyards. The Aztecs disputed every foot of the pathway and from overhead rained arrows, stones and boulders upon the invaders. Many Spaniards were swept over the brink and fell into the courtyard where the Aztecs made short work of them. Seeing the predicament of Cortes, Velasquez de Leon, who commanded the musketeers at the base of the pyramid, ordered them to pick off the leading warriors so as to permit the Captain General to reach the summit. As Cortes with his captains had reached a point half-way to the platform and in the centre of the eastern side of the pyramid, two great logs, each forty feet in length, prepared for that purpose, were thrown over the edge of the temple platform. There was no shelter available. In another moment the Spaniards would have been crushed or swept into space, when,

as through divine intervention, the logs suddenly turned and slid
harmlessly butt foremost down the slope. Disappointing as this
was to the Aztecs they did not lose heart and every step of the
ascent was marked with the blood of defender or invader. About
fifty Spaniards following Cortes fought their way to the temple
platform where over six times their number of frenzied warriors
fell upon them. The Homeric combat thus placed in high relief
against the sky, drew the attention of the combatants below who,
as if by mutual accord, ceased fighting while watching with bated
breath the struggles of their leaders. The roofs of Mexico were
black with spectators. The figures of the Spanish captains in their
distinctive armour were familiar to the Aztecs who gleefully anticipated the death of the Christians on the very altar of Huitzilopotchli. Surely nothing could be more fitting and no omen more
propitious than that the White invaders were at last to pay the
penalty for their impious treatment of the Gods.

The combatants knew they must win or die; there would be no
surrender and no prisoners. The Indian warriors were massed
around the temple of Huitzilopotchli, the Spaniards formed in line
at the far edge of the platform where the staircase from below led
to the sacrificial stone. Finding that by sheer weight of numbers
they could not hurl the newcomers over the edge the Indians
retired momentarily, the better to use their arrows and slings. During an instant's lull in the fighting, two young nobles, unarmed,
ran to Cortes who was standing close to the edge of the platform
and throwing themselves on their knees with extended hands
begged for mercy. He had lowered his sword and turned to order
that the youth's lives be spared when his treacherous antagonists
seized him, one about each knee, attempting to hurl him over the
brink. Impeded though he was by his crippled left hand, he crushed
the head of one assailant with the hilt of his sword and loosening
the frantic grip of the other, hurled him to the fate he had destined
for the Captain General. Although the Aztec losses were greater
than those of their White enemies, the latter would soon have been
so reduced in number that even the prowess of Cortes and his captains could not have withstood the pressure. Just at this moment
the sun, which had been hidden by clouds, appeared, throwing its
rays full in the eyes of the defenders. This unexpected advantage

gave the Spaniards the victory. Reanimated they rushed forward, brushing resistance aside. The warriors who did not seek martyrdom by leaping into space died in the last struggle before the chapel. Only two or three priests cowering behind the altar were spared. A great moan of terror and sorrow burst from the surrounding multitudes as the hated invaders stood triumphant, breathless, upon the platform of the temple sacred to the Aztec Gods. Wrenching aside the golden curtain covering the doorway, the Spaniards found the altar laden with human hearts. About lay Spanish helmets, evidence that some of their fellows, captured in the preceding battles, had met the ghastly fate of Aztec prisoners. Rage combining with holy zeal lent strength to the Spanish arms, and the enormous bloody image of the leering Huitzilopotchli was torn by force from its resting-place and sent hurtling into the abyss where it was shattered into bits. Tezcatliopoca immediately followed his colleague and a column of smoke arose in the still air as the Spanish torch avenged the massacre of the prisoners. The crowds which had beheld the death of their champions were silent now with stupefaction. Huitzilopotchli had failed them, had failed himself. When the bloody image of the War God hurtled over the edge of the platform, the Aztec religion received its death blow. Much blood, White and Red, was to be shed before its devotees acknowledged the fact, but the multitude never regained their blind confidence in their deities.

Nonetheless, shaken as they must have been by the defection of their Gods, Cuitlahuatzin and Quauhtemotzin were determined to be revenged in this world at least on the White strangers. Before they could rally their stricken troops, Cortes and his men passed unmolested through the remaining warriors in the courtyard and regained their place. This great victory had not been without loss to the Spaniards, forty-six of whose number were killed and many wounded.

Cortes again proposed peace. Standing on the battlements so fatal to Moctezuma, with Doña Marina at his side as interpreter, he pointed out to the Aztec chiefs standing in a hostile row beneath them that the white man was more powerful than their gods but that he would refrain from destroying the city if he was granted a safe conduct through the Mexican Empire in eight days' time. To this the chiefs replied with furious gestures that they possessed twenty-five thousand warriors to every Spaniard and proposed to exterminate the invaders then and there. Cortes withdrew and the battle was resumed.

Many of the soldiers of Narvaez who had come to Mexico to find a paradise were in a mutinous mood, asking for deliverance from this accursed place at any cost. This task was almost impossible, in fact would have been impossible to any except the men that composed the legion. Surrounded by half a million bloodthirsty enemies, hampered by the baggage and wounded, progress impeded by pits dug in streets and causeways, bridges destroyed, Cortes knew how desperate was his condition and how few of the Spaniards could hope to see Cuba again. As soon as it was known to the Indians that the Spaniards had abandoned the palace, the empty fortress would be overrun and the fugitives would have no place to return. The progress of the column would become slower and more difficult each mile as its strength was reduced by wounds inflicted on the soldiers and allies who would thereafter have to be carried. The greatest obstacle was the lack of bridges without which the artillery, horses and heavy baggage could not cross the canals. Had Moctezuma remained alive his presence might have provided an avenue of escape but with this influence removed and the violent Cuitlahuatzin Emperor, they were dealing with a man bereft of all save the determination to exterminate the newcomers.

Since there was no help for it, Cortes prepared to abandon Mexico. A large portable bridge was made of stout planks to be used to cross the canals and gaps in the causeways. Of the three routes, Cortes had decided on that of Tlacopan as it was less than half the length of the others and broken by only three gaps. The portable bridge was carried by four hundred Tlascalan Indians and guarded by one hundred and fifty Spanish soldiers to protect the bearers from Indian attacks while the structure was placed in position and later removed.

While preparations for departure were under way, a messenger arrived from Cuitlahuatzin requesting the release of the two chief priests captured during the battle in the temple that they might arrange a peace between the Indians and Spaniards. Duped by the apparent sincerity of this message or to gain time for his own preparations, Cortes released the prisoners who disappeared into the city to be seen no more. Cuitlahuatzin required their presence for his coronation as successor to Moctezuma which was about to take place.

To open the way for his retreat Cortes sallied forth on June 29 at the head of half his force and, taking the enemy by surprise, rapidly seized the street leading to the Tlacopan causeway past the first seven canals and within sight of the lake. The broken bridges were restored and the cavalry rushed down the length of the avenue, riding down Mexicans emerging from the cross streets to attack the foreigners. By afternoon, however, an overwhelming force gathered in every side street, in the lake and on the roofs, and so exhausted the Spaniards that Cortes ordered a retreat. The enemy dashed at the very feet of the horses and succeeded in upsetting a number of them and blocked the Spanish retreat at one of the canal crossings. Cortes, gathering his few mounted followers, turned about and charged into the horde of warriors defending the passage, crushing them beneath the hoofs of his horses and striking off heads as far as his brandishing sword could reach, until the last man had crossed the canal. The Captain General held his position despite the desperate efforts of the Indians to capture him as the supreme sacrifice to Huitzilopotchli. When the army had crossed, he put spurs to his horse and leaped the gap amid a storm of arrows, being wounded twice in the left leg.

The battered Spanish troopers returned to the palace more discouraged than ever—it was time to leave. One of the soldiers, Botello, an amateur astrologer of note who had foretold the greatness of Cortes while the latter was still in Cuba, picked the following night as an auspicious time for departure and said that he himself would find his death in the struggle. The last part of his prophecy at least was correct.

Cortes ordered all the gold belonging to the Crown brought out and piled in the great hall of the palace.[14] Eight horses and eighty Tlascalan servants placed at the service of the Royal Treasurer, Gonzalo Mejia, were loaded with treasure. A large number of ingots remained and a notary was called in who took formal notice of the inability of the treasurer to remove all of the gold. Cortes offered the remainder to the troops. The veterans contented them-

selves with the lighter jewels,[15] while the soldiers of Narvaez
rushed to rescue the heavy bars. The precious weight was to cause
the death of many of them this same night.[16] It is said that Cortes'
personal fortune had been sent during the truce to Tlascala where
it was kept safe for him, but there is no proof of this.

At midnight on July 1, 1520, Mass was celebrated by Father
Olmedo asking the protection of the Almighty for the Spaniards.
The gates were thrown open and the army marched out into the
silent city through a driving rainstorm, leaving the fortress for the
last time. Gonzalo de Sandoval, who had so valiantly confronted
the might of Narvaez, set his face into the darkness, leading two
hundred of the more active Spanish infantry with Diego de Ordaz,
Francisco de Lugo and twenty horsemen; next came the artillery;
then the portable bridge, guarded by two hundred Tlascalans and
one hundred and fifty Spaniards, and its attendants. The treasure
was guarded by a group of soldiers under Alonso de Escobar.
The Captain General with Cristobal de Olid, Alonso de Avila and
one hundred men were in the centre where they could render aid
to any section of the column as required; followed by the baggage,
Doña Marina, the children of Cortes, and the prisoners, including
Cacama, guarded by thirty Spanish soldiers and thirty Tlascalan
warriors; the remainder of these valiant allies were distributed
throughout the column. The rear of the column, the most dangerous post in a retreating army, was covered by thirty cavalry
and one hundred foot-soldiers; close behind followed two horsemen, Juan Velasquez de Leon and Pedro de Alvarado. After them
the empty street reechoed the footfalls of their horses. The Spanish retreat was under way.

The army had passed six blocks[17] and was close to the causeway when, as the portable bridge was being placed in position to
cross the first canal, the alarm was given.[18] Instantly from all
quarters streamed the Indians and war cries resounded in the
streets, while in the fortress of Tlatelulco, at the land end of the
causeway, the war drums sounded as the garrison put out in
canoes to dispute the passage of the Whites. The Spanish army
was thus taken in front and rear, the open bridges proving death
traps. An immense host of Indians fell upon the fugitives; confused in the darkness and obliged to reconstruct their ranks to

protect the baggage and the wounded, they were unable to give their customary good account of themselves.

Despite furious Indian attacks the bridge was placed in position and about half of the army including part of the artillery crossed in safety. Alvarado faced about and drove the attackers back down the main street. By canoes in the canals, over the roofs and from side streets, swarms of warriors descended upon the little column. Panic seized the soldiers of Narvaez and many of them were crowded off the bridge into the canal to meet death by drowning or at the hands of their enemies. Native historians of the Conquest state that one hundred Spanish soldiers, despairing of advancing against such odds, returned to the palace where they resisted siege for three days. Exhausted by hunger, they were captured and sacrificed at the coronation of Cuitlahuatzin. Sandoval reached the causeway and spurring his horse, followed by his troops, succeeded in clearing it of enemies as far as the first bridge over the lake. Where the stout timbers had been was a great gap, bottomed by black water. Fresh legions of warriors swarmed over the causeway from either side. The causeway was approximately twenty feet wide and, due to the great length of the column, the first soldiers had reached Sandoval before the rear guard had passed over the bridge of the canal. The bridge guard and the carriers stopped to remove their structure, but the weight of the artillery had so imbedded it in the mud that they could not stir it. Finally, when more than half of the escort had been killed, Captain Magarino, entrusted with this vital duty, succeeded in pulling the timbers loose from the embrace of the earth, but the Aztecs jumped upon the loose structure in such force as effectually to wreck it. The Spanish army was thus trapped in complete darkness on a narrow causeway with deep water and overwhelming numbers of bloodthirsty enemies on every side. The destruction of the bridge caused panic in the army and the ranks surged forward regardless of discipline. Sandoval and his troopers jumped their horses into the water, where many of them were lost in hand-to-hand battles with the Indians. The commander and Ordaz crossed safely and commenced clearing the further abutment of Indians. All this time the continuous rain of arrows and javelins, fired at close range by unseen enemies, decimated the Christians. Only when warriors, brave to foolhardiness, clambered from their canoes upon the causeway could the Spaniards even the score.

As Cortes spurred his way through the mob to aid Sandoval, he was seized by Indians in canoes as his horse plunged into the lake and only through the superhuman efforts of Cristobal de Olid and the Tlascalan chief, Texmaxahuitzin, could he free himself from their grasp. Sandoval as before made his way down the causeway and found to his great dismay that the next opening, also bereft of its bridge, was deeper and wider than the preceding. The fearless Captain forced his horse over the brink, crushing a Mexican canoe in his fall, and followed by five horsemen and one hundred foot-soldiers cleared the passage. Leaving most of his men to guard the land approach to the causeway, Sandoval returned to the open channel to aid his compatriots in crossing.[19]

A precarious hold having been obtained on the last segment of the causeway, Cortes returned to visit his rear guard, fighting his way through the flow of panic-stricken fugitives. Arriving at the first channel, he found a bridge had been constructed in his absence. And what a bridge! Spaniard and Tlascalan, men and women, baggage and gold, armour and weapons were packed into the gap until it formed a solid mass across which the remaining soldiers were rushing heedless of the groans of their dying comrades. Terrible as was the loss at the first bridge, the second and wider gap exacted a more fearful penalty. A great fleet of Mexican war canoes was clustered about the gap like sharks about a ship anchored in a tropical harbour. A continuous rain of arrows filled the air. The first faint light of dawn appeared, showing a single beam still hanging across the gap. This proved almost invariably a fatal snare for the Spaniards as the soldier making his precarious way across the slippery log was the target for a thousand archers. In this gap horses and men, who had fought their way across the first bridge, sank, never to rise. The dawn increased the difficulties of the Spaniards as the enemy could see the state to which they had been reduced and took fresh courage therefrom. Wave after wave of Indian warriors swept over the embankments of the causeway to grapple with their exhausted foes and drag them alive into the canoes for sacrifice. Here Juan Velasquez de Leon, struck by an Aztec lance, fell and was drowned under the weight of struggling bodies. The Noche Triste was indeed a "Night of Sorrow" to the invaders.

The rear guard under command of Alvarado had been almost exterminated. Attacked on all sides, they had resolutely held every water crossing until the column had passed. As Cortes neared the first gap in the causeway with its ghastly bridge, he came upon his chief captain, unhorsed, unhelmeted, bleeding from many wounds and fighting like a madman against overwhelming odds at the head of his handful of followers. The light was strong now and the Indians raised a great shout, confident of capturing this famous leader as a sacrifice. Cortes and his five horsemen charged the enemy, giving Alvarado a respite during which his men, all on foot, threw themselves into the deep channel where several drowned. To protect them, Cortes, followed by the other horsemen, plunged into the lake, scattering the Aztecs but leaving Alvarado alone on the causeway. On the instant silence fell. Behind him the Aztecs advanced quietly, their lances ready. Before him and on the sides the canoes drew nearer. The hunt was over—the captive in their hands. They wished to take him alive to the greater honour of Huitzilopotchli. Alvarado picked up a long Chinantec lance lying at his feet, abandoned by some flying soldier, turned to face his enemies, and then grasping the pike firmly in his hands, rushed at the abutment, planted the sharp point on a slippery piece of wreckage in the water and vaulted high in the air to safety on the far side. The Indians stared in awe. Surely this was "Tonatiuh" (Child of the Sun); no mortal man could have made so great a leap. To this day the site of the feat is known as the "Salto de Alvarado" (Alvarado's leap).

FOOTNOTES FOR CHAPTER FIVE

[1] Diaz del Castillo, *Conquête de la Nouvelle-Espagne*, p. 347.

[2] Bancroft, *Annals of Early Mexico*, p. 407, reverses the commissions of these two captains but without quoting his authority.

[3] Bancroft and other partisans of Moctezuma have endeavored to show that the Emperor took no part in the conspiracy and subsequent uprising, but it is generally believed that, with the Spanish forces in Mexico City reduced to a handful, he made a desperate attempt to regain his untrammelled sovereignty. Had his efforts been more open they would probably have been success-

ful. As it was he incited the priests and people secretly while preserving an appearance of friendship with the Spaniards that he might be secure in his own person yet emerge successful from the storm he was stirring up.

4 Also called Texcetepuca.

5 Prescott, *History of the Conquest of Mexico,* Vol. II, p. 281, is mistaken in comparing the ceremony to that of the bloody Huitzilopotchli, the Aztec God of War.

6 The bigoted Bancroft, so ready to condemn the Spaniards that he loses track of facts and circumstances, says (*Annals of Early Mexico,* p. 414) that the Spaniards were welcomed to the courtyard with demonstrations of joy by the unsuspecting nobles. Nothing could be further from the truth, as Bancroft must have known, for the bloodthirsty nature of the Aztecs and their determination to rid Mexico of the Spaniards and to use their bodies for the propitiation of their gods did not change overnight.

7 Prescott, *History of the Conquest of Mexico,* p. 276.

Diaz del Castillo states thirteen hundred infantry and ninety-six cavalry.

Cortes himself, *Cartas de Relacion de la Conquista de Mejico,* Vol. I, p. 127, says seventy horsemen and five hundred foot-soldiers.

8 Diaz del Castillo, *Discovery and Conquest of Mexico,* p. 409, states that ten thousand Hectors and as many Rolands would not have been able to break through the Indian hosts.

9 When Cortes returned to Spain it is related that, while at the Court, he made some disparaging remarks regarding the conduct of a Spanish column which had retreated before a superior army of Moors. A number of the courtiers replied angrily that Cortes was accustomed to drive off twenty-five thousand Indians with ten Spaniards and that he did not encounter worthy opposition. It is therefore worthy of note that Bernal Diaz del Castillo, recounting the events of this day, states: "I do not know why I write thus so lukewarmly, for some three or four soldiers who were there with us and who had served in Italy swore to God many times that they had never seen such fierce fighting, not even when they had taken part in wars between Christians and against the artillery of the King of France or of the Great Turk nor had they then seen men like those Indians with such courage in closing up their ranks." Diaz del Castillo, *op. cit.,* p. 410.

10 Duran, *Historia de Indias,* p. 468.

Acosta, *Historia de Indias,* p. 523.

11 Cuitlahuatzin must have considered this effrontery on the part of the foreigner.

12 Bancroft, *Annals of Early Mexico,* p. 446, states both chapels were on the east end of the platform while Prescott, *History of the Conquest of Mexico,* Book II, p. 325, says at either end of the platform, which seems more probable.

13 Lorenzana, *Historia de Mejico,* p. 204.

14 Diaz del Castillo, *Discovery and Conquest of Mexico,* p. 420, says this amounted to more than seven hundred thousand pesos.

15 Diaz del Castillo states he obtained four finely carved pieces of jade which he afterwards sold for a large sum.

16 Antonio de Solis estimates that two million gold pesos were lost on the retreat from Mexico City.

17 Bancroft states that the first five canals had been filled in during the preceding day with debris from the burning houses on either side.

18 "By a woman," says Bancroft, while Prescott and Diaz del Castillo state the alarm was given by an Indian guard on the causeway, which would seem natural.

19 Diaz del Castillo, *Discovery and Conquest of Mexico,* p. 420, states that Cortes and all his horsemen and Tlascalans passed safely over the mainland without stopping to aid the remainder of the army. This is untrue as regards Cortes and obviously impossible in regard to the heavily laden gold carriers, most of whom perished.

VI

DESTRUCTION OF MEXICO

A S THE sun rose on the morning of the fatal "Noche Triste" Cortes, seated at the foot of a great tree, still standing today, surveyed the sorry remnant of his army. All of the artillery, powder and stores were lost and he could see the Aztecs gleefully searching the causeway for gold and baggage of the defeated. The Spanish swords and spears, especial prizes to the Aztecs, were used by their new owners in the succeeding battles. Of the thirteen hundred Spaniards that had left the palace of Axayacatl at midnight not more than five hundred and fifty remained alive. Four thousand Tlascalans had perished, over two-thirds of the allied contingent. The rear guard under Alvarado had been almost exterminated—four White soldiers and eight Tlascalans alone surviving. Twenty-four horses remained, many crippled by wounds. Cacama, Cuicuitza, Lord of Tuzcuco, and the other prisoners had been killed by their countrymen in the darkness and confusion. Doña Marina and Doña Luisa, sister of Xicotencatl and wife of Pedro de Alvarado, were among the survivors, owing their lives to the desperate efforts of the Tlascalan chiefs. Every soldier bore wounds, some were without weapons, their armour dented and broken, smeared with mud and blood. Beaten, exhausted and discouraged, only the ceaseless exhortations of Cortes, Alvarado, Olid, and Avila prevented the Spaniards from disintegrating into helpless groups. Cortes' sole refuge was Tlascala, across mountains and deserts. What reception would he meet returning penniless and defeated, he who had heretofore been invincible? All depended upon the loyalty of the Tlascalan Council of State, and they did not fail him.

Taking counsel with the Tlascalan chiefs, Cortes decided upon a little-travelled highway leading through isolated regions and set out, attacked in front and rear by forty thousand of the victorious enemy. The Spaniards were entirely without food and the nights were very cold, bringing great suffering to the wounded. The army ate two horses killed in battle, cactus pears, roots and grass. The march of the fugitives was paralleled by great bodies of Aztec troops keeping just out of range and filling the air with exultant shouts.

At midnight on July 7[1] the Captain General broke camp, hoping to elude his pursuers. The wounded were placed in the centre of the column, borne in hammocks by Tlascalan servants or making their way with difficulty on crutches. The road led through a rocky pass blocked with boulders, cactus and thorn bushes. Beyond lay a desert bounded by the mountains of Tlascala.

At dawn the army surmounted the pass. At their feet lay the town of Otumba crowded at this time with pilgrims to the Great Fair held there annually. In the far distance the sun gleamed on the peaks of Tlascala and the tired soldiers cheered at the sight of sanctuary. But only for an instant. As the light strengthened, on the plain below appeared countless dancing tips of fire that the rays of the morning sun reflected from the spear points of the finest army met by the White men in the New World.[2] Here in the very shadow of safety the Spaniards were to be exterminated. To make certain of this laudable object, Cuitlahuatzin had ordered the Aztec Governors of Otumba, Tectihuacan and Calpulalpan to join their forces to the legions pursuing the fugitives. More than forty thousand warriors awaited the Spaniards in the valley of Otumba. So great was the array that it stretched across the entire horizon dotted by the glittering banners of the chiefs. The army was led by Cihuacatzin, Governor of Teotihuacan, the splendour of whose suite was eclipsed only by that of the Emperor of the Mexicans himself. Behind the Spaniards on the heights overlooking the battlefield appeared ten thousand additional warriors, come direct from Mexico City to make sure that the trap was sprung. Even Cortes believed his last hour had come.[3] He could not retreat; to turn aside was useless as the enemy would be upon him in an hour's time. Since there was no hope for it, he formed his twenty horsemen into four groups of five each to protect the front, rear and flanks of his column and with the banner of the Cross carried before the Spanish army advanced resolutely down the mountain side to where their numberless enemies awaited their coming with a

great cheer and clashing of weapons. As we have said before, in
this battle of Otumba the Whites had no artillery, no firearms of
any kind; the entire strength of the Spanish column did not exceed
two thousand five hundred men including two thousand Tlascalans,
who Diaz says "fought like lions on this crucial day." The Azetcs
were well fed, rested and whole; the Spaniards were wounded,
exhausted and starving. The battle was of Cuitlahuatzin's making
as Cortes' only desire at this moment was to reach Tlascala. Elsewhere in the world's history where a resolute handful had confronted and defeated great masses of men, the smaller party had
usually been firmly intrenched, as witness the heroic defence of
the Spartans at Thermopylae.[4]

Approaching the battlefield, Cortes revised his orders, directing
the four groups of horsemen to charge the enemy at separate
points to break up the Indian formation. Orders were given not to
stop to spear individual enemies but to hold the lances firmly
pointed at the level of a warrior's face to open paths through the
native ranks. To conserve the strength of the foot-soldiers and to
inflict greater damage on the enemy, Cortes ordered them to
abandon the sweeping overhand sword thrusts and to aim for the
abdomen of their opponents that each would effectually disable an
adversary. As the Spaniards reached the open ground the Indians
rushed upon them, impeding themselves by their very eagerness
to gain the front rank for the first blow at the hated invaders.
The tiny army was swallowed up in the ocean of their enemies.
In a moment swirls and whirlpools disrupted the onward moving
surface of the human ocean. As the twenty horsemen at full gallop
tore their way through the native ranks, the infantry followed in
the gap thus created and finding a level spot formed a hollow
square with the wounded in the centre. Again and again the cavalry charged while the infantry fought shoulder to shoulder, par-
rying the innumerable blows of their antagonists. Heaps of dead
lay before the line of Toledo blades. The enemy withdrew slightly
to reform their ranks, whereupon Cortes moved his small force
forward, but the only result was that the Indian waves engulfed
them deeper than ever. The contest had lasted several hours when
the cavalry, exhausted by their exertions and the heat, had ridden
into the square to rest. The Indians' advantage in manpower

seemed about to carry the day. Cortes' horse, struck in the mouth and rendered unmanageable, was being exchanged for another when the injured animal broke loose and flew at the Aztecs riderless. Now if ever the Aztecs believed that horses were imbued with demons as the raging beast struck with all four feet, causing great confusion in their ranks. Sandoval and three other horsemen dashed to retrieve the animal and were engulfed by the enemy, until rescued by the remaining cavalry.

Seeing that his enemies were on the point of exhaustion and defeat, Cihuacatzin, Generalissimo of the Aztec army, approached closely to view his moment of triumph. Standing in his stirrups, the desperate Cortes was at this instant searching far and wide over the battlefield seeking an expedient, no matter how rash, to turn the tide. In another hour no Spaniard save only those destined for sacrifice would remain alive, and Cortes well knew the fate reserved for him. Suddenly, directly before him appeared the litter of the enemy General, glittering with gold and quetzal feathers, surmounted by the gold banner of his rank and surrounded by splendidly costumed warriors, the flower of the Aztec nation. No sooner had Cortes seen his enemy than his decision was made. Turning to Alvarado, Sandoval and Olid who stood beside him, panting with their exertions, he exclaimed: "There is our mark. In the name of God and St. Peter, gentlemen, let us close with him!"[5] Putting spurs to his horse and followed by the Captains, Cortes burst like a cannonball through the Aztec ranks, the ferocity of his charge carrying him through the very guard of Cihuacatzin. The horse of Cortes, mad with rage at the spurring of his rider, reared on its hind legs, crashing through the litter of the Mexican General and bringing him ignominiously to the ground. A young soldier, Juan de Salamanca, ran his lance through the prostrate chief and picking up the fallen banner presented it to his General.[6]

Horror-stricken, the nobles of Cihuacatzin fled in all directions, their panic communicating itself to the Aztec army. Electrified by the sudden change of fortune, the Spaniards sprang at their enemies, the horsemen dashing at full gallop wherever the standard of an Indian leader waved, cutting down the chiefs and throwing their followers into hopeless confusion as the closely packed ranks

strove to escape from the fatal spot. The battle continued but
the initiative and the ascendancy were now the Europeans'.
Wherever groups of warriors offered determined resistance, the
cavalry smashed through their ranks and the infantry completed
the rout. As the first shadows fell across the field of Otumba, Cortes recalled his tired troops, scattered far and wide over the plain
pursuing the enemy, and camped for the night on a nearby hill,
crowned by a strong temple. From the nearby town, food and
firewood were secured. In this greatest battle of the Conquest, an
immense number of Aztecs, contemporary historians say not less
than twenty thousand, were killed. As the destruction of the idol
of Huitzilopotchli had destroyed the Aztec religion, the battle of
Otumba crippled the Mexican military power.[7] For nearly a year
more Cortes was to meet superior Aztec armies in battle, but never
again were the natives imbued with supreme confidence. They
fought fearlessly and desperately but no longer with faith in their
ultimate victory. Nearly all of the Tlascalan allies were killed at
Otumba, and Cortes, in gratitude to his valiant friends, gave the
survivors the rich spoils gathered from the slain.

On the next morning the march was resumed, and not too soon,
for another Mexican army, late for the rendezvous at Otumba, was
close behind. On that same night the Tlascalan border was reached
and the Spaniards were in safety among friends.

With the exception of Xiconacatl the Younger, all the Tlascalan
chiefs hastened to welcome Cortes, condoling with him over the
loss of his men and offering him the entire resources of the Republic to reconquer Mexico. The Tlascalans were in no wise discouraged by the defeat of their White allies and were for immediately
pursuing the Mexican army returning from Otumba, but Cortes
persuaded them to await a more favourable opportunity. The
banner captured from Cihuacatzin was presented to the Tlascalan
Prince, Maxixcatzin, all Tlascala rejoicing in the possession of
this trophy. Cortes was lodged in the palace of Maxixcatzin where
the injury to his head developed into brain fever. Finally, after
a crude operation was performed and pieces of bone removed, he
rapidly recovered. Pedro de Alvarado was feasted in the palace
of his father-in-law, Xicotencatl. The army remained twenty-two

days in Tlascala, healing its wounds and regaining its strength while the commander made plans for his revenge.

No sooner had Cortes recovered than he was faced with a multitude of problems. Small parties of Spaniards had been slaughtered throughout the Empire, while the former followers of Narvaez were in a mutinous mood, demanding a return to Cuba. Cortes knew that a retreat to the coast would mean the disintegration of the expedition, the loss of the Totonac and Tlascalan friendship and probably the death of all the Spaniards. Defying the mutineers to leave he overawed them and they subsided, muttering.

Both sides made frenzied preparations for the inevitable renewal of the campaign. Spanish and Tlascalan columns ravaged outlying Aztec provinces, destroying the garrisons and inciting the captive peoples to revolt. On his part Cuitlahuatzin was energetically following up his success. The City of Mexico was cleaned of ruins, provisioned and fortified while Aztec embassies besought an alliance with the Tarascan nation. Six of the principal Aztec chieftains appeared before the Tlascalan Council of State proposing an offensive and defensive alliance upon the sole condition that the Spaniards be exterminated or handed over to them. The Tlascalans with the exception of Xiconacatl the Younger, who was expelled from the Council for his stand, saw clearly the Aztec plan to separate their enemies that they might destroy them separately, and sent Cuitlahuatzin's envoys back empty handed.

While he was thus recapturing his reputation for victory and gaining the support of powerful Indian tribes, Cortes neglected no detail of his plan for the recapture of Mexico. The shipbuilder, Martin Lopez, who had escaped on the Noche Triste, set to work to build thirteen sailing vessels at Tlascala which were to be transported in pieces on the shoulders of carriers over the deserts and mountains to the shores of the Mexican lake. Sails, ropes and ironwork were brought from Villa Rica. Some of the Spaniards scoffed, believing the transportation of the vessels impracticable, but the Tlascalan chiefs, firm in their unbounded faith in their friend, the Captain General, promised to place the vessels in the lake if Lopez would construct them.

Another ally came to the assistance of the Spaniards—smallpox brought to Mexico by the Negro body servant of Narvaez.[8] It spread like a forest fire through the native towns, claiming thousands of victims daily. The Tlascalan Prince, Maxixcatzin, died of this malady as did the Emperor, Cuitlahuatzin, who is said to have contracted the illness from a Totonac maiden, seized by an Aztec raiding party and sent to his harem.[9]

Pedro de Alvarado was sent to Villa Rica to escort a number of malcontents and to consolidate the Totonac alliance. He busied himself to good account on this visit to the coast, impressing the crews and supplies of two small Spanish ships just arrived at the port, whose commanders were seeking to emulate the exploits of the Captain General. Scarcely had these recruits been sent to Tlascala than Alvarado persuaded two hundred soldiers, survivors of Francisco de Garay's latest expedition to the Panuco, to join his commander. These newcomers were provided with stores and powder which Cortes was greatly in need of. The Governor of the Canary Islands had fitted out a ship, not for making war upon native chieftains, but to trade with his fellow captains. In Villa Rica the ship's commander was pleased to find Alvarado an eager customer.

With the death of Cuitlahuatzin the throne passed to Quauhtemotzin, he that threw the first stone at Moctezuma. This prince was twenty-three years of age, educated as a priest, handsome and of fairer complexion than his relatives. Cuitlahuatzin, anxious to make his position secure, had put to death all the relatives of Moctezuma in his grasp, sparing only Quauhtemotzin[10] whom he despised as a rival. The latter was a nephew of Moctezuma and hereditary chief of Tlatelulco. He was married, incestuously we would believe, to the Princess Tecuichpo, daughter of Moctezuma, and to delude Cuitlahuatzin as to his real purpose, for ambition to occupy the Serpent Throne burned in the veins of this young man, had himself crowned King of Tlatelulco as Cuitlahuatzin was formally proclaimed Emperor. Quauhtemotzin added to the dignity of his coronation by personally sacrificing Spanish prisoners. This prince was so noted for his extreme ferocity that his followers trembled in his presence lest he slay them in blind rage. Such was the new antagonist of Cortes. His first act as Emperor was to dissolve the Council of State that no contrary opinions might be heard. He proclaimed a holy war against the Spaniards, offering great prizes for the delivery to him of White prisoners, removed much of the civilian population from Mexico, strengthened the garrisons on the frontier of Tlascala and provisioned his capital for the siege that he anticipated. He pretended contempt for Cortes but, prudent despite his years, prepared for defeat as well as the victory he publicly foresaw.

The Spanish force consisted of five hundred and fifty-nine infantry and forty horsemen with nine pieces of artillery. The powder supply was still limited; although some had been manufactured with sulphur taken from the nearby volcano of Popocatapetl. Taking a little-known short-cut through the dense forest on the flanks of the volcano of Iztaccihuatl,[11] Cortes appeared before Tuzcuco on December 31 and after only one skirmish with Aztec troops who were easily defeated captured the city.

Hearing that one hundred thousand Aztec warriors were gathered nearby, Cortes sent Alvarado to climb the great temple. From the height, the Captain could see the inhabitants of Tuzcuco hurrying away from the city in all directions while groups of armed men guarded the roads. Quauhtemotzin was prepared for war. After twelve days spent in consolidating his position in Tuzcuco and urged by the Tlascalans, eager to avenge the death of their comrades, Cortes set out along the lake shore for Iztapalapan with Alvarado, half of the army and the Tlascalan allies. The city of Iztapalapan was captured but flooded by the Aztecs, whereupon the Spaniards returned to Tuzcuco.

The fall of Iztapalapan resulted in immediate offers of alliance from the new Governor of Otumba and the Kings of Chalco, a tributary nation that had long desired the return of its lost freedom. Heretofore they had not ventured to approach Cortes and had indeed aided in the attack on the Noche Triste, but now that fortune smiled again on the Spaniards they took confidence and changed masters. Each day brought fresh acquisitions of strength to the Captain General. Some of these were highly valuable such as that of Ixtilxochitl, some were of little value and some doubtful in faith, but each represented a decrease in the Aztec power, another fissure in the edifice of the Mexican Empire. Many Aztec chiefs secretly wished for a peace that would leave them in control of their nation even though nominally vassals of Charles V, but Quauhtemotzin would listen to no compromise.

The Spaniards captured on the Noche Triste and forty-five others taken at Tuzcuco at the same time were sacrificed in the coronation ceremonies of Quauhtemotzin and his predecessor. Inhuman tortures were inflicted upon the captives before their hearts were torn out, a favorite device of Quauhtemotzin being to flay the prisoners alive. The skins were then carefully treated so as to keep them life-size and hung as ghastly effigies in the great temples, where upon occasion the priests and the Emperor himself donned these macabre garments in their frenzied invocations to Huitzilopotchli. Perhaps these evidences of Spanish mortality gave Quauhtemotzin a feeling of superiority over his White antagonists or perhaps he feared his fate in their hands, but in any event he refused any interview with the Captain General.[12]

Word having been received that the brigantines were ready for transportation, Cortes sent Sandoval with fifteen horsemen and two hundred foot-soldiers to meet the Tlascalan escort. Eight thousand Tlascalan carriers escorted by twenty thousand warriors transported the brigantines. The procession was two miles long, and the inhabitants of the Aztec villages stared in awe at the strange sight. Meantime at Tuzcuco yards had been prepared for the assembling and launching of the vessels, eight thousand Tuzcucans having been employed fifty days in this labor, where Alvarado was stationed to protect the workmen against attempts to fire the yards.

On March 1, 1521, Cortes set out on a march about the four lakes of Mexico (or Tuzcuco), Xaltocan, Xochimilco and Chalco, the heart of the Aztec Empire, to subjugate and destroy the lakeside cities that served as outposts and supplied warriors, food and information to Quauhtemotzin. Fifteen thousand Tlascalans, three hundred Spanish infantry, twenty-five horsemen, as many archers and six small cannon were commanded by Cortes, Alvarado and Olid. Met by frenzied resistance the army pushed forward over broken causeways, flooded fields and impassable roads to capture the cities of Xaltocan, Tenayocan, Azcapuzco and Tlacopan. Where the inhabitants did not join the Aztec troops their homes were spared. Weeks of bitter fighting found the Spaniards and their allies recapturing Tlacopan daily from the apparently inexhaustible fresh levies of Quauhtemotzin. Returning to Tuzcuco by the same route, they found every step one to be gained by the sword. Scarcely had he arrived at Tuzcuco then Cortes was confronted with the necessity of rescuing the Kings of Chalco, recent converts to the Spanish cause, from Quauhtemotzin's wrath, a task which Sandoval accomplished with such ferocity that the stream flowing through the battlefield was so polluted with the blood of the Aztec slain for hours afterward that the Spaniards could not drink therefrom.

During the next month two hundred Spaniards, eighty horsemen and a great amount of arms and ammunition arrived from Santo Domingo, while the Chinantec Kings, delighted at the success of the Whites, sent a large number of their famous pikes. Cortes occupied himself with expeditions far and wide throughout the Valley of Mexico, reducing to submission the strong cities of the Tlayacapan Valley set in almost impregnable positions, protected by cliffs and canyons. Forty thousand native allies were engaged in these forays, the columns being commanded by Alvarado, Olid and two Spaniards newly come from Santo Domingo, Alderete and Melgarejo. The high point in this campaign was the capture of the important lake city of Xochimilco, approximately ten miles distant from Mexico City. After the initial seizure by the Spaniards, Quauhtemotzin sent twelve thousand warriors in two thousand canoes to the support of his defeated garrison, while an equal number hurried over the Tlacopan causeway. On the morning of the third day the Aztec army exceeded fifty thousand men and two bodies of ten thousand each were proceeding from Tlacopan and the southeast. An attack from the water was beaten off, although four Spaniards captured alive were carried to Mexico and personally sacrificed by Quauhtemotzin. The bloodthirsty chieftain sent the arms and legs of the slain to the tributary chieftains in the surrounding cities, stating that such would be the fate of all enemies of the Aztecs. The battle of Xochimilco raged for three days, the Spaniards withdrawing into the confines of the city as the enemy was reinforced by twenty thousand additional warriors. Finally to prevent its use as a base for Indian attacks during his contemplated siege of Mexico and exasperated by the

Indian habit of slipping through canals and over the roofs of houses to attack his soldiers, Cortes gave the city to his followers, White and Red, to pillage after which it was burned. So great was the loot that many of the soldiers could barely walk under the weight of the gold and embroidered mantles taken. As the Spanish army marched out, the Aztecs retired after a sharp skirmish, for their losses during the three days' battle, replaced though they had been by fresh recruits, had been so great as to cause even the bravest to pause before the ready blades of the Whites.

Returning to his base at Tuxcuco, Cortes occupied the city of Coyuhuacan, afterwards his residence, seized and destroyed the fortress of Xoloc, set astride the Iztapalapan causeway and with his cavalry advanced along the highway over the waves to draw the attention of the Aztecs while his army, heavily laden with the spoils of Xochimilco, gained the shelter of Tlacopan. Leaving Azcapuzalco, a great body of Aztec warriors fell upon the column and carried off two of the favorite pages of Cortes. Furious at his loss, the Captain General and his cavalry hid themselves in ambush in a defile and when the Mexicans pursuing the Spanish column rushed through the narrow space, the horsemen fell upon them, spearing and riding them down. In a few moments over one hundred of the leading warriors were stretched lifeless upon the ground and the golden ornaments on their armour, among the richest yet seen in the hostile ranks, made a large addition to the spoil. As the army was now approaching the domain of Chalco, the Aztec legions fell away and the Spaniards returned to Tuzcuco without further molestation, to find that a conspiracy had broken out among the Spanish garrison at the base. The plotters planned to murder Cortes, Alvarado, Sandoval, Olid and Andres de Tapia. The plot was stifled and the leader, a private soldier named Villafane, executed.

On April 28, 1521, the fleet was ready and after consecration and a gala review the thirteen small vessels put out into the lake. Now at last Cortes was able to cope with the canoe fleets of the Mexican Emperor. The Tlascalans gazed in exultation at the strange birds, their allies. With eight hundred eighteen Spaniards, three large and thirteen small cannon, eighty-seven horses, the fleet, and fifty thousand Tlascalan warriors, Cortes advanced to the investment of Mexico, defended by a resolute enemy five times as numerous.

Alvarado, commanding half of the native contingent, one hundred fifty Spanish foot, thirty horse, eighteen archers and crossbowmen, set out for Tuzcuco on May 21 to capture the Tlacopan causeway which had proven so fatal on the Noche Triste. The blond Captain was a prime favourite with the Tlascalans, all of whom clamoured to follow the Child of the Sun. At the crucial moment, Xicotencatl deserted his command and returned to Tlascala. Seized en route, he vented imprecations upon the Council of State and the Captain General, who sensing the grave danger that a defeat would be followed by thousands of imitations, hanged the deserter high in the marketplace of Tuzcuco.

While engaged in filling the canals of Tlacopan and levelling houses to permit of manœuvres by his horsemen, Alvarado was unexpectedly attacked by a large Aztec army heretofore hidden in the hinterland, while other hordes in canoes struck the Spanish base from the lake. It was the battle of Mexico all over again. The long lances of the Spaniards were useless in the narrow streets against enemies who crept stealthily up the canals and over the flat roofs. Not until May 30, when Cortes at the head of his fleet swept down upon the city, was Alvarado free of his tormentors.

To distract Quauhtemotzin's attention, Sandoval recaptured and burned Iztapalapan while the Captain General and the fleet fought a desperate battle with the garrison of a steep rocky islet off the city, the Penon del Marques. At the head of one hundred and fifty soldiers, Cortes climbed hand over hand up the rocky sides, covered by gun-fire from the brigantines, and after a desperate fight, put the garrison to the sword, sparing only women and children.[18] While he was regaining his ships the Mexican war fleet was seen approaching, enraged by the sight of the burning city. The Spanish vessels lay in an irregular line, their sails flapping idly against the masts. Suddenly with one of those strokes of fortune or miracles which never seemed to fail the Christians, the wind blew from dead astern and the fleet sailed full tilt into the enemy lines. Few of the Aztecs had ever seen these water monsters in action before and some thought them living beasts. A volley from the guns preceded the onslaught and through the powder smoke emerged the prows and sails of the little fleet, crushing and sinking the canoes before them.[14] The Indians were panic-stricken and fled in all directions for safety. The water was covered with broken and sinking canoes, bodies of the slain and struggling survivors who begged their fellows in vain for places in canoes still unsunk. The pursuit continued for twelve miles. The cannon and archers did scarcely less execution than the prows of the vessels which continually rammed and sank enemy canoes. Several of the vessels penetrated to the very mouths of the widest canals, picking up fugitive chiefs as they strove to swim ashore. With this great battle, control of the lake passed definitely to the Spaniards. A large number of Aztec canoes had been destroyed and they were definitely impressed with their inferiority in naval combat. Quauhtemotzin, however, was not discouraged. He called the leading nobles in counsel to ratify his measures for defence of the city. Four thousand captives, mostly Chalcans, died in honor of Huitzilopotchli. The gratified God promptly responded through the lips of the Emperor that within a few days the Indian allies of Cortes would become discouraged and leave for home whereupon the Spaniards would fall easy victims. A number of the older chiefs, discouraged by the outcome of the naval combat and the isolation of Mexico, were for peace or at least a truce, but Quauhtemotzin would not hear of it and supported by the younger chiefs and warriors intensified his efforts.

Under cover of the battle, Olid seized the causeway fortress of Xoloc, whereupon Cortes cut the dike and passed several of his vessels to the far side where they created a diversion, keeping large Mexican forces engaged and disrupting the food supply. Quauhtemotzin was reduced to importing provisions by night as no canoe could hope to escape the swift sailing monsters. Masters of Xoloc, Iztapalapan was no longer a vital position. Sandoval was accordingly despatched to seize the village of Tepeyacac, at the mainland end of the only causeway yet in Mexican hands. A general attack was now undertaken, Cortes advancing from Xoloc, Alvarado along the Tlacopan causeway and Sandoval from the north, while part of the fleet attacked the city and the remainder protected the flanks of the attacking columns. The brigantines proved invaluable in this action as their cannon-fire drove the Mexicans from the gaps while the working parties built bridges for the artillery and the allies in their eagerness swam across. Behind the fighting men labor battalions of Tlascalans and Tuzcucans tore down the ramparts protecting the gaps in the causeways and even parts of the highways themselves to effectually and permanently fill the chasms. On this day Sandoval and Alvarado did not reach the city, being occupied in repairing the causeways while fighting off their tireless enemies.

Cortes, however, penetrated into the capital followed by the men of Olid and eight thousand native auxiliaries. Straight ahead the avenue led to the fatal square dominated by the great pyramid of Huitzilopotchli, surrounded by the palaces of Moctezuma, Axayacatl and the new edifice occupied by Quauhtemotzin. The street was protected by barricades and the canals yawned free of their customary bridges. The Captain General fought his way along the avenues, crossing three canals, but not until after sending for two of the heavy guns which, transported across the new bridges in the causeways, destroyed the barricades and their defenders. As before, the roofs were thronged with archers and slingers and the canals with canoes. After a furious combat the last canal was crossed and the Spaniards rushed through the temple enclosure. This space was packed by warriors before whom danced frantic priests, their hair matted with the blood of self-inflicted wounds, shrieking imprecations at the invaders and encouragement to their warriors. No progress was made against the horde until the guns were brought up whose projectiles opened a path to the very foot of the pyramid. The Spaniards rushed through the narrow lane thus created but the pressure of humanity was too great to overcome. From all sides, from the roofs and the heights of the pyramid, arrows, stones, spears and darts fell upon them in such number that they were forced to retreat, literally swept out of the square by the weight of numbers. The enemy was composed of the followers of Prince Quauhtin, noted for his skill and ferocity, and accounted the most valiant warriors in the Mexican army, who formed the bodyguard of the Emperor. These intrepid fighters even captured the guns. At this desperate moment the horsemen who had been delayed on the causeway suddenly came up and at the sight of the dreaded beasts the Aztecs drew back momentarily.

Charging at full gallop through the enemy ranks the horsemen once more opened a path to the pyramid up whose steep sides Cortes followed by a number of others rushed to the very temple of Huitzilopotchli. The image destroyed by the invaders had been replaced in full splendour. In an instant the Spaniards had snatched the golden mask and jewelled headdress from the idol and hurled it into space, accompanied by the guardian priests. As night was coming on the Christians retired, fighting their way step by step back through the city and across the causeway to the fortress.

Although Cortes had won a notable victory he saw that unless he could retain the positions gained, his nightly retirements would cancel all his advantage and result in the useless sacrifice of his men. He must retain the advances which meant either encamping in the city itself, exposed to continual attacks which would exhaust his army, or destroy buildings as captured, filling in the canals and leaving the Aztecs no shelter. The levelled space would provide a suitable battle-ground for the cavalry. Recognizing the dire necessity of the destruction of the city (which as he wrote to the Emperor was one of the finest in the world) Cortes gave orders that close behind his battle-line companies of native sappers should wreck the captured edifices.

Nor had Quauhtemotzin reason for self-congratulation on the events of this day. He had seen his vaunted defences pierced and the Holy of Holies of his empire violated by the hand of the intruder. True, the Spaniards had retreated but he knew only too well that they would come again on the morrow.

Each morning as the Spaniards advanced from their mainland camps they found the gaps in the causeways, filled under fire the previous day, enlarged and deepened by the tireless enemy. Christian attacks destroyed the palaces of Axayacatl and Moctezuma but no permanent advance was recorded. Alvarado was impatient with this caution on the part of his commander and encamped his men on the causeway itself. It was the height of the rainy season and his soldiers without shelter, unable to remove their armour for weeks at a time and wet to the marrow by the cold rain, endured agonies during the ninety-three days of the siege. For them there was no rest by day or by night, for Quauhtemotzin had entirely revised the Aztec rules of war and attacked relentlessly and tirelessly at all hours. He filled forty of the largest war craft with his fiercest warriors to convoy other fleets of canoes bringing food at night through the besiegers' lines. These fighting canoes aided by the stakes and nets set to trap the brigantines scored an initial success, ambushing two Spanish vessels and killing the captains Portillo and Pedro Barba. To offset this loss, Cortes decoyed the war fleet toward his main naval force and inflicted so severe a punishment upon the warriors, few of whom escaped, that Quauhtemotzin desisted from further attempts to dispute the mastery of the lake.

As the siege proceeded and hunger made itself felt in the capital, Quauhtemotzin gradually withdrew his force toward the northern part of the city, the district known as Tlatelulco, where the principal market and one of the great temple pyramids were situated. This portion of the city was reached directly by the causeway to Tepeyacac[15] and lay to the left of the entrance of the causeway from Tlacopan along which Alvarado was advancing. In the southern part of the city, including the great temple and the imperial palaces, Quauhtemotzin abandoned resistance except for surprise attacks and ambushes. At this time the force of the besiegers had risen to one hundred thousand men while the Aztecs, decimated by the daily battles and desertion, were scarcely greater in number.

By June 23, Cortes had cleared the city of enemies from the head of the Iztapalapan causeway to the great temple and was advancing along the street from the temple leading to the Tlacopan causeway that free communication might be established with Alvarado.

The question of food was a most serious one, particularly for Alvarado's division. These troops, encamped on the very battle-lines, subsisted on herbs, cherries and corn cakes (tortillas) prepared by their Indian servants, as the causeway was too choked with fighting men and war material to permit of the construction of barracks and kitchens. The incessant rainfall and damp clothes had reduced the vitality of the soldiers to such an extent that fresh wounds would no longer close and became infected by the next day. Alvarado resorted to the desperate expedient of searing the cuts with boiling oil and even the tips of lances heated red hot.[16] By June 20 he had fought his way into the city, destroying the houses as he advanced, preferring to camp in the ruins exposed to the storm and cold rather than risk surprise and ambush in the buildings. As he set foot on the island he turned left along a street leading to the market of Tlatelulco instead of advancing along the main avenue to the palace of Moctezuma. The success of Cortes had aroused the envy of the other divisions which determined to equal his prowess by capturing the remainder of the city and if possible the person of the Emperor.

The enemy attacked in such numbers that Alvarado, who had left his horsemen on the mainland to protect the lines of communication, was obliged to bring them up. In the following week's fighting, thirty-three Spaniards were captured alive and sacrificed by Quauhtemotzin. Bernal Diaz del Castillo himself was seized and only rescued in the nick of time by Alvarado who came thundering onto the scene on horseback and rode down the captors of the future historian. Tonatiuh was seriously wounded in this battle but no Spaniard had time to pause for wounds that did not literally cripple him. In fact, such was the disinclination of the Christians to leave the battle-line, that when Alvarado decreed that the soldiers more seriously wounded but still able to move should superintend the filling-in of canals and the construction of bridges, almost open mutiny arose in his ranks, as no Spaniard wished to be counted a laggard when face to face with the enemy.

When news came to him of Alvarado's losses, the Captain General passed over by brigantine to his subordinate's camp lest the impetuous nature of the latter might have led him into a trap. He was astonished by the progress made by his favourite commander. In his account of this day's fighting the Captain General wrote Charles V :[17]

June 24: When on my return to camp in the evening I heard of Alvarado's losses, I decided to go to his camp on the following morning and reprimand him for what had happened and see how far he had advanced and where he had placed his camp. When I arrived there I was astonished to see how far he had penetrated into the city and the formidable bridges and passes which he had captured and having seen them I could not impute much blame to him and after talking over what was to be done I returned to my own camp.

Cortes vainly proposed an armistice, anxious to spare the city and its inhabitants, reduced to eating the bodies of the slain, friend and foe alike. Cannibal as the Aztecs were, this food was neither strange nor revolting to them; the bodies of the Spaniards being reserved for the tables of the Emperor, his generals and the chief priests. Cortes withdrew the force of Sandoval, leaving only a picket to hold the Tepeyacac causeway, and sent the Captain to join Alvarado with half his men, while the remainder reinforced the Captain General. The assault in force, which it was hoped would overcome the frenzied resistance of the enemy, was pushed directly northward from the Great Pyramid by the forces of Cortes, while Alvarado drove forward in a northeasterly direction along his highway. The battle of June 30 ran strongly to the Spaniards until, rendered careless by their unexpected gains, the lieutenants of Cortes neglected his instructions to fill all canals as captured. Alderete, leading the advance, was within sight of his goal, the pyramid of Tlatelulco, and could hear Alvarado's battle in the distance, when he was overwhelmed and thrown back by a countercharge of desperate warriors. Forced to retreat across the last bridge, the beams broke beneath the weight of the struggling mass, throwing Tlascalan and Spaniard alike into the deep water at the mercy of the enemy. In an instant the roofs of the surrounding houses were packed with Aztecs. The retreat across the canal was another Noche Triste. Soldier and native ally were drowned in the canal or dragged away for sacrifice. Even the royal banner, jealously guarded emblem of Spanish sovereignty, was snatched from the hands of its dying holder. Cortes himself was overthrown and seized by frantic Aztecs and only the superhuman efforts of Olea, the Captain General's personal attendant, who literally chopped away Indian arms curled about the body of his master, saved him. The avenue so lately captured with ease swarmed with warriors while overhead shrilled the note of the trumpet of Quauhtemotzin, a sacred symbol reserved for sounding in great emergencies. Brilliant as their efforts had been before, the Aztecs fought like madmen now, seeing the very heart of their city invaded by the Spaniards. On this day the invaders lost forty Europeans and one thousand Tlascalans killed. Almost as serious was the loss of one cannon and many crossbows and muskets which could not be replaced. Nearly all of the Spaniards were wounded and Cortes' bodyguard almost exterminated. As the defeated column retired over the causeway, Indians on nearby roofs threw three freshly severed Spanish heads at the Christians, shouting that on the morrow the remainder would be served likewise.

On the same morning Alvarado advanced against dense masses of Indians who disputed every foot of progress. After making some headway the opposing warriors were suddenly replaced by fresh squadrons in brilliant uniforms who hurled five bleeding heads at the Whites, shouting that they had just killed Cortes and Sandoval and were here to settle accounts with Tonatiuh.[18] For a moment the Spaniards were overcome, believing that it was indeed the Captain General's head they saw before them. The soldiers wavered and but for the frantic efforts of Alvarado who threw himself into the forefront of the fighting, panic might have ensued. The sudden increase in the number of his opponents together with repeated shouts that Cortes had been defeated, induced him to order a retreat as he had penetrated far beyond the point made secure by the destruction of the adjoining houses. To assure room for manœuvres and prevent confusion on the narrow causeway, he sent his Indian allies off first who retreated in good order and cleared the causeway for half its length while the Spaniards formed a rear guard and fought their way back step by step.

Cortes sent Andres de Tapia along the lake shore to learn what had befallen Alvarado, while the gallant Sandoval, mounted on the finest horse in the Spanish army burst his way through enemy skirmishers to the Captain General's headquarters. Each division was cheered to learn that the other commanders were safe, but the day had been a sad one for the invaders. Sixty-two Spaniards had been captured alive in addition to the killed and wounded. Two cannon and seven horses had been lost. Cortes himself was so seriously wounded that he retired from the campaign for several days, his division being commanded by Sandoval. As the rays of the setting sun lit up the pyramid of Tlatelulco, a great burst of barbaric music sounded and the horror-stricken soldiers of Alvarado, less than a mile from the scene beheld with their own eyes the sacrifice of their comrades taken in the day's battle. Lest the present writer be accused of painting the terrible picture in too sombre colours, the following description is quoted from Bancroft whose pro-Aztec bias is notorious :[19]

Then a space was cleared and a long file of naked men stood revealed. A cry of horror burst from the watching soldiers. There could be no mistake. Distant as was the temple, the glare of the fire clearly revealed the white hue and bearded faces of their comrades, bound for sacrifice and plumed. Now they were made to march forward and with blows to dance before the idol to which they were consecrated. Ah, to be a helpless looker-on at such a time! Again they formed in line exhausted and then one was seized by several priests and borne struggling to the stone of sacrifice. He was thrown upon his back and held down by the limbs while the high-priest with ceremonious flourish raised the glittering blade. The gazing soldiers clutched each other's hands in agony, as their eyes followed the instrument and saw it plunged into the breast of the victim. They seemed to hear his stifled cry, to feel the knife in their own hearts and, realizing that they were still safe, thanked Heaven for their escape.

Victim after victim was carried to the stone, some with frantic struggles, others resigned and still others weighed down in helpless fear of what they beheld. Heart after heart was torn from the gaping breasts and held before the idol, while the bodies were cast down the steps. The skin, particularly of the head and upper body was removed and used as a dress for festive occasions, and the flesh was hacked to pieces, the limbs for the banquet table, the trunk for the beasts. After a while came darker-hued victims and now the Tlascaltecs and other allies shuddered. To them the sacrifices were not so terrifying as to the Spaniards, but they could not unmoved behold the cruel death of their countrymen. Then came more processions, music and idolatrous rites, followed by fresh companies for the sacrifice, white and dark; and so passed the night until the horror palled on the gazers and many expressed the opinion that the priests were pretending sacrifice by producing the same bodies upon the stone several times to inspire greater fear. This belief was strengthened when they observed similar ceremonies take place on other minor temples, and by the continuance of the sacrifices for several days. The offerings at the minor temples consisted chiefly of the lower class of allies. All the pyramids, however, received a quota of heads from Spanish, leading native and equine victims, wherewith to decorate their summits.

Aware that the sight of the sacrifice, purposely intensified for Spanish edification, must have deeply stirred the breasts of the survivors, the Mexicans took advantage of this to attack the camp of Alvarado during the night. "Behold the fate in store for you all!", they cried, casting in half-roasted pieces of flesh from white and dusky bodies. "Eat, for we are satiated."

The Spaniards were badly demoralized and the allies wavering. The native legions melted away overnight; only the Tlascalans remained faithful. The entire city was again in Aztec hands and great fires blazed nightly in celebration. Hunger stalked the Spanish camp as the lake cities lapsed into neutrality or opened secret negotiations with Quauhtemotzin, requiring Cortes' utmost efforts to restore them to their allegiance. But the fleet retained its iron grip upon the lake, no supplies reached the starving capital and victory became a mockery to the haunted Emperor. He ordered a simultaneous sortie by all causeways; the cannon mowed bloody lanes through the closely packed Aztec troops and the attempt was abandoned. The chief priest tried his hand. On the morning after the great victory he proclaimed a divine portent that within eight days' time the invaders would be completely destroyed. Circulated among the lake cities, their wavering inhabitants decided to wait and see. Hunger fought for Cortes, superstition for Quauhtemotzin. Fatal error, that definite time. Eight days passed, the Christians sat firm in their camps on the lake, the brigantines maintained their ceaseless patrol, the Gods withheld their bolts: the allies flocked again to the standard of Spain. Quauhtemotzin's last trump had failed.

Cortes now decided that the entire city of Mexico must be destroyed if Quauhtemotzin would not surrender. He would not again expose himself to a defeat in the narrow streets trapped between canals. The Mexican Emperor refused a final request for a truce and the work of destruction was under way, Cortes personally setting the example carrying stones with his own hands to fill breaches in the causeways newly made by the Aztecs. Protected by soldiers each building captured was levelled, over fifty thousand allies being occupied in the work of destruction.

While Cortes advanced over the many-times-trodden road from Iztapalapan to the Great Pyramid, Alvarado fought his way to the marketplace and temple of Tlatelulco. On July 24 the temple was captured, idols destroyed and sanctuaries burned but during the afternoon the Spaniards were forced to retire before continuous enemy attacks. The following week was spent in continual fighting in the streets, while the labour companies slowly and relentlessly advanced behind the cover of the battle-front, foot by foot, destroying the capital of Quauhtemotzin. During these days great numbers of women and children starved until they were literally living skeletons, came to the Spanish lines begging for food and were passed through to the mainland. On July 26, while Cortes was struggling forward from the Tlacopan causeway, the enemy before him was suddenly seized with panic and fled down the side streets or leaped into the canal. In an instant Alvarado followed by four other horsemen came flying down the street; for the first time the two wings of the Spanish force had established contact. Quauhtemotzin's days were numbered. The avenue leading to the marketplace was garrisoned by a large force of Tlascalans and the buildings on either side razed. When Alvarado cut through to join his conquest to that of Cortes, over seven-eighths of the city was in the hands of the invader, but the Emperor showed no signs of yielding. The Captain General sent Alvarado to seize a quarter consisting of about one thousand houses, which the fiery Captain did, capturing the entire section, killing a great many Aztecs and taking twelve thousand prisoners. Only his threat to use force against his allies prevented the Tlascalans from instantly slaughtering the captives, such was their rage against the Mexicans. So desperate had the fighting been in this quarter in the preceding days that the invading soldiers were almost stifled by the odour of decaying bodies. Wounded and dying lay scattered on the roofs, in the houses and in the streets, too weak to move, gazing at their conquerors with lacklustre eyes.

The general battle continued for three days, the besieged losing streets and squares but steadily refusing an armistice or an interview with the Emperor. Beyond patience at a series of evasive replies brought by Aztec nobles, Cortes exclaimed, "Since they will not have peace, let them have war!" and loosed the Tlascalans, who in their eagerness swept over the housetops and, reversing their rôles, speared the fleeing Aztecs in the streets below with their long Chinantec lances. The defenders fought bravely, desperately, hopelessly, the narrow streets were piled high with the bodies of the dead. When the sun went down on the third day

over forty thousand Mexican warriors had fought their last battle. Following this defeat the chief advisor of Quauhtemotzin
appeared and after delaying Cortes for five hours with pretended
negotiations, during which a stream of women and children poured
from the besieged quarters, suddenly departed stating that the
Emperor would never present himself. Furious, Cortes attacked
in full force, whereupon for the first time large bodies of Aztec
troops surrendered. In fact this surrender was evidence of their
trust in the Captain General's word, since he had promised to spare
the lives of deserters. In Aztec warfare prisoners were invariably
reserved for sacrifice and the edict of Cortes enslaving them but
sparing their lives seemed to the helots of Quauhtemotzin an
escape from Avernus, even though their traditions made them
despise mercy to the vanquished. But while the Indian legions
were surrendering to the Spaniards, their fellows meeting the
Tuzcucans and Tlascalans were not so fortunate. The native
allies left no enemy alive within range of their weapons until
Cortes, sickened by the carnage, strove to put an end to the battle.

On August 13, 1521, Quauhtemotzin fled his capital by water,
to be captured by Diego Holguin, master of a brigantine. The
imperial canoe was laden with the choicest flowers of the harem
and a quantity of gold. Overtaken by the enemy, the Aztec begged
for mercy. The ferocious executioner of Spaniard and Tlascalan
had not elected to die in defence of his sacred city but was fleeing
desperately from the fate he left his deserted warriors to face. As
Quauhtemotzin conducted by Spanish soldiers passed along the
ruined streets of Mexico to face his conqueror all resistance
ceased while Aztec and invader alike dropped their weapons to
witness the passing of the man whose determination to be Emperor
had cost the destruction of the city and the lives of over two hundred thousand persons. Gone were the proud mien and glittering
regalia. The knife that had torn the hearts from helpless Spaniards
was missing from his belt. The hands that had exultantly held
aloft newly severed Spanish heads while the blood of the victims
streamed over his sacred person, hung abjectly at his sides. To his
intense surprise, Cortes instead of slaying him on the spot as
he must have expected, received him with much courtesy, a company of soldiers being drawn up at salute and a table laden with

food and backed by an improvised throne awaiting him. The fallen Emperor begged Cortes to slay him with his sword, fearing more refined tortures, but the latter reassured him with fair words, saying that according to his lights the Mexican had fought well for his faith but that none could withstand the God of the Spaniards and that since there was no help for the past, he, Cortes, would forget the suffering caused by the obstinate determination of Quauhtemotzin. The Emperor, his harem and suite were placed in safe keeping while the Aztec quarters were given over to the allies for pillage. Mexico had fallen, the handful of Spaniards had conquered. Huitzilopotchli and his companion gods vanished forevermore to the setting of a furious thunderstorm that burst over the city on the last day of the Conquest.

FOOTNOTES FOR CHAPTER SIX

[1] Prescott says, *History of the Conquest of Mexico*, Vol. II, p. 402, July 8. Diaz del Castillo says July 14. This was an error in his reckoning as he was ten days late in his calculation of the return from Cempoala.

[2] Diaz del Castillo, *Conquête de la Nouvelle-Espagne*, p. 375.

[3] Lorenzana, *Historia de Mejico*, p. 148.

[4] The present writer has been unable to find an instance similar to the Spanish attack at Otumba, the nearest being that of the great defeat inflicted on the Earl of Essex, supported by thirty thousand of the finest troops in Queen Elizabeth's army by the Irish chieftain, Rickard O'Toole, with less than three thousand clansmen.

[5] Bancroft, *Annals of Early Mexico*, p. 501.
Prescott, *History of the Conquest of Mexico*, Vol. II, p. 399.

[6] The arms of the Salamanca family bear an Aztec plume in commemoration of this deed.

[7] Prescott, *History of the Conquest of Mexico*, Vol. II, p. 402:
"It was undoubtedly one of the most remarkable victories ever achieved in the New World. And this not merely on account of the disparity of the forces but of their unequal condition. For the Indians were in all their strength while the Christians were wasted by disease, famine, and long-protracted sufferings; without cannon or firearms, and deficient in the military apparatus which had so often struck terror into their barbarian foe; deficient even in the terrors of a victorious name. But they had discipline on their side, desperate resolve and implicit confidence in their commander."
Bancroft, *Annals of Early Mexico*, pp. 503-4:
"Obviously this battle was the most important so far in the New World; and it must ever be regarded as one of the most remarkable in history. The natives were probably much less numerous than the estimates of the boastful victors

(200,000), still they were immensely superior in number and condition to the Spaniards, enfeebled by recent defeat, by wounds, and want. Further, the latter had no firearms wherewith to terrify the natives, only swords and pikes. Their main advantage lay in their horses, their discipline, and the genius of their leader, all strengthened by the enthusiasm born of a national pride and a certain knowledge that failure meant utter destruction."

[8] Said to have been named Francisco Eguia.

[9] The Mexican author, Efemio Mendoza, in his biography of Cuitlahuatzin, gives the date of his death as November 26, 1520.

[10] Also called Guatemoc.

[11] "The White Woman."

[12] The sentimentalists who have exalted the character of Quauhtemotzin and Cuitlahuatzin, ascribing to them all the virtues and painting Cortes and Alvarado in the blackest colours, may meditate on the Aztec sacrificial ceremonies and ask themselves were they in Cortes' place, the ghastly relics of his slaughtered soldiers before his eyes, would they have spared Quauhtemotzin as Cortes did. After his capture and while en route to Honduras with Cortes as a hostage, Quauhtemotzin was detected in a conspiracy against the Spaniards and hanged in Campeche. His execution, however, was caused by his attempted revolt and not for his treatment of the Spanish prisoners. The humane attitude of Cortes is more remarkable when there no longer existed as in the case of Moctezuma reason for his politic handling of the imperial captive. The execution of Quauhtemotzin immediately after his capture would have in no wise imperilled the Spanish position, as the Aztec power was thoroughly broken. Historians have held Quauhtemotzin up as a model of desperate bravery. The present writer has no desire to take from the Indian Emperor such good qualities that he may have possessed. Physical bravery is an attribute not governed by race, sex or geography and the letters of Cortes attest abundantly to the courage of the Aztecs. Inhuman cruelty practised in the name of religion by the Aztecs well merited the destruction of the Mexican Empire. No such religion could exist in the sixteenth century, and those who overlook the bloodthirsty traits of the Aztecs and remember only their romantic aspect permit sentiment to cloud their reason.

[13] This rock is now known as "El Peñol del Marques" for Cortes, who was granted the title of "Marquis of the Valley."

[14] Cortes estimated the number of canoes at five hundred, while Bernal Diaz del Castillo states that during the attack on the rocky island the number had been greatly reinforced and not less than four thousand canoes and twenty-five thousand warriors confronted Cortes in this naval engagement.

[15] Now the suburb of Guadelupe.

[16] Diaz del Castillo states that when oil was not available, fat taken from the bodies of dead Indians was used for this purpose.

[17] As translated by Maudsley.

[18] Diaz del Castillo differs from other historians in permitting Sandoval to retain his original command and attack from the Tepeyacac causeway.

[19] Bancroft, *Annals of Early Mexico*, p. 657.

PART TWO

THE CONQUISTADOR

1524 — 1541

VII

CONQUEST OF GUATEMALA

August 1521 — July 1524

THE fall of Mexico marked the end of the period of preparation in Alvarado's career. Heretofore the chief lieutenant of Cortes, he now began on an ever-increasing scale to undertake expeditions on his own account. For something over a year these were directly under the control of the Captain General and the subsequently formed Audiencia of Mexico and not until the expedition to Guatemala[1] was Alvarado Captain General in his own right. Hereinbefore in tracing his career it has been necessary to recount much of the life of Cortes; hereafter reference will be made to the Conqueror of Mexico only where his conduct or instruction affected Alvarado.

On the day following the surrender of Quauhtemotzin, the Aztecs evacuated Mexico City, over seventy thousand men, women and children filing disconsolately across the Tlacopan causeway. Those of the allies not required for the cleaning and rebuilding of the city were dismissed to their homes amply compensated by part of the booty while the chiefs were confirmed in possession of their provinces. As soon as order could be restored the Spaniards' first thought was to secure the gold of Quauhtemotzin. In this they were greatly disappointed,—only a little over a million dollars' worth being recovered. To this day the disposal of the remainder, which contemporary historians valued at five times that found, remains a mystery. Some of it is said to have been sent by Quauhtemotzin early in the siege to be placed in safekeeping in the mountains of Michoacan where it is thought the fugitive Emperor was en route when captured. Much more is supposed to lie lost in the depths of the lake or hidden beneath the ruins of the Aztec palaces. It is probable that a large amount was discovered and secretly taken to Spain, indeed many of the soldiers accused Cortes of this practice. The army murmured so loudly that Quauhtemot-zin must know where the treasure was and so threateningly did their attitude become that Cortes, with little reason to love the monarch, delivered the prisoner into the hands of Alderete who tortured the Emperor to some extent but not to compare with the

Quaubtemallā.

Panel from the Tlaxcala Tapestry, Now in Mexico City, Showing Pedro de Alvarado's Conquest of Guatemala, Accompanied by Tlascalans.

savagery the latter was accustomed to mete out to his prisoners. A considerable amount of gold was obtained from information given by the Emperor from wells in his palace and from nearby parts of the lake, but the army remained greatly disappointed.

To the most remote reaches of the Empire and beyond it to the people of the hostile nations, north, west and south spread the stupendous news of the destruction of the Aztec power. Emissaries and ambassadors thronged the camp of Cortes protesting their fealty to Charles V while the King of the Chinantecs came in person to see with his own eyes the ruins of the capital of his dreaded foe. It is worthy of note that this monarch had kept four Spaniards sent by Cortes to establish an agricultural colony during the truce with Moctezuma free from harm and now brought them with him as living evidences of his friendship for the Christians.

Pedro de Alvarado was sent to Oaxaca to subdue an Aztec Prince who believed his luck better than Quauhtemotzin's. The Captain made short work of the rebel, washed the streams for gold and so glowing was his report of the country and its resources that Cortes determined to select that province for his own residence when peace should have been finally established throughout the Empire.[2] Alvarado's optimistic report hid a multitude of difficulties and disappointments. The region, though rich in agricultural land and timber, yielded little gold and was unhealthy, the White settlers being tormented with vampire bats, mosquitoes and innumerable insects.

The force at Alvarado's command consisted of one hundred and eighty Spanish soldiers, including thirty-five horsemen and a small force of native auxiliaries. He bore orders to requisition twenty crossbowmen from Captain Francisco de Orozco, who had pacified the province of Guaxaca[3] through which the expedition was to pass. Alvarado left Mexico early in the year 1522, having been in charge of the rebuilding of the capital during the closing months of the previous year. En route he received instructions from Cortes to subdue several Aztec villages which were reported risen in arms, but found them quiet and continued his journey without incident until arriving at Tutepeque, the chief city of the tribe. The newcomers were well received and lodged in the palace of the King and the surrounding buildings. The priest, Olmedo, who accompanied the expedition, cautioned Alvarado against accepting these lodgings as the thatched roofs overhung the narrow streets, and the wooden construction of the houses would serve admirably as a pyre if the chiefs meditated treachery. Alvarado immediately moved his troops to the outskirts of the city. Approximately two hundred thousand dollars in gold had been

collected when Cortes sent urgent instructions that all the treasure
was to be immediately forwarded to Mexico as the last shipment,
including the loot taken from Quauhtemotzin, had been captured
by the French en route to Spain. Alvarado complied, to the rage
of his soldiers, a number of whom conspired to kill him and his
brothers when they should be taken off guard. One of the mutineers confessed the plan to Father Olmedo who promptly advised
the Captain. When he received the news, Alvarado was some
distance from the city, accompanied, as it happened, by most of
the conspirators. Pleading a sudden illness, he returned immediately to Tutepeque to seek medical aid. Immediately upon his
arrival, his health was restored, and placing himself at the head of
his brothers and the loyal troops, he fell upon the plotters who,
outnumbered, surrendered without fighting. They confessed their
guilt, revealing that it had been planned to stab Alvarado and
his brothers that same night as they lay asleep. The Indian chiefs
were also parties to the plot, having agreed to aid the mutineers
in case the Captain escaped and doubtless planning in their own
minds to take advantage of this division of the newcomers to make
an end to both parties. Alvarado held a summary courtmartial and
executed two Spaniards, ringleaders in the conspiracy. The Indian
King was reduced to prison, where he died in two weeks' time.

Alvarado founded the city of Segura de la Frontera which, by
authorization of Cortes, was moved together with its Spanish inhabitants from its previous location on the Tlascalan frontier,
and appointed Mayors and Aldermen.[4] He now proceeded to
Mexico to deliver the gold but in his absence rebellion broke out
again and nearly all of the inhabitants deserted the city, making
their way to Guaxaca, Soconusco and other provinces. Even in
Mexico City the gold found was insufficient to satiate the Spanish
appetite and rumours always painted the new lands richer than
their present habitation. The Spaniards gone, the Indians proclaimed their independence and Alvarado was forced to return in
haste with new troops, put down the uprising and capture a number
of the mutineers. Tried and condemned to death, they appealed to
Cortes who ordered them brought to Mexico where a second courtmartial heard the case. Sentenced a second time, he commuted the
sentence to banishment to Cuba. The province was repacified, but

such was the climate that it was impossible to find settlers and for a number of years no further Spanish activity was undertaken in this region. A Governor without subjects, Alvarado was recalled to Mexico to take part in the Panuco campaign.

Ever since the landing of Cortes at Villa Rica, Francisco de Garay, Governor of Jamaica, had spent his force and resources in vain attempts to conquer the Panuco.[5] His expeditions had suffered mutiny, shipwreck and massacre and one of them, as we have seen, deserted to Cortes. Late in 1521, after the destruction of the Aztec Empire, messengers from the King of the Indian nation inhabiting the Panuco arrived in Mexico asking Cortes for protection against neighbouring tribes and against the forays of Garay. Delighted with the excuse, he proceeded in person to the region and fought a number of severe battles with Indian armies, numbering as many as sixty thousand warriors. While the pacification was under way, the Jamaican Governor formed a confederacy with Diego Velasquez and Diego Columbus, looking to the conquest of the Panuco and if possible the overthrow of Cortes. Scarcely had the Captain General returned to Mexico City than he was apprised of the landing of Garay in person at the head of a large expedition. Accompanied by Alvarado, Cortes set his face again for the coast.

As the Captain General was about to leave Mexico, two Spaniards arrived from the Province of Soconusco,[6] stating that the inhabitants who formerly had displayed a most friendly feeling, sending a number of their principal men to make submission to Cortes, were in a state of rebellion. A messenger from the chief arrived almost simultaneously stating that it was not they but their immediate neighbours to the southward[7] who were exhibiting a warlike attitude. To hold this territory, Cortes detached Alvarado, giving him eighty-four horsemen, two hundred infantry and four pieces of artillery together with full powers and instructions to investigate the controversy and save the provinces for Spain. Before the expedition could set out, however, information from Villa Rica that Francisco de Garay had landed in the Panuco with one hundred and twenty horsemen, four hundred foot-soldiers and much artillery, caused Cortes to postpone the expedition, and Alvarado and his men accompanied the Captain General. Garay followed the tactics of Narvaez, proclaiming himself Governor of the Panuco by royal decree and stating that he had come to liberate the natives from the slavery established by Cortes. This touching consideration on the part of Spanish captains for the natives conquered by some other conquistador is one of the few touches of comedy in the drama of the conquest of the New World. Many relatives and partisans of Diego Velasquez were among the expedition which as a whole was bitterly hostile to Cortes, envious of his success and anxious, if possible, to wrest from him the Empire of the Aztecs. Garay hoped and expected to find another Mexico in the Panuco, and if not, there would be nothing to prevent him, so he fondly hoped, from marching on Mexico.

On the way to the coast, Cortes' horse fell, injuring his rider who was confined to bed for several days. Alvarado led the force forward, and when two days on the road met a messenger newly arrived from Spain bringing a royal order addressed jointly to Cortes and Garay, ordering the latter to abstain from any interference with the Captain General. Having thus law as well as priority on his side, Cortes determined to act in a politic rather than a warlike manner if possible and sent his chamberlain in hot haste to overtake the column and order its impetuous commander to follow and observe the moves of the Jamaicans but not to come into armed conflict with them without express orders from him. Cortes also sent a copy of the letter from Charles V to Garay by an Indian runner, requesting an answer.

So rapidly had Alvarado moved in his desire to inflict punishment upon the envious enemies of his commander, that the chamberlain, Diego de Ocampo, did not overtake him until far into the Province of Guastecas[8] and already in touch with the outposts of the Jamaican Governor. Gonzalo Dovalle, who afterwards settled in Guatemala and was a persistent enemy of Alvarado, at the head of twenty-two horsemen was visiting the towns on the coast whose savage population had lately been subdued, agitating against Cortes, levying taxes of gold and threatening to hang the Spanish officials left by the Captain General in the Panuco. Upon Alvarado's approach, Dovalle placed his men in ambush but, informed of the trap by a friendly Indian, Alvarado surrounded the Jamaicans and calling the commander to him asked the reason for his warlike preparations, as neither he nor Cortes had any desire to attack the newcomers but rather to help them. Taking a leaf from the book of his politic commander, he politely requested Dovalle and his men to deposit their arms with him as an evidence of good faith, to which the Jamaican agreed, having no choice. Shortly thereafter the chamberlain of Cortes caught up with the column and informing the Captain General of the state of affairs the latter played his rôle of welcoming all his countrymen after his lieutenants had effectually demonstrated his power, as Sandoval had done at Villa Rica, sending orders to return the arms and horses to Dovalle and to leave him free to go his way provided he desisted from molesting the native population.

Meantime the fleet of Garay lay in the mouth of the Panuco River within ten miles of the town of Santisteban which Cortes had founded during his recent pacification of the country. For two months the ships lingered, their captains exchanging threatening notes with Cortes' lieutenant, Pedro de Vallejo, who, emulating Sandoval, showed no fear of superior numbers or armament. This fleet was commanded by Juan de Grijalva who had led the expedition of 1518. Little by little the crews grew impatient at the interminable waiting and the arguments of Vallejo reinforced by tales of the Conquest made way, and the fleet without firing a gun submitted to the jurisdiction of Cortes. Francisco de Garay, who was then some sixty miles distant along the coast in two other ships, came under full sail the moment the news of the defection reached him, only to be confronted with the letter from Charles V, directing him to interfere in no way with the conqueror of Mexico. He agreed to assemble his men and return to Jamaica but his followers refused absolutely and, confronted with this mutiny and the loss of six of his ships, destroyed by a storm, the Governor set out for Mexico where Cortes warmly received him. The greater portion of his men were later incorporated into the Mexican force and Garay's son married the daughter of Cortes' first wife. While the Governor was absent in Mexico his force divided into small groups of five and six, wandering about the country molesting and pilfering the natives, until they rose in revolt, killed many of the strangers and except for the energetic action of Alvarado would have destroyed all of the Spaniards in the province.

The conquest of additional territory was ever the first thought of Cortes, and as soon as the safety of Mexico permitted, late in the year 1523, he returned to his project of adding the nations inhabiting the territory bordering the South Sea,[9] to the Empire of Charles V. Pedro de Alvarado was sent overland to conquer the northern tribes while Cristobal de Olid proceeded by sea to Habana where he obtained a large number of recruits and a great store of supplies for the campaign in Honduras. Of the latter expedition it is sufficient to say that tidings brought to Mexico that Olid had deserted the Captain General for Diego Velasquez motivated Cortes' terrible march overland through the wilderness of Peten.[10]

In his letter to Charles V written from Mexico City on October 15, 1524, the Captain General details his preparations and mentions a letter from Alvarado written from Tehuantepec[11] on January 12, 1524, as being the last word he had heard at that time from the future conqueror of Guatemala, although he was already advised of the alleged rebellion of Olid. Cortes had only a faint idea of the extent of Central America and in his cited letter to the Emperor he wrote: "I consider it certain according to information I have concerning the country and its configuration, that Pedro de Alvarado and Cristobal de Olid will meet unless the strait divides them. Many journeys would have been made to that country and I should have acquired much knowledge of it had not the disturbance occasioned by the arrival of armadas (of rivals) prevented." Alvarado was well equipped, commanding one hundred and twenty cavalry with forty extra horses, three hundred foot-soldiers of whom one hundred and thirty possessed crossbows or muskets, a small number (not more than four hundred) of native auxiliaries and a group of Mexican chiefs. Four small cannon and a large quantity of munitions added greatly to the strength of the column.

The Captain General becoming aware of the ingratitude of Charles V, took pains in this letter to set forth some account of the expense he had personally been put to in the various expeditions of pacification. Of the preparations for the Guatemalan campaign, he wrote as follows:[12] "Your Royal Excellency may consider it certain that the smallest of these expeditions which have just been fitted out has cost me more than five thousand pesos of gold; and that the two under Pedro de Alvarado and Cristobal de Olid have cost me more than fifty thousand pesos[13] without reckoning other charges on my estates which are not carried to the account." It appears that prior to the expedition of Alvarado, Cortes had sent two Spaniards on a reconnaissance who visited the Quiche and Cakchiquel nations of Guatemala[14] and that the latter had sent emissaries to the Captain General offering submission to Charles V. The Quiches, however, a warlike nation allied to the Aztecs and bitter enemies of the Cakchiquels, refused any dealings with the Whites, and it seems improbable that the Spanish scouts would have ventured within the frontiers of the Quiche kingdom. Alvarado bore instructions to secure submission by peaceful means wherever possible but to insist upon the adoption of the Christian religion. He was also to proclaim the Spanish civil laws and to liberate slaves destined for sacrifice. To aid him in the religious phases of his mission, the priests Juan Godinez and Juan Diaz accompanied the column.

En route the Captain was ordered to subdue certain villages of Tehuantepec who had risen against the royal Intendent, Guelamo. A few days were spent in this campaign, the natives being easily pacified, before the column proceeded to the neighbouring Province of Soconusco, sparsely peopled, the Indian population not exceeding fifteen thousand persons. He was received in peace, a small amount of gold collected, and the march continued to Tonala where opposition in force was encountered, in the form of a Quiche army six thousand strong sent by their king to attack the foreigner before he set foot on Quiche soil. These Indians had never seen horses nor artillery before and despite a brave resistance were utterly defeated. Following instructions of Cortes, Alvarado sent a number of the chiefs, taken prisoners during the battle, to carry a message to the Quiche King. He stated his authority gave him the right to subdue by force of arms those who would not willingly pay homage to Charles V and that he regarded their attack on his force as treason since their envoys had lately offered submission to Cortes.[15] However, if the Quiches would now recognize their error and give him free passage through their territory, their late

attitude would be forgiven, but if they persisted he would overthrow and enslave them.

As Alvarado was now approaching the frontier of the Aztec
Empire, his career as a conqueror opened before him with antagonists differing in race, character and customs from the Mexicans.
The inhabitants of Guatemala were largely descended from Maya
stock mixed with the blood of Aztec, Toltec and other northern
races. The total population of the country is in dispute,[16] a French
author inclining to a population of fifteen millions, which seems
to the present writer much too great. The present-day population
of the Republic of Guatemala is slightly in excess of two million
people of whom more than half are of undiluted Indian blood,
descendants of the tribes conquered by Alvarado. The three principal nations of Guatemala, the Quiches, Cakchiquels and Tzutuhils, inhabited the highlands of the continental divide running
parallel and close to the Pacific Coast. This is a healthy and very
productive region where at the time of the Conquest cacao, at once
a beverage reserved for priests and chiefs and a form of currency,
was cultivated. The elevation ranges from three thousand to twelve
thousand feet with a temperate climate, cold in winter, producing
an active and warlike population. The country drops sharply to
the Pacific coastal plain, so that the Tzutuhil kings in their citadel
on Lake Atitlan, a bottomless volcanic bowl, could see the blue
waters of the Pacific far below and fifty miles distant. The scenery,
as Alvarado reported to Cortes, was the most magnificent encountered by the Spaniards since landing in Mexico. Sixteen volcanoes,
alive or extinct, rear their heads above the clouds in a column
marching along the Pacific from Ayutla to the frontier of El Salvador. These volcanoes, quite naturally, were the dwelling-places
of the Indian Gods.

The Quiche nation was divided into three tribes, each composed
of four clans. The dominant clan, that of Cajuek, was descended
from the Demi-God Balaam-Quitze, "the Smiling Tiger." The
capital of the nation was near the present town of Santa Cruz
Quiche,[17] almost due north of Atitlan, while the Cakchiquels early
in the fourteenth century moved from the northwest to settle in
Iximche, now Tecpan, close to and west of Santa Cruz Quiche.
The three principal nations thus were in close touch, although

between the Cakchiquels and the Quiches war had been almost continuous for several centuries. The separation of the Quiches and the Cakchiquels, of the same parent stock, took place about the year A.D. 1000.[18] The former receiving a strain of Aztec blood, had imported the ferocious religion of Huitzilopotchli and sacrificed large numbers of slaves annually in his honour. This custom and the close proximity of the other tribes[19] giving rise to boundary disputes were the principal causes of the wars.[20]

The monarchy of the Quiches was absolute and hereditary but not in the form customary in the Old World. The King who bore the title of "Ahau-Ahpop"[21] shared his power with his brother or cousin occupying the post of "Ahpop-Camaj." To this Prince were confided certain duties and in the absence of the King he became Regent. On the death of the King the Regent succeeded him and the eldest son of the former King became the "Ahpop-Camaj," while the son of the former Regent, who during the life of the King had been the high priest, now stood next in line for the honour of the "Ahpop-Camaj." The House of Cajuek, with rare exceptions, had possessed the throne for the past eight centuries so that the Quiche monarchy was one of the oldest known on the American continent.[22] Both the Quiches and their rivals possessed a remarkably accurate calendar, heritage from the Mayas, and a system of jurisprudence far superior to that of the Aztecs. The weapons and armour employed by the Guatemalans were similar to those which the Spaniards had known in Mexico.

The capital city of the Quiches, then called Utatlan or Gumarcaaj, excited the admiration of the Spaniards by its size and almost impregnable location. Surrounded on all sides by deep cañons, there were only two ways of entry, one by a flight of thirty steep steps easily defended, and the other over a narrow stone-paved causeway crossing the cañon which could be destroyed in a few moments by its defenders. The entry by the causeway was guarded by a fortress four stories in height, an unusual elevation for an Indian structure, built of great stones, while a pyramid, called by the Spaniards the Watch Tower, over one hundred feet high, was located at the top of the staircase entrance. The ruins of this city which still remain show in their extent and size evidences of the energy and engineering skill of the Quiches.[23] Bancroft compares this city to Mexico in wealth and splendour, though the amount of gold amassed by the Quiche Kings was vastly inferior to that of Moctezuma. The ruins of the royal palace are one thousand feet in width by twice that distance long. It was built of cut stone in contrasting and harmonizing colours giving the effect of mosaic. The great building contained barracks, harem, gardens with fountains and a profusion of tropical flowers, baths and miniature lakes as well as the royal apartments. Close around, separated by narrow stone-paved streets running over the uneven surface of the capital, stood the stone palaces of the nobles, only less striking in size and splendour than that of the King, while the houses of the common people were crowded between the palaces and the battlements overlooking the surrounding cañons. At the time of its destruction Utatlan is estimated to have had a population of sixty thousand persons with as many more residing in towns and villages dotting the surrounding hills.

The religion, laws and customs of the Cakchiquels, while similar to those of the Quiches, were more humane, and human sacrifice appears to have been sparingly practised. The Cakchiquel King bore the imposing title "Ahpozotzil" (the Bat King), from his family crest. An associate reigned with him but the succession in this nation appears to have been direct.[24] The associate or "Ahpoxahil" (Prince of the Dancers) led the Cakchiquel armies in war.

The Cakchiquel nation was composed of four clans, descended from the God Hunahpu, one of the "not dead but sleeping" heroes dear to all mankind, awaiting his country's call in an icebound sepulchre high on the Volcan de Agua. In addition to the three principal nations, many other tribes, allied by blood and from time to time conquered by the Quiches or Cakchiquels, divided the country between them. Among them were the Queches, Pokomans, Chortis, Xincas, Manes, Pipiles, Populucas, Lancandons, Chontles and Poponchis.

The war between the Quiches and the Cakchiquels, which broke out about the year 1400, lasted for over sixty years resulting in the triumph of the latter. The Quiches, though retaining their independence, lost much in wealth and manpower and a number of confederate nations, especially in the south and east of the present republic, passed under the sway of the victors.

However, in 1497 a civil war broke out between two branches of the Cakchiquel nation during which the Quiches reconquered portions of their lost provinces and regained their former position as most powerful of the Guatemalan tribes. In the years 1510 and 1512, Moctezuma II sent emissaries to the Guatemalans, striving to bring them into the Aztec confederacy, but no definite treaty appears to have been arranged and none of the nations ever formed part of the Empire. While Moctezuma had communication by sea along the east coast of Central America as far as Colombia, where the imperial emeralds were secured, there was no road between Mexico and Guatemala prior to the arrival of Alvarado. Further south in Nicaragua the inhabitants appeared to have had an understanding with the Aztecs and spoke a Mexican dialect.[25]

As Warren Hastings in India, Tonatiuh found his task rendered easier by the discord between the Indian Kings. Playing one off against the other and aided by the terror caused by his horsemen and artillery, Alvarado conquered the three warlike nations in a campaign of one hundred days.[26] The rapidity of his conquest was the more remarkable since he was not aided by great forces of native allies.

The Conquest was preceded by signs and portents. The sacred Black Stone of Tzataha, an infallible oracle, was broken by an unseen hand and forever silenced. A Cakchiquel prisoner about to be sacrificed by the Quiches exclaimed that he would be avenged by men that were shortly to appear in the country, not dressed Indian fashion but clothed from head to foot in armour that no lance nor arrow could penetrate. These very terrible and cruel men should come shortly and destroy the capital of the Quiche nation and reduce the inhabitants to living as the beasts of the field, and the grandeur of Quiche would be forever past. Thus it was foretold and indeed came to pass. The war between the Quiches and the Cakchiquels broke out again in the year 1513 with great slaughter on both sides, the Cakchiquels capturing the city of their enemies, putting the population to death. In the year 1515 an invasion of locusts, still a plague in Guatemala, laid waste the fields and the capital city of Tecpan was destroyed by fire, while in 1521 and 1522 epidemics of unknown character reduced the population to such an extent that the survivors fled to the mountains, leaving the dead a prey to the buzzards. Among the victims were the Kings of the Cakchiquel nation and the principal warriors, their places being taken by Belehe-Qat as High King or "Ahpozotzil" and Cahi-Imox as his associate.[27] These chiefs, both of whom were very young, were in power when news came of the destruction of the Aztecs, followed shortly thereafter by Cortes' scouts who returned to Mexico accompanied by Cakchiquel ambassadors offering submission. In the months immediately preceding the Conquest the Cakchiquels and Quiches were at war, striving to exterminate each other, while the King of the Tzutuhils, driven from his throne, employed a Cakchiquel army to restore him to power, destroying thirteen towns in the campaign.

Such were the nations Alvarado was to overthrow, energetic, intelligent, ambitious, equally advanced with the Mexicans in the art of war and in some respects a superior people, especially physically. Their fatal weakness was their mutual jealousy and internecine warfare which rendered them a prey, though not easy victims, of the forthright Spanish captain. Cortes had chosen the right man for the job. In the pitiless give and take of Guatemalan warfare there was neither time nor place for politic consideration. The words of the Conqueror paint the story of the Conquest more vividly than is possible after the passage of four centuries. The colours are fresh on his palette and if he chooses his favourite tints, no conqueror has been accused of impartiality.

Of the four letters sent by Alvarado to Cortes at Mexico City after his departure from the capital in December, 1523, two forwarded from Tehuantepec and Soconusco on January 12 and early in February, 1524, have been lost. The remaining two, which appear hereafter, are not found in the standard chroniclers of the Conquest such as Remesal, Fuentes, Jimenez, Vasquez and Juarros, and appear to have been unknown to Bernal Diaz del Castillo. The two later letters were, however, published by Gaspar de Avila[28] and Gonzalo Barcia.[29] Their versions differ slightly in text and spelling and for the sake of accuracy I have followed the excellent translation of Mr. Sedley J. Mackie.[30] The first letter written about April 10, 1524, in Mr. Mackie's translation, reads as follows:

Sir: From Sonconusco I wrote to Your Grace all that had happened to me as far as that place and even something of what was expected to happen further on. And after having sent my messengers to this country, informing them of how I was to come to conquer and pacify the provinces that might not be willing to place themselves under the dominion of His Majesty, I asked of them as his vassals (for as such they had offered themselves to Your Grace) the favour of assistance and passage through their country: that by so doing, they would act as good and loyal vassals of His Majesty and that they would be greatly favoured and supported in all justice by me and the Spaniards in my company; and if not, I threatened to make war on them as traitors rising in rebellion against the service of our lord the Emperor and that as such they would be treated, and that in addition to this, would make slaves of all those who should be taken alive in the war. And having done all this and despatched the messengers, who were men of their own people, I reviewed all my men, both foot and horse. And the next day, on the morning of Saturday, I set out in search of their land, and after marching for three days through uninhabited forest, we pitched our camp and the scouts whom I had sent out captured three spies from a town in their country named Zapotitlan.[31] I asked them what they came for and they told me that they were collecting honey, but it was notorious that they were spies, as it later on appeared. Notwithstanding all this, as I wished to treat them reasonably before compelling them, I gave them another command and requirement as before, and sent them to the chiefs of the said town. To none of my requests did I receive any answer.

Arriving at this town, I found all the roads open and very wide, the highway as well as the crossroads, but the roads that ran to the principal streets were obstructed, and then I understood their evil intentions and that everything was arranged to fight us. There came a few of them sent to me and from a distance they told me I should enter into the town to lodge, intending that they might fight us at their convenience, as it had been ordered. That day I camped near the town until I would be able to reconnoitre the country to see the plans they had. Later that same afternoon they could not conceal their bad intentions and they killed and wounded some of the Indians of my army. When I was informed of this, I sent some of the horsemen to reconnoitre the country and they found many warriors with whom they fought, and that afternoon some horses were wounded.

Next day I went to examine the road by which we had to advance and also saw warriors, and the country was so thickly wooded, cov-

ered with trees and cacao plantations, that it was very favourable
for them and not for us, so I returned to camp. Next day I left with
all my men to enter the town. In the road was a river[32] difficult to cross,
at which the Indians had taken their position, and there, after a
struggle, we defeated them. On the high bank of the river, on a plain,
I waited for the stragglers because the way was very dangerous and
caused much trouble, although I carried the best outfit that could be
had. Being as I have said, on the river bank, they came from many
parts through the woods, and assaulted me again, and we resisted
them for a long while until we had carried all our baggage across.
And, after entering in the houses, we struck down the people, and
continued the pursuit as far as the marketplace and half a league
beyond, afterwards returning to the marketplace to camp. Here we
were two days reconnoitering the country. And at the end of that time
I left for another town called Quezaltenango. That day I crossed two
rivers with very steep, rocky banks, which we passed with much
difficulty, and commenced to climb a mountain pass[33] that was six
leagues in length; half way up I made camp that night. The pass was
so rough that the horses could scarcely climb. Next morning I continued and above a gully I found a woman and a dog sacrificed, which
my interpreter informed me was a challenge. Continuing our march,
we found in a very narrow pass, a stone barricade with strong palings,
but nobody in it. We had just got through the pass with the archers
and infantry in front of me, as the horses had not been able to keep
up with us on account of the roughness of the road, when there
appeared about three thousand or four thousand warriors above a
ravine and struck at the contingent of our friends and caused them to
retreat; then we defeated them. While up there, collecting the people
to rally them, I saw more than thirty thousand men coming towards
us. I thanked God that there we found some plains, and although the
horses were tired and fatigued from the pass, we waited some time
for them [the Indians] to arrive to throw arrows at us; and we
attacked them. As they had never seen horses they showed much
fear, and we made a very good advance and scattered them and many
of them died.

Then we awaited all our people and gathered together, and went to
camp a league away near some springs because there we had no water
and were suffering greatly from thirst, and as we were very tired, any
place was a good site to camp. As the country was flat I took the lead
with thirty horsemen. Many of us had taken along a relay of horses.
The rest of the men came in a body, and then I dismounted to drink

the water. While dismounted and drinking, we saw many warriors approaching and we allowed them to approach as they came over very wide plains; and we defeated them. Here we made another very big advance to where we found people awaiting us, one of them to two horsemen.[34] We continued the pursuit for a full league and they brought us to a mountain and there they faced us, and I put myself in flight with some of the horsemen to draw the Indians to the plains, and they followed us, until reaching the horses' tails. And after I rallied with the horsemen, I turned on them, and here a very severe pursuit and punishment was made. In this affair one of the four chiefs of the city of Utlatan was killed, who was the Captain General of all this country. I returned to the spring and there made camp that night, greatly fatigued, and several Spaniards and horses wounded.

Next day in the morning I left for the town of Quezaltenango,[35] a league away, and after yesterday's punishment I found it empty—not even a single person there. I camped and reorganized and reconnoitered the country, which is as thickly populated as Tlascala and equally cultivated and excessively cold.

At the end of six days that I had been here, one Thursday at noon, a great multitude of people appeared on many sides and, according to what I learned from them, twelve thousand were from this city and surrounding towns and the others they said could not be counted. From the moment I saw them, I put my men in order, and went out to give them battle with ninety horsemen, in the middle of a plain three leagues long. I left men in the camp to guard it and, at a gunshot from the camp and no more, we commenced to crush them and scatter them in all directions and followed them in pursuit for two leagues and a half until all of them were routed and nobody left in front of us. Later we returned against them, and our friends and the infantry made the greatest destruction in the world, at a river. They surrounded a bare mountain where they had taken refuge, and pursued them to the top, and took all that had gone up there. That day we killed and imprisoned many people, many of whom were captains and chiefs and people of importance.

And when the chiefs of this town found that their people were defeated, they took counsel with all the land and called many other provinces to them, and gave tribute to their enemies and induced them to join them, so that all might come together and kill us. And they agreed to send and tell us that they had wished to be friends, and that again they gave obedience to our lord the Emperor, so that I should enter the city of Utlatan,[36] where they afterwards brought me, thinking that they would lodge me there, and that when thus encamped, they would set fire to the town some night and burn us all in it, without the possibility of resistance. And in truth their evil plan would have come to pass but that God our Lord did not see good that these infidels should be victorious over us, for this city is very very strong, and there are only two ways of entering it; one of over thirty steep stone steps and the other by a causeway made by hand, much of which was already cut away, so that that night they might finish cutting it, and no horse could then have escaped into the country. As the city is very closely built and the streets very narrow, we could not have stood it in any way without either suffocating or else falling headlong from the rocks when fleeing from the fire. And as we rode up and I could see how large the stronghold was, and that within it we could not avail ourselves of the horses because the streets were so narrow and walled in, I determined at once to clear out of it on to the plain, although the chiefs of the town asked me not to do so, and invited me to seat myself and eat before I departed, so as to gain time to carry out their plans. But I knew the danger in which we were, and at once sent some men ahead of me to take possession of the causeway and bridge, so that I could get out on to the plain, and the causeway was already in such a condition that one could hardly get over it on horseback, and outside the city were many warriors, and as they saw me pass out on to the plain, they retreated, but not so much that I did not receive much harm from them. But I concealed it all so that I might capture the chiefs who were taking to flight and by the cunning with which I approached them, and through presents which I gave them, the better to carry out my plan, I took them captive and held them prisoners in my camp. But, nevertheless, their people did not cease fighting against me in the neighbourhood and killed and wounded many Indians who had gone out to gather grass. And one Spaniard who was gathering grass, a gunshot from camp, was slain by a stone rolled down the hill. This land is very full of gullies; there are gullies two hundred estados[37] in depth, and, on account of them, one cannot carry on war and punish these people as they deserve.

And seeing that by fire and sword I might bring these people to the service of His Majesty, I determined to burn the chiefs[38] who, at the time that I wanted to burn them, told me, as it will appear in their confessions, that they were the ones who had ordered the war against me and were the ones also who made it. They told me about the way they were to do so, to burn me in the city, and that with this thought (in their minds) they had brought me there, and that they had ordered their vassals not to come and give obedience to our lord the Emperor, nor help us, nor do anything else that was right. And as I knew them to have such a bad disposition towards the service of His Majesty, and to insure the good and peace of this land, I burnt them, and sent to burn the town and to destroy it, for it is a very strong and dangerous place, that more resembles a robbers' stronghold than a city. And to enable me to hunt out these people I sent to the city of Guatemala, which is ten leagues distant from this place, and ordered them on the part of His Majesty to send me some warriors (and this I did so that I could find out what their disposition was, as well as to strike terror into the land), and they were well disposed toward me and agreed to do so, and sent me four thousand men,[39] and with these men and those that were already with me, I made an expedition and chased them and threw them out of the entire country. And seeing the damages which they had suffered, they sent me messengers to tell me that now they wished to be good, and that if they had erred, it had been at the order of their chiefs, and that while their chiefs had been living they dared not do otherwise, but as now their chiefs were dead they prayed me to pardon them, and I spared their lives and ordered them to return to their houses and live as they had done formerly; and this they did, and at the present time I have them in the same condition as they were formerly, at the service of His Majesty. And for greater security I have liberated two sons of the chiefs, whom I placed in their fathers' positions and I believe that they will carry out faithfully all that tends to the service of His Majesty and the good of his lands. And as far as touches the war, I have nothing more at present to relate, but that all the prisoners of war were branded and made slaves, of whom I gave His Majesty's fifth part to the treasurer, Baltasar de Mendoza, which he sold by public auction, so that the payment to His Majesty should be secure.

I would wish Your Grace to know that the country is healthy and the climate temperate, and well populated, with many strong towns, and that this city is well built and wonderfully strong, and has much corn land and many people subject to it, the which, with all the subject towns and neighbourhoods, I have placed under the yoke and in the service of the royal crown of His Majesty.

In this country there is a mountain range of alum, another of copperas and another of sulphur, the best which I have yet seen and with a piece of it which they brought me, without refining or any such process, I made half an arroba of very good gunpowder; but whenever there should be a messenger there will be time for it.

On Monday, April 11, I am leaving for Guatemala, where I mean to stop but a short time, because the town which is situated on the water called Atitlan is at war, and has killed four of my messengers, and I think with the aid of our Lord soon to subdue it to the service of His Majesty.

According to my information I have much to do in the future and I am therefore in haste to winter fifty or one hundred leagues beyond Guatemala, where they tell me, and I have notice from the natives of this land, of marvellous and large buildings and wonderful cities that are there. Also they tell me that five days' journey beyond a large city that is twenty days' journey from here, is the end of this country, and they confirm it. If it is so, I am certain it is the strait.[40] May it please God to give me victory over these infidels so that I may bring them to His service or that of His Majesty. I should not wish to give this account piecemeal, but after everything is finished, because I would have much more to say. The Spaniards of my company, both horse and foot, have conducted themselves so well in the war that they are worthy of great thanks. At present I have nothing more of importance to say except that we are in the wildest country and people one has ever seen, and so that our Lord may give us victory I supplicate Your Grace to ordain that a procession be held in your city of all the priests and friars so that our Lord may help us. We are so far from help that if He does not help us, nobody can. Also be sure to inform His Majesty how we have served him with our persons and our properties at our own cost, for your own conscience' sake and so that His Majesty may grant us privileges. May our Lord protect the magnificent person of Your Grace for as long a time as you desire. From this city of Utlatan, April 11.

As I am on a long voyage and think I will lack horseshoes, if, during the coming summer, Your Grace could provide me with same, it would be very well, and His Majesty will be well served by it. They are now worth here 190 pesos a dozen and so we are trading them and paying for them in gold.[41]

I kiss the hands of Your Grace.

PEDRO DE ALVARADO

The second letter written late in July, 1524, at the time of the founding of the first city of Guatemala, shows Alvarado had changed his tone toward Cortes and thought himself nearly if not absolutely an equal of his chief:

Sir: Of the things that had happened to me up to Utlatan, as well in the war as otherwise, I gave a long account to Your Grace; and now I wish to give you an account of all the lands that I have travelled and conquered and of all other things that have happened to me, and this is:

That I, Sir, left the City of Utlatan and came in two days to this city of Guatemala[42] where I was very well received by its chiefs, that I could not have been better off in our parents' house, and we were so well provided with everything necessary that nothing was lacking. And at the end of eight days that I was in this city, I knew from the chiefs of it that seven leagues from here was another city[43] on a very large lake, and that it made war against this city, and against Utlatan and against all others in their neighbourhood, and that they were very strong on account of the lake and their canoes, and that from there they came out to make night raids on this land; and as the people of this city saw the damage that they received from them, they told me they were good people and in the service of His Majesty and that they did not wish to make war or go against them without my permission, praying me that I should help them. As I told them that I would send to call them on the part of our lord the Emperor and that if they should come I would command them not to make war nor do anything wrong in this land, as they had heretofore done, and if they did not come I would go with them to make war and punish them. I therefore sent them two messengers, natives of this city, whom they killed without any fear.

When I was informed and seeing their wickedness, I left this city to go against them with sixty horsemen and a hundred and fifty foot, in company with the chieftains and people of this land, and we marched so quickly that we arrived in the enemy's land on the same day. And no one came out to receive me in peace or otherwise, and when I was aware of this I started with thirty horsemen through the country to the shores of the lake, and when we came to an inhabited rock, which stood out in the water, we saw a company of men very near us, and I attacked them with the horsemen that were with me, and as we followed in pursuit they got on to a very narrow causeway which led to the rock, where we could not follow on horseback, so I and my companions dismounted, and on foot, together, and at the heels of the Indians, we reached the rock, so that they had no time to break down the bridges, for had they done so we could not have reached them. In the meantime many of my men who had been marching behind me came up to us, and we gained possession of the rock, which was thickly inhabited, but all the people threw themselves into the water to swim to another island. And many of them escaped, because my allies, who were bringing three hundred canoes across the lake, did not arrive soon enough. And that afternoon I left the rock with all my men and we camped in a maize field where we passed the night.

And the next day we commended ourselves to God and set out for the town on ahead of us, which was very strong on account of the many rocks and palisades about it, and we found it deserted. And as they had lost the fortress which they had in the lake, they did not dare to face us on land, although a few of them waited for us at the end of the town; but owing to the roughness of the ground, which I have already mentioned, no more people were killed. We encamped there about midday, and commenced to reconnoitre the country, and we captured some of the native Indians, and I sent off three of them as messengers to their chiefs, advising them that they should come and render obedience to His Majesty and submit themselves to the Imperial Crown and to me in His Majesty's name, or otherwise I should still carry on the war and follow them and seek them in the mountains. These chiefs replied to me that hitherto their land had never been broken into nor entered by force of arms, and that since I have forced an entrance they would be glad to serve His Majesty in any way I might direct them, and soon afterwards they came to place themselves at my orders, and I gave them to understand the greatness and power of our lord the Emperor, and that they should appreciate that for all that had passed, I, in His Royal name, would pardon them, and that from now on they should behave themselves and not make war against anybody in the neighbourhood, as all were now vassals of His Majesty; so I dismissed them, leaving them safe and peaceful, and returned to this city. At the end of three days after my arrival there, all the chiefs, principal people and captains of the said lake came to me with presents and told me that now they were our friends and considered themselves fortunate to be vassals of His Majesty and relieved of hardships, wars and differences that they had amongst themselves. And I received them very well and gave them some of my jewels and sent them back to their country with much affection, and they are the most pacific that are in this land.[44]

While I was in this city, many chiefs of other provinces of the south coast came to give obedience to Their Majesties saying that they wished to be their vassals and did not wish to war with anybody, and that therefore I should receive them as such and favour them and maintain them in justice. And I received them very well, as was proper, and told them that they would be favoured and helped by me in the name of His Majesty.

And they told me of another province that is called Yscuintepeque[45] that is somewhat more inland, that would not allow them to come to give obedience to His Majesty, and not only this, but that other provinces of that part of the land were well disposed and wished to come in peace, and that those people would not allow them to pass, asking them where they were going, and saying they were crazy and that they should allow me to go there and then all would make war on me. And as I was assured that this was so, as well by those provinces as by the chiefs of this city of Guatemala, I left with all my people, both foot and horse, and remained encamped for three days in a desert. Next morning when we entered the outskirts of the said town, that is very heavily wooded, we found all the roads closed and very narrow—really only pathways—because they did not trade with anybody and had no open road. And I sent the crossbowmen ahead because the horsemen could not fight there on account of the many marshes and wooded thickets. And it rained so much that on this account their watchmen and spies had returned to the town; and as they did not think I would arrive amongst them that day, they were somewhat careless and did not know of my sally until I was in the town amongst them; and when I entered, all the warriors were huddled together in houses because it rained so much, and when they wanted to form they had no time, although some of them still waited and wounded some Spaniards and many of the friendly Indians that were with me, and because of the thick woods and rain, they escaped into the forest, so I had no opportunity to do them any damage except to burn their town. And then I sent messengers to the chiefs, telling them that they should come to give obedience to Their Majesties and to me in their name, and if not, I would do great damage to their land and lay waste their maize fields. They came and gave themselves as vassals of His Majesty, and I received them and ordered them to be good in the future; and I remained eight days in this town. And to this place there came many other towns and provinces in peace, who offered themselves as vassals of our lord the Emperor.

And wishing to explore the country and know its secrets so that His Majesty may be better served and possess and rule more lands, I determined to leave here, and went to a town called Atiepac,[46] where I was received by the chiefs and natives who are of a different language and race; and at sunset without any reason it was suddenly depopulated and cleared out, and one could not find a man in all the town. And in order to prevent the rigour of winter catching me there and impeding my journey, I left them, and passed on without stopping, taking all provisions and equipment with my army because my wish was to explore a hundred leagues further, and on the way accomplish whatever might happen until I had explored them fully, and on the return fight them and pacify them. And the following day I left and went to another town called Tacuylula and here they did the same as the people of Atiepac, receiving me in peace and hiding an hour afterward. And I left here and went to another town which is called Taxisco, which is very strong and has many people, and was received as by the previous ones; and I slept there that night. And next day I left for another very large town that is called Nacendelan, and fearing those people as I did not understand them, I left ten horsemen as a rear guard and ten more with the baggage, and continued my march. And I might have gone two or three leagues from the said town of Taxisco when I heard that warriors had come out and fought with the rear guard and had killed many friendly Indians and taken a large part of the baggage and all the strings of the bowmen and all the iron that I carried for the war, and they could not resist them. And at once I sent Jorge de Alvarado, my brother, with forty or fifty horsemen, to look for all that they had taken, and he found many armed people in the fields, and he fought with them and defeated them, and could recover nothing that had been lost because the clothes had already been torn in pieces and each one wore a loin cloth of it in the war. And having arrived at this town of Nacendelan, Jorge de Alvarado returned, because all the Indians had fled to the mountains. And from here I again sent Don Pedro with foot-soldiers that he might search the mountains for them and see if he would be able to bring them to the service of His Majesty, and never could anything be done on account of the great thickness of the forests, and so he returned. And I sent Indians of their own country to them as messengers with requirements and orders, and warning them that if they did not come I would make them slaves, and with all this they did not wish to come, neither the messengers nor themselves.

And at the end of eight days that I had been in this town of Nacendelan, there came a people in peace called Pasaco,[47] which was on the road by which we had to go, and I received them and gave them of what we had and I entreated them that they be good. And next morning I left for this town, and at its entrance found the roads closed and many stakes thrust in, and when I was entering into the town I saw certain Indians cutting a dog in quarters in the manner of a sacrifice, and in the said town they made an uproar, and we saw a great multitude of the people of the country, and we attacked them, breaking them up until we drove them from the town, and we followed them for another town called Mopicalco[48] and was received in exactly the same way as in the others, and when I arrived at the town I did not find a living person. And from here I left for another town called Acatepeque where I found nobody, it being entirely abandoned rather.

And following my idea, which was to explore the said hundred leagues, I left for another town called Acaxual,[49] which is on the coast of the South Sea, and when I had arrived within half a league of the said town, I saw the fields full of its warriors with their plumage and insignias and with their offensive and defensive arms, in the middle of a plain where they were awaiting me, and I arrived within a bowshot of them, and there I waited until all my people had arrived, and after we had gathered, I went about half a bowshot towards the warriors and there was no movement or alteration in them that I could tell, and it seemed to me that they were somewhat near to a woods where they could shelter from me, and I ordered that all my people retreat (who were a hundred horsemen and a hundred and fifty foot, and about five or six thousand friendly Indians), and so we were retreating, and I remained in the rear guard to make the people retire. The pleasure they had on seeing me retire was so great that they followed me, even up to the horses' tails—the arrows that they shot passed in front of us. And all this took place on a plain where neither for them nor us was there anything to stumble over. And when I had retreated a quarter of a league to where each one had to fight instead of running away, I turned on them with all my people and broke through their ranks. And the destruction that we made amongst them was so great that in a short time none were left alive, because they came so heavily armed that those who fell to the ground could not get up, and their arms are corselets of cotton three fingers thick, reaching to their feet, and arrows and long lances, and when falling, the foot-soldiers killed all of them. In this encounter many Spaniards were wounded, myself amongst the rest. They shot an arrow at me that passed through my leg and entered my saddle, from which wound I remained lame, as one leg remained shorter than the other a good four fingers.[50] And I was forced to remain five days in this town to cure our wounds.

And at the end of that time I left for another town called

Tacuxalco,[51] to where I sent as scouts Don Pedro and other companions, who caught two spies who told us that ahead were many warriors of that town and others nearby, awaiting us, and to make certain, they went forward to see the said people, and saw a great multitude of them. At this time Gonzalo de Alvarado, who was leading the advance, arrived with forty horsemen, because I was coming, as I have said, suffering from a wound, and he made front until we had all arrived. As soon as we all had arrived and all the forces were gathered, I mounted a horse as best I could, in order to be better able to arrange the attack. And I saw that they had a body of warriors ready and formed in battle against the enemy, and I sent Gomez de Alvarado with twenty horsemen to attack them on the left hand, and Gonzalo de Alvarado with thirty horsemen on the right hand, and Jorge de Alvarado should attack them with the rest of the army. To see them from afar was terrifying, because most of them had lances thirty palms long, all raised high. And I mounted a hill to better see what happened and I saw that all the Spaniards arrived at within a quoit's length of the Indians and that neither the Indians fled nor the Spaniards attacked, so that I was afraid of the Indians who so dared to wait. The Spaniards had not attacked them because they thought that a field that lay between them was a marsh, and after they saw it was firm and good, they attacked the Indians and defeated them, and were following in pursuit through the town for more than a league; and here they made a great massacre and punishment. And as the people thereafter saw that we defeated them in the plain, they determined to hide and leave us the towns. And in this town I rested two days, and at the end of that time I left for a town called Miaguaclam,[52] and also they left for the woods like the others. And from here I left for another town called Atehuan[53] and there the chiefs of Cuxcaclan sent me their messengers to give obedience to Their Majesties and to say they wished to be his vassals and be good. Thus they gave their obedience to me in Their Majesties' name, and I received them, thinking that they would not lie like the others. And arriving at this city of Cuzcaclan[54] I found many Indians who received me, and the whole town empty. And while we were making camp, there did not remain a man of them in the town, and all went to the hills. And as I saw this, I sent my messengers to the chiefs there to tell them that they behaved badly, and to understand that they had given obedience to His Majesty and to me in his name, assuring them that if they came I would not make war against them nor take their property, but merely bring them to the service of God and His Majesty.

They sent me word they did not know either of them, that they did not wish to come, and that if I wanted anything from them, they were there waiting with their arms. And when I saw their evil intentions, I sent them an order and requirement on the part of the Emperor, in which I required and ordered that they should not break the peace nor revolt, as they had already given themselves as his vassals, and if not, I would proceed against them as rebellious traitors and rebels against the service of his Majesty, and that I would make war against them, and all that were taken alive would be slaves and would be branded, and that if they were loyal, they would be favoured and protected by me as vassals of His Majesty. And to this, neither the messengers returned, nor was there any answer from them. And as I saw their wickedness, and because that country should not remain without punishment, I sent the army to the woods and mountains to look for them, who found the warriors and fought with them, and Spaniards and friendly Indians were wounded. And after all this, a principal of this city was made prisoner, and for greater justification I returned him again with another order, and they answered the same as before. And then, as I saw this, I proceeded against them and against the others that had made war against me, and called them by proclamation, and still they would not come, and as I saw their rebelliousness, and the proceedings were closed, I sentenced them, as traitors, to death, both the chiefs of these provinces and all others that had been taken during the war, and might be taken henceforth, until such time that they would give obedience to His Majesty, should be slaves and be branded. And that from them and from their value, they should pay eleven horses that had been killed in conquering them, and all those that might thereafter be killed, and for the arms and other necessary things for such a conquest. After these Indians of this said city of Cuxcaclan I was for seventeen days, and never by the expeditions I ordered to be made, nor the messengers I sent them, as I have told, could I attract them, on account of the great thickness of the woods and the great mountains and broken ground and other great powers that they had.

Here I learnt of very great countries inland, cities of stone and mortar,[55] and learnt from the natives that this land has no end, and to conquer it, as it is large and of very great cities, much time is required, and on account of the rigorous winter that was beginning, I did not go farther to conquer, but rather decided to return to this city of Guatemala, and to pacify, while returning, the country that I had left behind. And so I did, and laboured with them, but never could attract

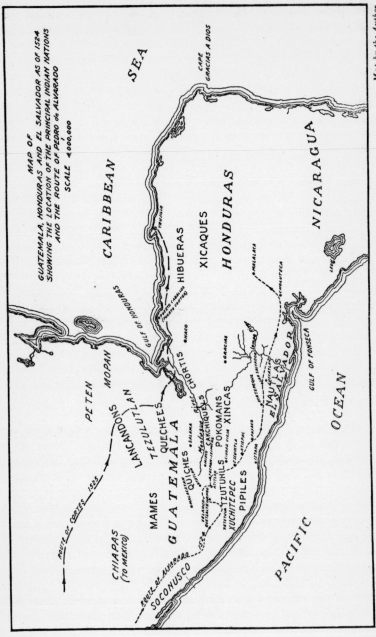

MAP OF
GUATEMALA, HONDURAS AND EL SALVADOR AS OF 1524
SHOWING THE LOCATION OF THE PRINCIPAL INDIAN NATIONS
AND THE ROUTE OF PEDRO de ALVARADO
SCALE 1,000,000

CARIBBEAN SEA

CAPE
GRACHAS A DIOS

NICARAGUA

HONDURAS

XICAQUES

HIBUERAS

GULF OF HONDURAS

TRUJILLO

PUERTO CABALLOS
(PUERTO CORTES)

NACO

GRACIAS

CHORTIS

RIVER

MOPAN

PETEN

LANCANDONS

TEZULUTLAN

QUECHEES

QUICHES

MAMES

GUATEMALA

CHIAPAS
(TO MEXICO)

SOCONUSCO

ROUTE OF ALVARADO 1524

CAKCHIQUELS

POKOMANS

TZUTUHILS

XUCHITEPEC

PIPILES

XINCAS

MALALACA

CHOLUTECA

EL
SALVADOR

NAU

GULF OF FONSECA

PACIFIC OCEAN

ROUTE OF CORTES 1525

Map by the Author

them to the service of His Majesty, because all this southern coast where I went, is densely wooded and the mountains are near, where they have a refuge. So it is that I am come to this city on account of the heavy rains, where, for the better conquest and pacification of this land, so great and so thickly inhabited, I made and built in the name of His Majesty a Spanish city[56] which is called the city of Our Lord Santiago, because this is the centre of all the country, and there are more and better arrangements for the said conquest and pacification, and to populate the surrounding country. And I elected two Alcaldes Ordinarios and four Regidores, as Your Grace will see by the election.

At the end of these two coming winter months,[57] which are the most rigorous of all, I will leave from this city in quest of the Province of Tepalan that is fifteen days' journey from here towards the interior, which, according to my information, is a city as large as that of Mexico, of large buildings of rough stone and mortar, and flat roofed. And apart from this there are many others, and four or five of them have come here to me to give obedience to His Majesty and they say that one of them has thirty thousand inhabitants. I do not wonder at it because, as the towns of this coast are so large, the interior of the country may have what they say. This coming summer, God willing, I expect to go forward two hundred leagues, where I think His Majesty will be well served and his estate augmented. And Your Grace will have news of other new matters. From that city of Mexico to where I have travelled and conquered there are four hundred leagues, and, believe it Your Grace, that this land is more populated and has more people than all the lands that Your Grace has governed up to now.

In this country we have found a mountain range where there is a volcano that is the most terrifying thing ever seen, that throws from its mouth stones as large as a house, burning in living flames, and when they fall they break in pieces and cover all the mountain with fire.

Sixty leagues beyond this we saw another volcano, which threw out very terrifying smoke that rose to the sky and which has a width or circumference of half a league. Nobody can drink the waters of any of the rivers that come down from there because they are sulphurous, and there is specially one large river which comes from there, very beautiful and so hot that it could not be crossed by certain people of my company who were making a certain raid. They went to look for a ford and they found another, cold river that entered into this one, and there where they joined they found a temperate ford where they could cross.

Of the things of these parts there is not more to advise Your Grace, but that the Indians tell me that from this southern sea to that of the north there is a winter's and a summer's travel. As the Indians say so it is of course to be understood that the journey is made on foot.

Your Grace gave me the honour of the Lieutenancy of this city, and I helped to gain it and defended it when I was there, with the danger and suffering that Your Grace knows, and if I might have gone to Spain, for what I have served His Majesty he would have confirmed me in it and granted me other favours. They tell me that His Majesty has disposed of it, which does not surprise me, as he has no notice of me, and for this, nobody is to blame but Your Grace for not having given an account to His Majesty of how I have served him since you sent me here. I pray Your Grace to give him an account of who I am and of how I have served His Majesty in these parts, and where I am and what I have conquered recently, and the will that I have to serve him, and will have in the future, and how, in his service, I am lamed in one leg, and of how little return I and these hidalgos[58] that are in my company have received up to the present and the little profit that we have made so far.

May Our Lord prosperously increase the life and very magnificent estate of Your Grace for a long time.[59]

From this city of Santiago, the 28th day of July of 1524.

PEDRO DE ALVARADO.

The burning of the Cakchiquel Kings was not an unusual punishment in the sixteenth century. The same generation had sent Savonarola to the flames for a purely academic rebellion and death by burning was a common sentence in Europe for the next two centuries. Moreover Alvarado had but seized the weapon forged by the Quiche Kings for the extermination of the Spaniards. The invader's statement that the Kings had plotted to burn their city when he and his men were asleep in the palace is confirmed by native historians of the Conquest. The Quiche Prince, Cailil-Balaam, attending a council of war after the battle of Xelahuh,[60] proposed that the invincible strangers should be invited to the capital, honours showered upon them and submission tendered and then while they slept the city set afire. To the desperate minds of the Quiche chiefs the loss of their capital would be amply compensated by the destruction of the "Donadus" (Children of the Sun).[61] The narrow streets and thatched roofs of the city of Utatlan lent themselves admirably to the plan which was instantly decided upon. The women and children were sent to neighbouring villages while the warriors and slaves filled the houses surrounding the royal palace with bundles of dry wood and reeds. On the appointed night the warriors would surround the city and a Spaniard escaping from the flames would break his neck falling into the surrounding cañons or be impaled on a lance point of volcanic glass.

All being in readiness the Quiche ambassadors stood before Alvarado in Xelahuh, tongues in their cheeks and honey on their lips, inviting the Captain General to visit the capital of their Kings.[62] Alvarado, delighted and apparently suspecting nothing, hastened to accept and set out for Utatlan on the following day accompanied by many Xelahuh warriors really or outwardly reconciled to the invaders. One of these overhearing details of the plot on his arrival in the capital, gave Alvarado warning, although the aspect of the city, the absence of women, the furtive demeanour of the courtiers and a half-completed breach in the causeway had already aroused Spanish suspicions. Scarcely had he arrived than Alvarado determined to make his way out of the trap by force if necessary. Politic for the moment he declined an invitation to an immediate feast stating that the horses were sacred animals which would be infuriated if they were kept overnight within walls and that he must first see to their comfort in the meadows beyond the cañons. The army spent the night in the open and on the morrow when the chiefs approached to repeat their treacherous invitation they were seized as Alvarado relates. Some writers[63] have supposed that the Kings were imprisoned under a promise that their lives would be spared if a great ransom were paid. According to this story, which formed one of the charges against Alvarado in his trial in Mexico City in 1529, after the treasure was delivered the Kings were executed. The charge, however, was triumphantly combated by the Captain General who showed clearly that the execution took place on the day after the capture, as was logical, as the effect would have been entirely lost if the attempt at burning the Spanish army and the retribution were not almost simultaneous.

So impressed was Alvarado by the treacherous nature of his antagonists that on entering the city of Guatemala, where he was very well received, he feared another trap, and scarcely was he lodged in the palace of the High King than he appeared before the chiefs asking the reason for their meditated treachery, pointing out that he had seen the mutilated bodies of many Indians lying beside the road on his entry into the city, which he took, in accordance with the Quiche custom, for challenging sacrifices. The astounded King, fearful lest he arouse the wrath of this superior being, replied pacifically that the dead were Tzutuhil warriors killed in an attack on the city the night before and that the good faith of the Cakchiquels was abundantly proven by their contingents which joined the Mexican allies in hunting down fugitive bands of Quiche warriors. Mollified, Alvarado returned to his headquarters, which, however, he moved from the palace assigned to him to a strong position on the outskirts of the city, more susceptible of defence.

When the Captain General returned to Tecpan, Guatemala, after the campaign against the Tzutuhils referred to in the first paragraphs of his second letter, an episode occurred regarding which partisan historians have written violently conflicting versions. A Cakchiquel Prince had as wife the maiden Xuchil. Struck by her beauty, Alvarado sent for her on the pretext that he wished information regarding the cities along the South Sea, and imprisoned her in his palace.[64] The husband finding that words and even tears would not free his bride, made Alvarado a gift of a large amount of gold which the Spaniard accepted but did not release the princess. So runs one version, while Alvarado, testifying in his own defence, said that Xuchil was neither young nor a princess but a slave of some fifty years of age, captured from one of the southern tribes and for that reason he sent for her to obtain information about her native country. He added naïvely that had the woman been young and of high rank it would not have been necessary for him to kidnap her as it was well known that the Indians willingly gave their wives and daughters to the Spaniards. Whatever the truth of the story, the arbitrary acts of the triumphant soldiery sowed doubt and discontent, the seed of rebellion, in the minds of the heretofore docile Cakchiquels.

FOOTNOTES FOR CHAPTER SEVEN

[1] December 1523.

[2] Bancroft, *History of the Pacific States,* p. 119, states that while on this expedition Alvarado reached the Pacific Ocean and wading in waist deep, claimed the water and any coasts washed thereby, for Spain.

[3] The regions pacified by Alvarado and Orozco are both within the limits of the present Mexican State of Oaxaca.

[4] By the Spanish custom, towns had two Mayors with equal and joint powers.

[5] The present Mexican State of Tamaulipas.

[6] This territory covered parts of the present Mexican State of Chiapas.

[7] In the present Republic of Guatemala.

[8] The Huasteca region of the Mexican Gulf Coast in the States of Vera Cruz and Tamaulipas.

[9] Central America.

[10] Olid was murdered by Francisco de las Casas in Naco, Honduras, in 1524.

[11] A town situated on the isthmus of the same name in Mexico.

[12] Folsom, *Despatches of Cortes to Charles V,* p. 402.

[13] The Guatemalan historian, following Prescott's calculations (see footnote 4, Chap. IV) estimates the cost of these two expeditions to Cortes at 535,000 Guatemalan pesos of 1880, the year in which Milla wrote. This would be equivalent to $267,000 in United States currency. The present writer believes, however, that the first cost of these expeditions in United States currency was about $80,000.

[14] Folsom, *Despatches of Cortes to Charles V,* p. 405.

[15] In this Alvarado was mistaken as the Quiche nation did not submit prior to the Conquest.

[16] Genet and Chelbatz, *Histoire des Peuples Mayas-Quiches,* p. 16.

[17] The Quiche name of their capital at the time of the Conquest was "Gumar-kaaj," which Alvarado's Mexican warriors translated Utatlan and it appears thus in the letters of Cortes.

[18] Genet and Chelbatz, *Histoire des Peuples Mayas-Quiches,* p. 210.

[19] The Quiches appear to have settled in this region since about the sixth century while the Cakchiquels of Toltec extraction had come at some later period up the valley of the great river, Usumacinta, from the Gulf coast of Mexico. This little-known river, the largest between the Mississippi and the Orinoco, drains the almost unexplored forests of Peten and Chiapas and forms a large part of the border between Mexico and Guatemala.

[20] Rodas y Villacorta, *Manuscrito de Chichicastenango.*

[21] "The Dark Lord."

[22] "While it is true that about the sixth century of our era, the Quiches found themselves at the crest of their material and spiritual wave—whereat their civilization and magnificence of life rivalled that of the Oriental splendours and exotic luxuries of ancient Asiatic Empires—it is equally true that even up to the time of the Conquest, they retained power and grandeur greater, and skill

in arts, science and affairs of government more profound, than those possessed
by their contemporary races the Aztec to the north, the Incas to the further
south, and the Mayas to the east,—the only three peoples then on this continent who were in any just manner to be compared with them." *Anales de la
Sociedad de Geografia e Historia de Guatemala,* March 1926.

[23] Bancroft, *History of the Pacific States,* p. 643.

[24] Brasseur de Bourbourg, *Histoire des Nations Civilisées de l'Amérique
Central.*

[25] According to tradition Nicaragua was conquered by the eighth Aztec Emperor, Ahuitzotl. Milla, *Historia de la America Central,* p. 27.

[26] Equal to the conquest of Roumania by Field Marshal von Mackensen.

[27] *Annals of the Cakchiquels.*

[28] "La cuarta relacion q' Fernado Cortes . . . envio al muy alto y muy potentissimo invictissimo Señor don Carlos," printed at Toledo by Gaspar de Avila,
October 20, 1525.

[29] *Historiadores primitivos de las Indias Occidentales,* Mexico City, 1479.

[30] *Documents and Narratives concerning the Discovery and Conquest of Latin
America,* The Cortes Society, New York, 1925.

[31] Zapotitlan was situated in the present Department of Retalhuleu. At the
time of the Conquest it was inhabited by Quiches, and it was here that Alvarado
first came in contact with that tribe.

[32] The Samala River.

[33] Santa Maria de Jesus. It is on the present highway from the coast to Quezaltenango. Up to this time Alvarado had been marching through a tropical country
at an elevation above the sea of only a few hundred feet.

[34] The meaning of this passage is obscure. Alvarado is possibly illustrating
the bravery of the Indians.

[35] Quetzaltenango, which is an Aztec name applied to this place by the
Mexican Indians accompanying Alvarado, was called in language of the country,
Tzakaha. Its altitude is about eight thousand feet. When Alvarado surmounted
the pass, he had reached the great interior plateau of Guatemala, varying in
height from five thousand to eight thousand feet above sea level, and dotted
with volcanic peaks and mountain ranges as high as thirteen thousand feet.

[36] The capital of the Quiches, called Utlatan by Alvarado, is now known as
Utatlan.

[37] An estado is equal to slightly over five and one-half feet.

[38] Oxib-Queh and Belehe-Tzy, the two Kings of the Quiches.

[39] In the *Annals of the Cakchiquels,* four hundred.

[40] Ever since the discovery of the South Sea by Vasco Nuñez de Balboa in
1513, the Spaniards had been looking for a strait connecting it with the Atlantic.

[41] Since there is no record of merchants accompanying the army and as iron
was not found in Guatemala, it is evident that some canny soldiers foresaw the
opportunity of trading with their fellows and loaded slaves with the metal. The
legionaires were not regularly enlisted soldiers but rather gentlemen adventurers.

[42] Tecpan Guatemala.

[43] Diaz del Castillo, *Conquête de la Nouvelle-Espagne,* p. 576.

[44] Atitlan is the Nahua name given to the capital of the Tzutuhils. It was
located on the south shore of the lake of the same name. Practically all traces
of the ancient site have disappeared. The modern town of Atitlan is near the
place.

[45] There is no record of the Tzutuhils ever having rebelled against the Spaniards.

[46] Probably the modern Esquintla.

[47] Here the expedition crossed the present Guatemala-El Salvador frontier.

[48] Nahuizalco, near the present city of Santa Anna.

[49] Like many other Indian towns it has disappeared. At Atiepac, Alvarado entered the country of the Pipiles, a branch of the Nahuan or Mexican people.

[50] Juarros says that ever thereafter Alvarado wore a built-up shoe with a cork sole four inches thick, but no other writer mentions this and the Captain General's subsequent activity belies it.

[51] This place was at or near the present port of Acajutla, one of the principal ports of Salvador.

[52] The ruins of this town, which was very large and important at the time of the Conquest, are about one-half of a mile from the present town of Sonsonate.

[53] Atehuan is today called Ateos. Here, Alvarado entered the government of Cuzcatlan.

[54] Cuzcaclan, or Cuzcatlan, is a Nahuan name. It was the capital of the large and powerful tribe of Pipiles, of Nahuan or Mexican origin, which at that time ruled the country between the rivers Paz and Lempa. It was situated about five miles to the south of the present city of San Salvador.

[55] Probably Copan in Honduras.

[56] The first capital of Guatemala was founded at Iximche on July 25, 1524.

[57] The rainy season which lasts in Guatemala from May to October is known as winter and the dry season as summer.

[58] Noblemen, here used as gentlemen.

[59] Captain Bernardo de Vargas Machuca, the author of *Milicia y Descripcion de las Indias* printed in Madrid in 1599, wrote in 1612 a refutation of the strictures of Las Casas against the conduct of the Spaniards in the conquest of Latin America contained in his *Brevissima Relacion*.

[60] Bancroft, *History of the Pacific States,* p. 633, states that this word means "Governed by Ten"; that the city had ten chiefs, each of whom possessed eight thousand houses, giving the city a population of over three hundred thousand which appears exaggerated to the present writer.

[61] A corruption of the Mexican word "Tonatiuh," Alvarado's nickname, which the Quiches heard from the Aztec auxiliaries.

[62] It appears that at about this time Alvarado received the commission of Captain General of Guatemala from Cortes, as in his second letter he makes definite mention of such appointment.

[63] Bancroft, *History of the Pacific States,* p. 648.

[64] In the Republic of El Salvador.

VIII

PACIFICATION

July 1524 — July 1528

WHEN Alvarado returned on July 21, after an absence of forty-five days, from the conquest of territory comprised within the present Republic of El Salvador described in the latter portion of his second letter to Cortes, he was ready to found a capital for the new province and with a view to central location, selected a site immediately adjacent to the Cakchiquel capital. The city as planned was located in a corn-field from which it took the name of Iximche, the Cakchiquel word for corn. Tecpan Guatemala, deprived of its rulers and a large part of its population during the subsequent revolt, dwindled to a village now known as Tecpan. The etymology of the word Guatemala has long been in dispute, over nineteen definitions, some of them ridiculous in the extreme, having been advanced. The word, however, appears to derive from the Cakchiquel name for the Volcan de Agua (water volcano), "Guhatezmalha."[1] The most prevalent though erroneous version of the derivation of the name is that it is a corruption of the Mexican Indian words "Cuauh" and "Temalli," meaning dead tree. Others have claimed that Guatemala in one or another Indian language meant "forest," "captive eagle," "the place of pines," "milk tree," and "spring of yellow oil." Alvarado clearly wrote Guatemala in the present spelling while the scribes of the newly founded city[2] occasionally wrote Goathemala.

On July 25, 1524, St. James' Day, the army was drawn up on parade on the site selected and after a solemn High Mass, celebrated by Father Godinez, the city was formally declared founded. Alvarado using his authority as Captain General and Lieutenant Governor, appointed Diego de Roxas and Captain Baltasar de Mendoza as joint Mayors, and as Aldermen the Knight Pedro

Puertocarrero, Hernan Carrillo, Juan Perez Dardon and Domingo de Zubiarreta. The trampled cornfield with only a Cross and a few hastily erected wooden huts to represent its future glories was solemnly given the high sounding name of "Muy Noble e Muy Leal Ciudad de Santiago de los Caballeros de Guatemala," (the very noble and very loyal City of St. James of the Knights of Guatemala). No sooner had his soldiers become settlers and land-owners than a multitude of complaints, demands and importunities vexed the not over-patient Captain General. He was to find that the art of governing was much more difficult than the conduct of headlong campaigns in which he was so proficient. A town crier being needed, one was selected by lot, who refused to obey on the pretext that he did not know the art, until threatened with one hundred lashes, whereupon he sulkily asked for lessons and agreed to serve.[3] The new city, however, did not prosper. It was too high, too exposed, too cold, distant from the mines, from suitable timber and difficult to defend.

Shortly after his return from Salvador, Alvarado levied a heavy tax payable in gold upon the Cakchiquel nation, stating that his Imperial master would be wroth if his new vassals did not display in a concrete manner, their gratitude for receiving the protection of Spain. The Kings hastened to comply, sending messengers throughout the kingdom and setting the example by despoiling themselves of their personal treasures even to the gold rings, symbolic of their sovereignty, worn in the royal noses. However willing the tribute, the amount collected was small and Alvarado resorted to threats. A Cakchiquel priest rendered envious by the prestige of the Christian religion and determined to restore the supremacy of his Gods at all costs, appeared before the distracted monarchs, hands raised high above his head, crying that he was the personification of the lightning and as such would reduce the Christians to cinders. The population must be ready to leave at once and when the voice of thunder reverberated through the streets, Kings and commoners alike should make for the depths of the forest across the river. He would do the rest on the following day.[4] The canny cleric was running little risk in this part of the prophecy as during July and August thunderstorms are nightly occurrences in the hills of Guatemala. Despite the overwhelming evidences of the power of the White Man's God as exemplified in the prowess of his believers, the Bat King retained sufficient faith in Hunahpu to risk the expedient. On the night of the twenty-sixth of August the city was evacuated and at daybreak the Spanish patrols coming from their nearby town to water their horses in

Arms of the City of St. James of the Knights of Guatemala.

the river, stared in surprise and suspicion at the deserted city. No smoke rose from the houses, no one moved in the streets. But the Cakchiquels were deceived; the sun arose in majesty, shone throughout a cloudless day and sank peacefully to rest. The promised lightning had not destroyed the impious invaders who, per-

turbed by the desertion but outwardly calm, remained in Iximche.
Alvarado waited ten days, sending friendly messages to the Kings
asking for the return of the people to their homes, but in vain.
The Cakchiquels replied that they were determined to fight to the
last and, calling the nation to arms, commenced a bloody war
against the Christians. These hitherto quiet people proved the most
dangerous enemies found by the Spaniards in Guatemala. From
all sides and at all hours the Spaniards were attacked, stragglers
cut off and patrols overwhelmed. To add to his difficulty, Alvarado had dismissed his Mexican auxiliaries laden with presents
just prior to the rebellion. The Cakchiquels sent embassies to the
Tzutuhils and Quiches asking their aid against the invader, but
the latter nations, blinded by their desire for revenge, joined the
Spaniards, taking the Cakchiquel armies in the rear. This turn of
fortune greatly aided Alvarado, giving his men much needed rest
and strengthening his position as the rivals destroyed each other.
The Cakchiquels dug pits and trenches before their battle positions
in which sharpened poison stakes were planted. Covered with
leaves and grass, these proved death traps to the Spaniards, many
horses and men being impaled thereon. As the Christians charged
the Cakchiquels loosed clouds of arrows shouting, "Here is the
gold you wanted, Children of the Sun."

Unable with his small force to maintain his base at Iximche
while engaged in punitive expeditions, Alvarado abandoned the
town in December 1524, moving his headquarters to a site given
by the chroniclers of the Conquest as Xepau. The location of this
town, which had only a fleeting existence, is not exactly known,
but it is supposed to have been in the territory of the Tzutuhils
then allied with the Europeans, somewhere in the vicinity of Lake
Atitlan. Shortly after the removal to Xepau, Alvarado received a
welcome reinforcement of two hundred Spaniards sent by Cortes
as the Conqueror of Mexico set out on his march to Honduras.
Three months thereafter another group of equal size arrived,
attracted by reports of great treasure to be won in the new country
and despairing of fortune in Mexico where continual quarrels
between Cortes and the newly arrived royal officials made life
difficult for the settlers.

With the assistance of the newcomers, Alvarado was able to

make an end of the Cakchiquel rebellion and proceeded against the Pokomans, a strong tribe allied to his late antagonists. The Pokoman citadel was Mixco, situated on an almost impregnable height in the valley of the Motagua, the principal river of Atlantic drainage in Guatemala. This stronghold, the ruins of which still remain, was built on a peninsula overlooking the junction of the Pixcayatl and the Motogua. On three sides the battlements hung over space, leaving an entrance over a strip of land so narrow that not more than two invaders could approach abreast.[5] Alvarado sent his brother, Gonzalo, at the head of ninety Spaniards and two thousand auxiliaries to take the fortress. Finding the position too strong for a direct attack, Gonzalo de Alvarado sat down to starve out the defenders, nearly succeeding in accomplishing the same result for his force. Stung to desperation by the stalemate, the Spaniards attacked the enemy but were repeatedly repulsed and prepared to abandon the siege when the Captain General arrived. He would listen to no such counsel. He could not leave this stronghold so close to his capital in the hands of a warlike enemy, and retirement would bring every Indian chief, heretofore defeated, to arms again. He accordingly laid siege to Mixco with his entire force but the sole result was the wounding of many of the besiegers while no impression was made upon the fortress. Three weeks passed fruitlessly and, hoping to take the enemy unaware, Alvarado had long scaling ladders prepared. Placed at the lowest point in the overhanging walls, the Spaniards rushed up only to be received with so furious a counter-attack that men and ladders crashed in a heap on the river bed.

While the captains, almost in despair, were seeking a new method of attack, a native army twelve thousand strong was seen approaching along the Motagua Valley. This force was composed of Chignautlans, allied to the defenders of Mixco. Alvarado believed that the garrison would descend from the heights and take him in the rear while his force was engaged with the newcomers, but the Pokomans remained idly in their fort, interested spectators of the battle. The valley was broad and level with a floor of firm sand whereon grew cactus and mesquite forming an ideal theatre for the operations of the cavalry. The horsemen set out on a wide circuit to gain the Indian rear while the latter, believing their antagonists in flight, threw themselves upon the infantry and native allies with fierce shouts, wounding a number of the Spaniards and killing many of the auxiliaries. Although this was their first sight of horses, they fought furiously as the cavalry overwhelmed them, clinging desperately to the manes and tails of the animals and trying to overthrow them by main force. Many of the Indians found their deaths from the steel-shod hoofs of the charging horses. A horseman, Garcia de Aguilar, was surrounded by four hundred of the enemy and despite the frantic efforts of the Spaniard and his mount, that with hoofs and teeth lunged at the screaming savages, he was at length torn from his saddle, falling beneath the horse. So great was the press of bodies and so valiantly did he defend himself that the Indians, dodging the plunges of the maddened animal, could not dispatch the Spaniard. In his crouching position, his sword and dagger took toll of warrior after warrior as the rear ranks pressed them forward, literally against his blade. As even his superhuman strength had reached its limit, six comrades, seeing the turbulent mass of warriors, rode at full tilt into the crowd, rescuing Aguilar in the very nick of time. The courage and strength of the lone horseman so impressed the enemy that, discouraged, they retired from the field leaving over two hundred dead behind them.

On the next day envoys arrived from the Chignautlan King offering submission. They brought a small amount of gold but, more important, revealed to Alvarado a secret exit from Mixco through a cavern opening in dense woods near the river bank.

On the morrow after sending forty men to guard the mouth of the cave, the Spanish commander determined upon another assault on the fortress. The first Spaniard in line up the narrow path carried a shield, close behind him was a crossbowman, then another shield bearer followed by a musketeer. This order permitted the greatest possible protection to the assailants. On this day better progress was made and despite a continual shower of stones, one of which broke the leg of the foremost shield bearer, the invading column reached a wider place on the ridge so packed with Mixcan warriors, eager for a blow at the enemy, that those on the sides were crowded over the edge of the cliff by the pressure of their comrades. Here crossbows and swords found an opportunity for their deadly work. So furious was the fighting and so invincible the courage of the Indians that a rampart formed of mutilated bodies and severed arms and heads of the defenders formed before the Spaniards. Only by literally clearing the ground of the dead at their feet could the Whites advance along the narrow defile. After a struggle of several hours the defenders broke and fled, convinced that no warrior, however daring, could defeat the mail-clad Children of the Sun. Many leaped to their deaths over the cliffs, others, including women and children, sought escape by the cave to fall prisoners to the guard awaiting them, while the remainder seeing all avenues closed surrendered at discretion. The stronghold was destroyed and the inhabitants moved to the present village of Mixco built in a picturesque site on the edge of the Valley de las Vacas within six miles of the City of Guatemala.

After the reduction of Mixco, Alvarado marched to Salvador with part of his force to complete the conquest of that country. The book of Acts of the City of Guatemala, of May 6, 1525, mentions the existence of the City of San Salvador of which Diego Holguin was a Mayor.[6] While the Captain General was absent, his remaining followers were confronted with the revolt of the Zacatepecs, a nation formerly tributary to the Cakchiquels with domains lying east of Mixco in the dry country near the present town of Zacapa. To show their contempt for the Cakchiquel submission to the Spaniards, of whose power the Zacatepecs had no first-hand knowledge, the latter raided Cakchiquel villages carrying off women and children, sacrificing them on nearby hills in full view of their anguished countrymen. A delegation of Cakchiquel chiefs sent to remonstrate with the Zacatepecs were executed with the exception of one sent back with a message that they would believe in the powers of the Christians when they could bring the sacrificed back to life. They proposed to destroy the Cakchiquel race in revenge for past wrongs before the Spaniards could take the field against them. While Cakchiquel messengers were en route to Xepau to seek assistance from their conquerors, Zacatepec armies marched far and wide through their enemy's territory, exterminating the population that had escaped the hand of Spaniard, Quiche and Tzutuhil. Forty Spaniards, including twenty horsemen, one thousand Cakchiquels and two hun-

dred Tlascalans, newly arrived from Mexico to seek further glory
and spoils under the leadership of their White friends, set out to
meet the enemy. A six-day battle took place, the Zacatepecs fighting
with great courage and skill, copying the Spanish tactics of holding
a column in reserve for the crucial moment. On the last day the
Spaniards feigned a retreat toward a thickly wooded ravine where
the Tlascalans and artillery were posted in ambush. Drawn into
the trap the opposing army was slaughtered, the chiefs captured
and held as hostages while a garrison of Europeans and Tlascalans
commanded by Diego de Alvarado occupied Zacatepec.

In June 1525, Tepepul II, High King of the Quiche nation by
nomination of Alvarado, advised his patron that the plot to burn
the Spanish army in Utatlan had not been of his father's devising,
but was suggested by Cailil-Balaam, a Quiche Prince, at this time
King of the Mames. This nation of Quiche blood occupied an
extensive area along the Pacific Coast of Guatemala between Atitlan and Quetzeltanango and extending northwest to Huehuetenango. Glad of so valid an excuse to extend his conquest, Alvarado
sent his brother Gonzalo with forty cavalry, eighty Spanish infantry and two thousand Tlascalan and Guatemalan Indian warriors,
accompanied by three hundred sappers equipped with shovels,
adzes and axes, to undertake the campaign. The Captain General
himself remained in Xepau busy with innumerable problems of
administration. The column left Xepau early in July 1525 in the
height of the rainy season and with much difficulty made its way
over the flooded trails to Totonicapan, a Quiche town on the edge
of the Mame domain, selected to serve as a base of operations.
Continuing their march in a continual downpour of such force
that fires could not be made, the troops shivered in the cold of
the mountain country. The Rio Hondo, ordinarily a small stream,
was so swollen that several days were spent seeking a ford. Arriving before the town of Mazatenango, they found it fortified by a
palisade of heavy logs inside a deep trench designed to check the
horsemen. As Gonzalo de Alvarado was about to advance, his
native guides noted that the level ground before the town, to all
appearances firm, was a swamp in which horses and men would
sink to their deaths. Behind the palisade hordes of warriors
shrilled defiance while captains blew signals and orders on great

seashell horns. The invaders passed in safety around the treacherous ground and, attacking the city from the rear, took it after a battle lasting throughout the day in which the Indians suffered great losses. Leaving a garrison to protect his rear, Gonzalo de Alvarado continued his march to Huehuetenango. A short distance from the city an army of five thousand Mame warriors from Malacatan, marching to the assistance of their fellows, was encountered. The front rank of the native army, composed of archers, stubbornly resisted the charge of the Spanish cavalry for some time. Overcome at length by the Children of the Sun, from whose metal-clad bodies the arrows of the most expert archer glanced in vain, the Indians broke and fled for the shelter of the nearby forest, many remaining pierced by Spanish lances or crushed by the flying hoofs of the warhorses. Meantime the infantry and the Indian auxiliaries were engaged with the main body of the Mame army commanded by the Prince Can-Ilocab, and despite their superior discipline the invaders were driven back step by step before the Indian advance. The remnant of the archers dispersed, Gonzalo de Alvarado led his horsemen at full gallop, falling on the enemy flank, but the determined warriors armed with long lances valiantly repelled the charge, many of the horses being wounded.

Despite great slaughter, the Indian ranks stood firm and the Spaniards were rapidly tiring when Gonzalo de Alvarado, remembering the deed of Cortes at Otumba, pushed through the press to where the banner of Can-Ilocab waved. Followed by his horsemen, even the flashing hoofs of the horses, who seemed to partake of the spirit of the rider in battle and lashed out at the enemy with bone-crushing blows, made little progress until a sudden movement in the enemy ranks opened a lane at the end of which appeared the bodyguard of the Mame chieftain. Seizing the opportunity, Diego de Alvarado burst through the ring of warriors, his levelled lance piercing the body of Can-Ilocab. The fall of their Prince dispirited the Indians who abandoned the battle and fled in all directions leaving the ground carpeted with their dead. On the next day while the Spaniards continued their march, they were met by envoys from the chiefs of Malacatan, bringing presents of gold and the submission of their masters. Gonzalo de Alvarado sent a body of Tlascalan warriors to garrison the city while he continued his march to Huehuetenango.[7] Expecting a desperate resistance, Alvarado was agreeably surprised to find the town deserted, the houses stripped of food and furniture. Establishing his camp in the deserted palace, the commander sent patrols in all directions, one of which, commanded by Gaspar Aleman, falling in with three hundred Mame archers, killed a number of them and took three prisoners including a chief. From them Gonzalo de Alvarado learned that the Indians had withdrawn to the castle or fortress of Zaculeu situated on the crest of a steep hill surrounded by a river and deep cañons with only a narrow entrance well guarded by a stone rampart having a great slab of rock as its only door. Here, provided with a great quantity of food and surrounded by his finest warriors, Cailil-Balaam confidently awaited the assault of his enemy. It was not long in coming. After a demand for surrender had been contemptuously refused, the heralds being driven off with arrows, Alvarado advanced to the assault. Before his storming parties had reached their stations, six thousand Mame warriors emerged from the fort and fell upon the invaders, followed during the course of the subsequent battle by two thousand reserves. The field, a stretch of level ground beside the river, was well to the liking of the Spaniards and though outnumbered six to one, the Whites and their Mexican allies, who were protected by thick coats of quilted cotton, gained their accustomed victory after a hotly contested battle in which three hundred Mames and forty Tlascalans were killed while Gonzalo de Alvarado and eight other Spaniards were severely wounded. Three horses were killed in this fight, a matter of much concern to the Christians. From the bodies of the dead the Spaniards gathered large golden medals which the soldiers seized with shouts of joy as recompense for their arduous campaign. The natives returned to their fortress while Alvarado, doubting the ability of his army to take so strong a position by a direct attack, sat down to starve the garrison out. To prepare for the day on which he could undertake the assault if necessary, the White captain set his pioneers at work building a road by filling in the passage across a cañon so as to bring the lowest part of the battlements within range of his cavalry. The workers were protected by crossbowmen who picked off Mame archers seeking to halt the construction. While the small Spanish force sat in its makeshift huts and grumbled at the inaction, a horde of eight thousand savage warriors, inhabitants of the jungles to the west along the headwaters of the Usamacinta River, appeared innocent of clothes but covered with warpaint in startling design and fell upon the Europeans. The latter now had their fill of battle, but the barbarian ranks paid heavy toll to the horsemen and artillery until at evening the remainder, wounded and discouraged, fled across the river and disappeared from history.

Hunger made itself felt both within and without the walls as the cold rain fell in sheets and cloudbursts upon the just and unjust. By October both parties were at the point of exhaustion. The Mames had consumed their food, had eaten their leather shields and the bodies of the dead. The Spanish troops, enduring freezing temperatures in their drenched clothes without relief, offered little resistance to pneumonia and fever. The ranks of his native auxiliaries also dwindled daily and Gonzalo de Alvarado, desperate, sending his sick and wounded back to Huehuetenango, prepared to take the fort by assault. On the following night as he was completing preparations for an attack at daybreak for which storming ladders, wide enough to carry three men abreast, were ready, the alarm was given. Cailil-Balaam at the head of a party of troops protecting his nobles and family attempted flight from the fort. Driven back and wounded the heroic Prince surrendered the next day, his garrison so weak from hunger that they could scarcely walk. Gonzalo de Alvarado received the conquered chieftain kindly, embracing him, and stated that the only condition for the surrender required the natives to become Christians. The Spaniards took possession of the castle which was rendered useless and, leaving a garrison in Huehuetenango under command of Gonzalo de Solis, Alvarado returned to Xepau in December to report to his brother. Eighteen hundred Mames had died in the defence of their country.[8]

During the fall of 1525, Pedro de Alvarado engaged in some minor campaigns against the natives of the Province of Guazacapan.[9] Anxious to secure recognition of his status from the Conqueror's successor, he decided to leave for Mexico, a decision that was bitterly opposed by his own brothers and the officials of Xepau who feared that in the absence of the dread "Tonatiuh" the Indian nations would again rise in arms. The month of January 1526 was spent in petty details of administration, always vexatious to Alvarado, and at the end of January he nominated new Mayors and Aldermen to replace the incumbents. Early in February he received a letter from Cortes written from Trujillo[10] in which the Conqueror of Mexico made some reference to his expedition and announced his intention of returning to Mexico by way of Guatemala that he might view the results obtained by his subordinate. Alvarado was requested to meet him en route with carriers and to open a trail from Honduras to Mexico. While relieved as to the health of Cortes, his announced visit was not pleasing to the conqueror of Guatemala. None too firmly seated in power he was not yet ready to exhibit his handiwork. Many of his soldiers had complaints, well founded or otherwise, which they would ventilate in the presence of the Commander in Chief, and tales of his severity toward the conquered populations might bring reproaches from Cortes. Since he could not disobey, however, Alvarado put the best possible face on it and prepared to go to meet his chief. In the midst of his preparations a second letter came from Trujillo in which Cortes stated that events in New Spain had caused him to abandon his proposed march overland and return to Mexico by sea. He ordered Alvarado to proceed immediately to Honduras that all pending matters might be settled before he set out for his headquarters. The long, difficult journey through an unknown country seemed vastly preferable to Alvarado than receiving Cortes in the new conquered provinces and accordingly he gave orders for immediate departure. Gonzalo de Alvarado, covered with glory from the Mame campaign, received the post of interim-Governor, but mutiny broke out in the Spanish ranks. Most of the soldiers selected to accompany Alvarado to Honduras, tired of his continual campaigns and disinclined to visit a land said to possess no gold, rebelled and fled to Iximche, intending to return to Mexico. Pursuing them with his loyal followers he found the mutineers entrenched in the city of Tecpan and wishing at all costs to avoid a battle that might cause the restive Indians to revolt, sought to persuade the rebels to return to their duty. A few were won over but the remainder set fire to the city and, while Alvarado and his followers were engaged in fighting the flames, fled to the Quiche territory, carrying off with them the artillerymen and the Chaplain of the expedition. To make sure that the latter would not desert them they seized his priestly vestments. The Governor attempted no further pursuit and the mutineers continued to Mexico unmolested. At Soconusco they tried Alvarado *in absentia* by a kangaroo court which condemned him and his captains to suffer death.

Passing over this insult, if indeed he heard of it, Alvarado set out for Honduras taking the long road through Salvador as the country to the southeast around Esquipulas[11] was occupied by tribes still unsubdued. Crossing through Salvador to Choluteca in Honduras[12] he met a party of Spanish soldiers commanded by the Captain Luis Marin who had come overland from Trujillo by orders of Cortes. Bernal Diaz del Castillo who had remained in Mexico after the departure of Alvarado and subsequently accompanied Cortes to Honduras was with the detail under Marin and joined Alvarado, settling in Guatemala where he lived for many years. The two groups greeted each other joyfully. Tonatiuh had good reason for happiness, learning that Cortes, unable to wait because of the critical condition of affairs in Mexico, had sailed from Trujillo.[13] While still in Choluteca another party of Spaniards arrived from Nicaragua where they held that country for Pedro Arias Davila, Governor of Tierra Firme (Panama). Although the latter claimed Honduras as falling within his grant from Charles V, the parties met amicably. After several days of conferences, Alvarado sent an intimate friend, Gaspar Arias de Avila, to Panama to confer with Davila. The object of this journey is unknown although Diaz[14] states that it was in regard to a treaty of marriage alliance between Alvarado and the Governor of Panama.

Much relieved in spirits, the Captain General took leave of the soldiers of Governor Davila and, accompanied by the men of Luis Marin, returned to Guatemala. The march was a continual skirmish with Indians who hung on the flanks and rear of the little column, killing three Spanish soldiers and wounding many of the others. The entire Indian population of Salvador was in arms, but Alvarado, anxious to return to his capital from which he had received alarming news and troubled by the possibility that Spain would send royal favourites to take over his domain,[15] neglected to avenge himself upon the natives and hurried through the hostile territory. Nearing Xepau, he had more reason to worry, finding the inhabitants of Petepa, close to his capital, in rebellion. These people, belonging to the Cakchiquel kingdom, were divided into factions between which a civil war was raging, motivated by the friendship of the present chief for the Spaniards. The natives, who had fortified themselves in a strong position on the tops of several small hills, well protected by trenches and pits to prevent the use of cavalry, held out for three days before Alvarado was able to disperse them. The Spanish column continued its march to the valley of Panchoy, where after his death the Spanish capital of Central America was to rise.[16] Here they defeated a Cakchiquel army, pursuing the rebels to Tecpan. The Quiche and Cakchiquel Kings, now too late, making common cause against the invaders, were present in the Cakchiquel capital together with the Zacatepecs and several confederate tribes.

An army of thirty thousand Indian warriors occupied the city, before which, in the usual manner, trenches had been dug to prevent attacks by the horsemen. Despite their great number, Alvarado resolutely attacked the rebels, defeating them and forcing the evacuation of the city. Fearing an ambush, he retired to the abandoned Spanish capital of Iximche, where his tired followers rested, in small comfort, in ruined cabins exposed to the continuous rain. Anxious to continue his journey to Mexico, Alvarado sent messengers to the fugitive Kings, asking a peaceful arrangement but in vain. The native monarchs had had enough of the Spaniards and remained hidden in the fastnesses of the hills, safe from molestation. Finding his efforts useless, he marched to Olintepec where Gonzalo de Alvarado, acting Governor, had retired with his small force when the rebellion of 1526 made Xepau impossible to hold.

The uprising was motivated by a system of slavery introduced by the conquerors. To the credit of Spain, however, Indian slavery was abolished by Royal Decree in the year 1546. As rapidly as towns were conquered, the inhabitants, with the exception of the nobles and priests, were divided among the White soldiers. The word slavery was neither used nor officially countenanced. The Indians were confided to their White masters for religious instruction and if the teacher employed his charges in washing the streams for gold or in agriculture, such tasks, indirectly at least, placed them in the service of the White Man's God and kept the lately benighted heathen from idleness and consequent communion with the Devil. Each representative of the Crown arriving from Spain bore strict and sincere orders to abolish slavery if it existed. At times the officials found no evidence of the institution; occasionally a settler was detected in a flagrant breach of the Royal edict. In some such cases the slaves were later mysteriously discovered working for the benefit of the Royal officials or found their way back through devious legal proceedings to the yoke of their former master. Even the native chiefs, through coercion or for personal gain, exerted themselves to supply slaves. The sufferings caused by this system which brought death to many Indians unaccustomed to continuous physical labor and lacking adequate food and shelter, culminated in the rebellion of 1526 which confronted Alvarado on his return from Salvador. The straw that broke the camel's back was the demand from Gonzalo de Alvarado, addressed to the inhabitants of Tecpan, for two hundred Indian children from nine to ten years of age, each of whom must deliver daily to his Spanish master from the gold bearing sands of the river as much of the precious metal as would equal the size of his little finger. A child who could not secure his daily quota was in danger of being sent to a distant part of the country as a slave. If the daily delivery fell short of the demand, the parents were sent at night to make up the deficiency. For several weeks the afflicted inhabitants of Tecpan succeeded in meeting the requirements, supplementing the results of the children's search with a small amount of golden ornaments that had heretofore escaped the Spanish collectors. When the daily harvest fell far below the requirements, the Indians were threatened with death, apparently not by Gonzalo de Alvarado himself but by the local tribute collector.

Exasperated at this treatment of their people and feeling the Spanish yoke settling ever tighter about their necks, the Cakchiquel Kings, taking advantage of the absence of the feared

White Captain, provoked a rebellion. For five hundred miles north and south the country sprang into flames overnight, Cakchiquel, Quiche, Pokoman, Mame, Xinca and Pokomchi, forgetting ancient rivalries, rose simultaneously against the invader. Only the Tzutu-hils and the Quiches of Xelahuh remained passive. Tribute collectors and isolated Spanish garrisons were massacred, Indians friendly to the Spaniards were sacrificed and in an instant the entire structure of the Conquest tottered toward a fall. At this moment Alvarado returned from Salvador. The rebels, however, lacked arms and experienced leaders. Many were youths and aged, heretofore considered unsuitable as warriors, while the terror of the warhorse and powder dampened their ardour for combat with the Christian force. By August 1526, Alvarado had made such progress in the reduction of the rebellious tribes that he felt it safe to set out for Mexico, leaving the government of Guatemala in the hands of Pedro Puertocarrero and Hernan Carrillo, gentlemen distinguished by their courage and loyalty to the Captain General. Puertocarrero was the Sir Galahad of the Conquests of Mexico and Guatemala. No act of wanton cruelty or barbarity ever stained his character and on many occasions he sacrificed his opportunity and risked his life for the benefit of his commander or companions.[17]

On August 26, 1526, Alvarado accompanied by the Mayors and Aldermen of Guatemala, a number of his own followers and the troops of Luis Marin, departed for Mexico, not without hearing bitter reproaches from many Spaniards who felt his absence disastrous at this critical time.

On the departure of the Captain General, Puertocarrero and Carillo divided the government between them, the former assuming charge of the campaign against the rebellious Indians while the latter handled civil matters. Puertocarrero showed himself an energetic substitute for his chief, manufacturing powder with sulphur taken from the volcano Santa Maria near Quetzaltenango and carrying the war to the Cakchiquel Kings who had fortified themselves in the almost inaccessible region of Ruyalxot (Comalapan). After a two-months campaign the rebels were routed, their Kings escaping. This task completed, Puertocarrero marched immediately to Chiapas, where a new insurrection required his attention. Here he found a party of Spaniards from Mexico under command of the Captain Diego de Mazariegos who had made much headway in the pacification of the province. Displeased at the appearance of the Guatemalan, Mazariegos made overtures to the troops of Puertocarrero, many of whom deserted their leader and proceeded to Mexico. Puertocarrero returned with his remaining followers to Chimaltenango.

Alvarado was received in Mexico with much joy by his former commander who, object of the ingratitude of Spain, had been removed as Governor, the incompetent Marcos de Aguilar serving in his stead. Jorge de Alvarado, brother of the Captain General, a strong partisan of Cortes, was then in the capital, having contracted an advantageous marriage with the daughter of the Royal Treasurer, Alonzo de Estrada. Finding that his enemies were active not only in Mexico but in the court of the Emperor himself, Alvarado made preparations to sail for Spain, and that his possessions might be secure from Marcos de Aguilar in his absence, he appointed his brother, Jorge, as Lieutenant General and interim-Governor of Guatemala. Jorge de Alvarado and his new bride left immediately for his post, arriving on March 20, 1527, accompanied by several Dominican priests recently arrived from Spain. The Captain General, an ardent Catholic, anxious to supplant the religion of Huitzilopotchli with the doctrine of the Cross, continually sought the assistance of the religious orders in his conquests, and in his letters to the Emperor he makes numerous references to the ecclesiastics who accompanied him. Early in 1527, he sailed from Vera Cruz for Spain to give a first-hand account of his exploits to Charles V and settle scores with his numerous detractors.

Marcos de Aguilar, interim-Governor of Mexico, arriving with instructions to investigate the conduct of Cortes, naturally fraternized with the enemies of the Conqueror. His messages to Spain were carried by malcontents, among them Gonzalo Mexia, the first Royal Treasurer who had deserted Cortes after the Noche Triste and returned with Ponce de Leon. This personage preceded Alvarado to Spain and, armed with power of attorney from Aguilar, formally presented charges against the Captain General. Quoting hearsay, he accused Alvarado of having appropriated to himself great quantities of gold, pearls and other valuables; of illegally seizing the territory of the Indians; of refusing to divide spoils with his fellow adventurers; and, most serious in the eyes of the court, of withholding the Royal Fifth. The Council of the Indies, duly impressed and ever anxious to humiliate the conquerors of America, ordered Alvarado to appear for examination, requiring him to give bond that he would accept sentence and pay any judgements assessed against him. The avaricious Council had condemned him in advance. Fifteen thousand ducats was the penalty levied upon Alvarado for the crime of having conquered Guatemala for Charles V, and to make sure that the judgement would be executed, his baggage containing the gold he had brought from America was seized. The armchair warriors had won the first round but Alvarado had only begun to fight. Through a family friend he made the acquaintance of Francisco de los Cobos, newly appointed Secretary of the Council of the Indies in succession to the villainous Fonseca. De los Cobos, intimate and counsellor of the Emperor, impressed with the manner and bearing of the blond captain, his romantic history and perhaps by more concrete reasons, lent his influence to the defence. But even more valuable than the friendship of the Secretary was the affection of Doña Francisca de la Cueva, niece of the powerful Duke of Alburquerque. Noble, rich, and beautiful, with such a wife it would be a rash foeman indeed that would attack the Captain General of Guatemala. The marriage followed almost immediately.[18] The clouds rolled away, the Council of the Indies dismissed the charges, the Captain General was knighted, a rare honour at that time, and in addition received the title of "Adelantado." The Cross of the Order of Santiago shone on his breast and a royal decree signed at Burgos, December 18, 1527, named him Governor and Captain General of Guatemala and its dependencies, subject only to the orders of the King and without intervention from the authorities in Mexico. His salary was fixed at 572,500 maravedis annually.[19] Laden with honours far beyond his wildest expectations, Alvarado spent the next six months in Spain alternating between the court and the estates of the Dukes of Alburquerque. Not until July 1528 did the Captain General with his bride and a brilliant suite of courtiers, happy to bask in the reflected glory of the royal favourite that shone so brilliantly on Alvarado, embark for Vera Cruz en route to Guatemala.

FOOTNOTES FOR CHAPTER EIGHT

[1] Municipality of Guatemala, *La Romantica Ciudad Colonial,* p. 14.

[2] Extracts from the Acts of the City of Guatemala during its early days are given in the Appendix.

[3] "Manuscript of the Acts of the City of Guatemala," copied by Arevalo and Don Victor Miguel Diaz.

[4] *Annals of the Cakchiquels,* Chap. XXVIII.

[5] Juarros, *History of Guatemala,* p. 284, says that a garrison of two men, by rolling boulders down the steep pass, could keep an army from entering.

[6] The original Spanish town was founded on a site now known as Bermuda and removed after twenty years to its present location. No record remains of this expedition of Alvarado.

[7] On the site of the present city of the same name.

[8] Juarros, *History of Guatemala,* Book II, Chap. VI.

[9] The Province of Santa Rosa in the Republic of Guatemala.

[10] Located as at present on the Atlantic Coast of the Republic of Honduras.

[11] This town is still an object of veneration by the Indians who make annual pilgrimages from all parts of Central America to the city in April, a time at which persons not of Indian blood are decidedly unwelcome.

[12] One of the principal cities of the present Republic of Honduras situated within a few miles of the Bay of Fonseca on the Pacific Coast.

[13] The royal officials sent by envious courtiers to embarrass Cortes in Mexico had taken advantage of his absence to seize his property. Cortes sent Martin de Orantes by ship to Mexico, bearing letters conferring the government of the country upon Pedro de Alvarado and Francisco de las Casas, or, if they should be absent, as Alvarado was, on Alonzo Estrada and the Treasurer, Alborñoz. At the same time the Captain Luis Marin was instructed to inform Alvarado of conditions in Mexico and warn him that his assistance might be required to restore Cortes to his government.

[14] Diaz del Castillo, *Conquête de la Nouvelle-Espagne,* p. 747.

[15] Ponce de Leon, Conqueror of Florida, had recently arrived in Mexico to open an inquisition into the acts of Cortes. De Leon died almost immediately upon his arrival and was succeeded by Marcos de Aguilar who continued his investigation with manifest prejudice against Cortes and his friends, so that Alvarado had good reason for worry.

[16] The city now called Antigua was founded in 1542; destroyed in 1773.

[17] Milla, *La Hija del Adelantado,* states that Puertocarrero was in love with Doña Leonor, daughter of Alvarado by the Tlascalan Princess, Doña Luisa, but that the Captain General rejected Puertocarrero's suit, ambitiously seeking a more advantageous match for his daughter with Francisco de la Cueva, his brother-in-law.

[18] Milla, *Historia de la America Central,* p. 187, without quoting his authority, states that Alvarado was engaged to marry Cecilia Vasquez, niece of Cortes, but promptly forgot his promise when a more brilliant match became possible.

[19] Which Milla values at 2,068 Guatemalan pesos, equal to approximately $1,000 United States currency.

IX

INQUISITION

August 1528—December 1530

WHILE Pedro de Alvarado was absent in Spain, his brother, acting as Governor in his stead and urged by the settlers, tired of an ambulatory capital, set himself to finding a satisfactory site. In October 1527 the temporary headquarters were moved once more from Olintepec to the Valley of Almolonga at the foot of the Volcan de Agua occupying an Indian village now known as San Miguelito. Several locations were suggested, each seconded by ardent partisans, among them the present location and the valley of Chimaltenango. A commission appointed to examine the sites reported on November 20, setting forth the advantages and defects of each location. After much discussion, during which the proximity of the volcano was urged against San Miguelito by many of those present, a site known to the Indians as Bulbuxya, immediately adjoining San Miguelito but further down the flank of the mountain, was selected as it was provided with excellent water from springs and the nearby river, while the prolific vegetation gave abundant evidences of the richness of the soil. Here on November 21, 1527, in the presence of the Lieutenant Governor, Jorge de Alvarado, and the municipal officials, the permanent establishment of the capital was decreed.[1, 2] The ruins of this city are now known as Ciudad Vieja. Streets and avenues were laid out following the principal points of the compass and space set aside for public squares, churches, hospitals and public buildings. Disputes arose as the new settlers clamoured for the most favourable lands. Those who had performed signal services in the Conquest demanded recognition over newcomers from Mexico, until on April 18, 1528,[3] the plots were redistributed, horsemen receiving a "caballeria" six hundred paces wide facing the river and one thousand four hundred sixty paces long, running up the mountainside so that each owner possessed pasture and timber land. Foot-soldiers received half a "caballeria." In 1528, new uprisings of Indians occurred during which, especially at the capture of a fortified hill at Jalpatagua, Hernando de Alvarado and a number of other prominent Spaniards were killed.[4]

On May 26, 1528, Alvarado receiving intimations from the Council of the Indies that it was high time that he returned to his post, presented his royal commission for inscription in the Archives and shortly thereafter sailed for Mexico, accompanied by his bride, Francisco Marroquin, afterwards Bishop of Guatemala, Francisco de Castellanos, Francisco de Zorrilla, Gonzalo Ronquillo and a large number of other persons of quality. Castellanos bore a commission as Royal Treasurer, Zorrilla that of Auditor while Ronquillo as "Veedor" was a sort of Inspector General and Magistrate at once. These men were at first secretly and later, during his absence when they dared to be so, open enemies of Alvarado. At Vera Cruz a major disaster overtook the Captain General, the sudden death of his bride from a fever contracted on the unhealthy coast. Dazed and disconsolate the widower proceeded to Mexico City where he sent a copy of his commission to his brother Jorge, confirming the latter in his appointment as interim-Governor. The power given Alvarado and delegated to his brother was little less than absolute.

Scarcely recovered from the loss of his wife, another blow was in store for Tonatiuh. The Audiencia of Mexico, ruthlessly uprooting the friends of Cortes, turned their attention to his principal captain. Notwithstanding his marks of royal favour, the commissioners determined to ruin him, trusting that they could so bolster their animosity with fact that their sentence, determined in advance, would be approved by the Emperor. The Audiencia was at this time composed of Juan Ortiz Matienzo, the Attorney Delgadillo and Nuño de Guzman, who was himself tried for malfeasance in office in 1531. The magistrates outdid themselves in searching for evidence, forgetting their judicial rôles in their determination to ruin the friend of Cortes.

Every rumour and complaint, justified, trivial or false, was welcomed by these original muckrakers. From the mass of fact and fancy presented, the Audiencia formulated thirty-four separate accusations. These ranged from the childish complaint that in his youth Alvarado had worn the robe of the Order of Santiago belonging to his father, to accusations of ill treatment of the Indians. A list of the accusations is given in the appendix herewith.[5]

The serious charge which the commissioners counted on to win them favour in Spain was that Alvarado had withheld the Royal Fifth of gold and jewels seized during his various campaigns. Before reducing the accusations to writing, the commissioners heard ten witnesses claiming to know the life of Alvarado since his arrival in the Indies and able to throw light on any controversial points. These witnesses were carefully coached in advance by the Audiencia, giving testimony which resulted in the formulation of the thirty-four counts of the indictment. Alvarado answered these accusations point by point in detail and in writing, afterwards presenting thirty-two witnesses in his own behalf. Attached to his defence were certificates issued by the Royal Treasurer of New Spain, setting forth the amount in gold, silver and jewels delivered by Alvarado to the Treasurer as custodian of the Royal Fifth, which amounted to about $250,000 in our own currency.[6] Among the accusations being one that he had secretly taken a number of large jewels to Spain, the Captain General was able to demonstrate that he had given these to the Emperor who returned some of them upon the occasion of the Conqueror's wedding. Among the documents presented by Alvarado in his own defence were the confessions of the Quiche Kings relative to their plan to burn him and his army in Utatlan. So overwhelming was his defence that the Audiencia dared not convict him. Unwilling, however, to admit their evil intentions the commissioners abandoned the examination without a verdict and Alvarado emerged triumphantly from his Calvary. Impatient at the length of the trial and anxious to arrive in Guatemala as soon as possible so as to consolidate their position if, as they secretly hoped, he was convicted and deprived of his post, the royal officials set out for Guatemala. At the same time the Dominican Father Domingo Betonzas left Mexico to found the first convent of his order in the new province.

The enemies of Alvarado in Guatemala, uninformed of the progress of the interrogation, petitioned the Audiencia for a new Governor, alleging that Jorge de Alvarado had seized for his

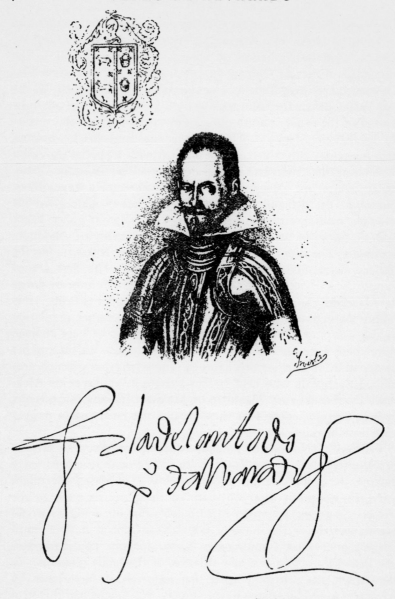

Portrait and Signature of "El Adelantado, P. de Alvarado,"
from the work of Ramirez.

brothers and self the best the country offered in slaves, mines and
agricultural lands. On August 14, 1529, Francisco de Orduña,
Secretary of the Audiencia of Mexico, presented himself to the
municipal officials of Guatemala, bearing a commission signed by
Guzman, appointing him as Captain General, Governor, Mayor
and Judge, instructing him to take over immediately the administration of the colony and to open an investigation into the acts of
the brother of Alvarado. The latter as substitute for his brother
held his power directly from the Crown with a special provision
prohibiting the Audiencia of Mexico from interfering in Guatemalan affairs, but for some unknown reason he gave way without
protest to the demands of Orduña. The latter made good his
triumph, naming Gonzalo Dovalle, former Captain under Francisco de Garay in the Panuco expedition and enemy of Alvarado,
as Mayor. The other municipal posts were distributed among the
settlers dissatisfied with the Captain General. The first act of
Dovalle was to declare all grants of slaves and territory by Jorge
de Alvarado void, but Orduña lacked the courage to carry this
radical suggestion into effect at the moment. Another regulation
of the usurping Mayor was that all dogs must be kept chained
since these were alleged to bite passing Indians with little or no
provocation. A further ordinance of the self-styled officials prohibited Spaniards who held Indian villages from Jorge de Alvarado, from employing Tlascalan or Mexican Indians as overseers
or intendents, alleging that these treated the Guatemalan natives
with brutality and contempt.

Pedro de Cueto, one of the new Aldermen, was sent to Mexico
to ask a reduction of the Royal Fifth to one-tenth, the petitioners
making the point that the great expense of working the mines
left them no profit after one-fifth of the proceeds went to the
Crown. Cueto was so burdened with debts that his creditors would
not let him leave the country even on an official mission until
Orduña intervened, granting him a moratorium. The envoy also
had instructions to ask a new division of the lands remaining to
the Crown, the petition stating that partition of these lands by
Alvarado would be odious to the signers. No sooner had this item
been included in the instructions of Cueto than some of the more
timid accomplices of Orduña were stricken with fright lest Alva-

rado appear to take revenge upon his enemies. Dovalle threatened the Aldermen with prison and only one refused to sign while two others did so with reservations. The Governor proceeded against Cristobal de Robledo who had been attached to the previous administration because Robledo had sent an account of the usurper's acts to Alvarado in Mexico, begging the Captain General to come at once to protect his followers and his own interest. Feeling the time appropriate, Orduña, acting through his illegal power from the Audiencia of Mexico, now declared all acts of Jorge de Alvarado and the previous administration null and void. Many of the colonists lost their lands by virtue of this decree, which roused the partisans of Alvarado to fury.

Such was the discontent in Guatemala that campaigns against the rebellious Indians languished, no captain desiring to absent himself from the city lest Orduña seize the opportunity to confiscate his property. A campaign against the Indians of Uzpantlan, half-heartedly undertaken by the Spaniards, resulted in their complete defeat, many Indian auxiliaries remaining in the hands of the victors who promptly sacrificed them to Exbalanque, a companion god of Hunahpu. When the news of this defeat reached Guatemala, the Governor and Francisco de Castellanos determined to take the field themselves but although large rewards were offered for volunteers, only forty foot-soldiers and thirty-two horsemen appeared to take part in the expedition. The usurper, who was not lacking in physical courage, sallied forth at the head of his column, accompanied by six hundred Tlascalan warriors. At the same time the inhabitants of Chiquimula, irritated by the bad government of Orduña, rose in arms and in the absence of the Mexican officials, Hernando Chaves and Pedro Amalin, veteran captains of Alvarado, led a column of sixty infantry, thirty cavalry and four hundred Mexican auxiliaries to suppress the revolt. During this campaign some of the most violent fighting of the Conquest occurred, the lieutenants of Alvarado distinguishing themselves in the capture of the great city of Copan, the original capital of the Mayas and now peopled by their valiant descendants, the Chortis. Not until after a long siege with great losses on both sides, was Galel, King of the Chortis, overcome.[7]

A new difficulty presented itself to Orduña. Martin de Estete, a captain in the service of Pedro Arias Davila, invaded El Salvador, alleging that the country formed part of Nicaragua, governed from Panama. The Spanish garrison of San Salvador consisted of some sixty men aided by a corps of Guatemalan Indian auxiliaries commanded by the Captain Diego de Roxas then engaged in the difficult task of subduing an Indian nation risen in arms along the Lempa River. Roxas finally succeeded in driving the enemy to the top of a heavily wooded mountain where he besieged them, not possessing sufficient men to carry the strong position by storm. The natives proposed a treaty to which Roxas showed himself agreeable but when the negotiations were far advanced his Indian servant warned the Captain that the desire for peace was a pretext to throw him off guard. The enemy had connived with his Indian allies to exterminate the Spaniards, the signal being a sortie of the besieged, whereupon the Guatemalans should attack the Christians from the rear. The Spanish Captain immediately seized the Guatemalan chiefs, forced a confession and hanged them in the act.

At this moment he received notice that a Spanish force advancing from the south was within two days' march of his position. Alarmed at this incursion of his countrymen into domains entrusted to his control, Roxas set out with eight Spaniards and a few Indians to ascertain the truth of the report. The partisans of rival Spanish Governors always entertained toward each other the tender consideration shown in like cases by strange bulldogs. A short distance en route they met Estete marching to San Salvador. The Nicaraguan Captain seized Roxas and his men. An Indian who escaped carried the news to the remainder of the force which retired to San Salvador, and a runner was sent to Guatemala begging assistance. The principal settlers joined in a council of war which sent a notary in full state to warn Estete to leave El Salvador forthwith as that territory was part of his master's domain. The Nicaraguan, widely known for his boldness and brutal treatment of the enemies of the Governor of Panama, replied insolently that he had Salvador and meant to keep it, that he was sending Roxas and his companions to Panama as prisoners and he proposed to eject all Spaniards except those of his own company from the province. When this message reached Guate-

mala, Orduña decided to refer the dispute to the Audiencia of
Mexico. Furious at this indifference to duty, the settlers demanded
that he go personally to confront Estete and expel him from El
Salvador. The Governor replied that he would make the journey
if he was furnished one hundred men to give due honour to his
rank. Only sixty responded and glad of the excuse, Orduña refused
to go. The Captain Francisco Lopez accepted the commission and
set forth in March 1530 for San Salvador. In the meantime Estete
had occupied the latter city and demanded that the municipal
officials receive him as Governor. Upon their refusal he founded
another village a short distance away, fully equipped with Mayors,
Aldermen, Constables and other officials. On the arrival of Lopez
in Salvador, the Captain prudently retired taking with him two
thousand Salvadorean Indians as slaves. Before leaving San Salvador he caused the Attorney for the city to be hanged because the
latter had opposed his conduct. At this arbitrary act a number of
Estete's soldiers deserted to the Guatemalans who set out in hot
pursuit of the boastful captain. After a chase of sixty miles the
quarry came in sight. As his men refused to fight, Estete fled
accompanied by three or four cronies and made his way to Nicaragua. The remainder of the soldiers gladly embraced the opportunity to serve in Guatemala, as the continual quarrels between
the Spanish chiefs in Nicaragua, accompanied by executions and
assassinations, gave little promise of a prosperous future.

Alvarado's friends had not left him in ignorance of the situation
and as soon as he learned of the invasion of Estete he set forth
for Guatemala and arrived early in April 1530. On the eleventh
day of that month he appeared before the municipal officials,
creatures of Orduña, demanding their recognition of him as Governor and Captain General. After some hesitation during which he
produced the original of his commission bearing the Emperor's
seal, the Mayors and Aldermen agreed to his demand, kissing the
Royal Seal and placing the commission on their heads, the customary sign of respect and obedience to Royal commands. Alvarado
took the oath, his right hand upon the Cross of the Order of Santiago. The Captain General showed himself an astute politician.
The officials ejected by Orduña appeared before him clamouring
for their positions while the others desired to retain them hoping

by their good conduct to evade punishment for their hostility
to the rightful Governor. Calling the officials and colonists together on April 30, he made an energetic speech setting forth that
the colony could not exist divided against itself. For this reason
no member of the municipal body selected by Orduña or those
ejected by him should be eligible to serve. The partisans of Orduña
surrendered their offices and Alvarado immediately selected successors from among the principal citizens of the colony, bound
to him by ties of long standing. To put an end once and for all
to the discord, he commanded an absolute cessation of all pending
political quarrels on pain of death to any person taking such quarrels away from his jurisdiction for settlement. In no other manner
could the tiny capital, consisting at this time of not more than
one hundred and fifty settlers, hope to maintain itself surrounded
by great masses of Indians, subdued but not submissive. There
were many who grumbled at the edict, but sotto voce, for it was
evident to all that Alvarado's word was law and the determined
character of the Governor was well known. Alvarado next turned
his attention to Orduña who had remained in the city by orders
of his successor, forbidden to leave under penalty of forfeiting
thirty thousand pesos of gold. Turning the tables the Captain
General ordered Orduña to trial for the acts which had exasperated
a large number of the colonists. While the indictment was being
drawn the prisoner fled in disguise and despite energetic pursuit
made his way to Mexico.

In June 1530, by appointment of the Captain General, Francisco
Marroquin succeeded Father Godinez as Chaplain of the army and
colony. Marroquin, afterwards Bishop, a man of strong personality,
played a prominent part in the progress of the colony, being one of
the strongest supporters of Alvarado and after the latter's death
acting for a short time as Governor.

As soon as the internal dissensions had been subsided, Alvarado
extended his conquest, sending his brother, Diego de Alvarado,
to found a city in the Province of Tezulutlan.[8] The Captain Luis
de Moscoso, who had rendered valuable services to the Conqueror,
was given command of the region beyond the River Lempa in El
Salvador where Roxas had recently encountered difficulties. Moscoso, an able Governor, pacified the Indians without resort to

force and established a prosperous colony. So great became Alvarado's fame as a conqueror of Indians that a German author ascribes to him the conquest of Costa Rica in 1530, evidently a mistake as this province had been conquered by the Governor of Panama several years earlier.[9]

The Cakchiquel Kings, Belehe-Qat and Cahi-Imox, fugitives in the mountains since their last defeat, tiring of the hopeless struggle, sent word to Alvarado asking pardon and expressing their desire to live in peace with the Whites. The Captain General accepted, desirous of crowning his conquest with an act of moderation. Accordingly, in August 1530, accompanied by a great number of their followers, the chiefs presented themselves in the capital, clothed with the now meaningless insignia of their rank, and were received with honours and demonstrations of friendship by the Spanish Governor.

FOOTNOTES FOR CHAPTER NINE

[1] *Anales de la Sociedad de Geografia e Historia de Guatemala,* December 1927.

[2] Stephens, *Incidents of Travel in Central America,* Vol. I, p. 278. Stephens' picturesque but inaccurate account is as follows:

"Resuming our ride, we came out upon a rich plain covered with grass, on which cattle and horses were pasturing, between the bases of the two great volcanoes; and on the left, at a distance, on the side of the Volcan de Agua, saw the Church of Ciudad Vieja, the first capital of Guatemala, founded by Alvarado the Conqueror. I was now on classic ground. The fame of Cortes and his exploits in Mexico spread among the Indian tribes to the south, and the Kachiquel Kings sent an embassy offering to acknowledge themselves vassals of Spain. Cortes received the ambassadors with distinction, and sent Pedro de Alvarado, an officer distinguished in the conquest of New Spain, to receive the submission of the native Kings, and take possession of Guatemala. On the thirteenth of November, 1523, Alvarado left the City of Mexico with three hundred Spaniards, and a large body of Tlascaltecas, Cholotecas, Chinapas, and other auxiliary Mexican Indians, fought his way through the populous provinces of Soconusco and Tonala, and on the fourteenth of May, by a decisive victory over the Quiche Indians, he arrived at the capital of the Kachiquel kingdom, now known as the village of Tecpan, Guatemala. After remaining a few days to recover from their fatigues, the conquering army continued their route by the villages on the coast, overcoming all that disputed their progress; and on the twenty-fourth of July, 1524, arrived at a place called by the Indians, Almolonga, meaning in their language, a spring of water (or the mountain from which water flows), situated at the base of the Volcan de Agua. The situation, says Remesal, pleased them so much by its fine climate, the beauty of the meadows, delightfully watered by running streams, and particularly from its lying between two lofty mountains, from one of which descended runs of water in every direction, and from the summit of the other issued volumes of smoke and fire, that they determined to build a city which should be the capital of Guatemala.

"On the twenty-fifth day of July, the festival of Saint James, the patron of Spain, the soldiers, with martial music, splendid armour, waving plumes, horses superbly caparisoned in trappings glittering with jewels and plates of gold, proceeded to the humble church which had been constructed for that purpose, when Juan Godines, the Chaplain to the army said Mass. The whole body invoked the protection of the Apostle, and called by his name the city they had founded. On the same day, Alvarado appointed Alcaldes, Regidors, and the Chief Alguazil. The appearance of the country harmonized with the romantic scenes of which it had been the theatre; and as I rode over the plain I could almost imagine the sides of the mountain covered with Indians and Alvarado and his small band of daring Spaniards, soldiers and priests, with martial pride and religious humility, unfurling the banners of Spain and setting up the standard of the Cross."

[3] "Manuscript of the Acts of the City of Guatemala," copied by Arevalo.

[4] "Manuscript of the Acts of the City of Guatemala," Session of September 16, 1528.

[5] Ramirez, *Proceso de Pedro del Alvarado*.

[6] Milla, *Historia de la America Central*, p. 209

[7] Stephens, *Incidents of Travel in Central America*, Vol. I.

[8] Herrera, *Historia General*, while Juarros, *Historia de Guatemala*, states that this city was founded at Olanchito in Honduras which seems scarcely possible as that district was at that time governed from Panama.

[9] Gunther, *La Epoca de los Descubrimientos*, p. 119.

X

NEIGHBOUR'S FIELDS ARE GREENER

(1532 — 1534)

ALVARADO had now completed the pacification of Guatemala but, by nature warrior rather than civil governor, he was irked by the constant quarrels between his subjects, between his subjects and the Indians, and the complaints of both directed against his government. The harvest of gold had been disappointingly small although he himself possessed five hundred Indian slaves working the placer deposits of the upland streams for the precious metal, and almost every sand bar in Guatemala had its contingent of natives turning the gravel for the benefit of a Spaniard.

From the time of his return from Mexico in April 1530, he had kept prominently in mind a proposal to discover and conquer the legendary Isles of Spice in the East Indies made to him by the Emperor during his latest visit to Spain. His Most Catholic Majesty had conferred the same right upon Cortes who had already sent two vessels to search for the islands but returned empty-handed. The Marquis of the Valley now proposed to Alvarado that the search should be a joint one, but his erstwhile lieutenant rejected the proposal rather bluntly and Cortes, feeling that he owed no further consideration to one who showed so little appreciation, fitted out two more ships that were lost at sea in 1531.

As Alvarado was undertaking the construction of three vessels at Iztapa on the Pacific Coast of Guatemala, the Cakchiquel King, Belehe-Qat, died at Solola, his last days saddened by the revelation that in aiding the Spaniards to conquer his hereditary enemies, the Quiches, he had effectually enslaved his own people. By the age-old custom of the Cakchiquel nation the succession derived upon the Prince Cahi-Imox, but Alvarado, wishing to demonstrate that there was a new law in the land, proceeded immediately to

Solola and selected as King the Prince Tzaya-Qatu who had become Christian and taken the name of Jorge. The legitimate heir returned to the former capital of Iximche, an object lesson of the loss of his nation's independence.

While the vessels were under construction, Alvarado undertook an active propaganda among the Spanish residents in Guatemala and Honduras, holding before their ever-credulous imagination the mirage of yet greater wealth and glory to be gained in the East Indies. In the midst of his preparations came the news of the conquest of Peru with the fabulous hoards of gold and silver wrung from the Incas by Pizarro and Almagro. The plans of Alvarado changed immediately. The Isles of Spice were distant, legendary and possibly barren of gold. The Spaniards had had many bitter disappointments on tropical shores where every prospect allured, but gold seemed always beyond the reach of their eager fingers. Peru had been proven by their comrades to be even richer than Mexico, and every Spaniard, ethics cast aside, longed to desert his plantation or gold mine and rush to wrest from Pizarro and Inca alike the treasures of Peru. To obtain certain necessary materials for his fleet, Alvarado had sent a vessel to Panama which returned at this time. The stories brought by the crew of the incredible discovery of Pizarro further inflamed the cupidity of Alvarado and his followers and no obstacle could prevent their expedition southward. At this time there were present in Guatemala three royal officials, respectively the Treasurer, Auditor and Inspector General, directly representing the Crown and the Council of the Indies. These functionaries were usually at loggerheads among themselves over questions of prestige, jurisdiction and personal aggrandizement. Now, however, they united against their common enemy the Captain General and wrote a long letter to the King in which, after accusing Alvarado of all of the crimes on the calendar, they protested particularly against his projected expedition to Peru, claiming that Guatemala would be left unprotected against Indian uprisings and the attacks of the pirates should he take with him the greater part of the Spanish garrison as well as several thousand converted Indian allies. They begged the King to send a new Governor immediately who would prevent him from depleting the Spanish forces in Guatemala and to molest and hamstring him in every way possible. To make sure of turning Charles V against Alvarado, they stated that the Captain General had spoken contemptuously of his position as Governor, saying that with his sword he could carve out a greater province, that he was autocratic and absolute in all his actions showing respect neither to the representatives of the Crown, to the Church nor to His Majesty himself.

Through his spies Alvarado was aware of the contents of this letter as well as of a similar one sent to the Audiencia in Mexico City, but continued his preparations nevertheless. When the fleet was ready he himself wrote to the Emperor stating that for the greater glory of His Majesty and Spain and at his own expense he had constructed three vessels and purchased five smaller ones from the Governor of Panama and provided them with necessary stores. He proposed to enlist five hundred Spaniards each having full armour, of whom one hundred were armed with crossbows, an equal number with swords and shields, fifty musketeers and the remainder equipped with lances and two-handed swords. Although he possessed two hundred horses, he did not intend to take these at this time but to send for them later as his vessels were already crowded, and finally that His Majesty need have no worry over the safety of Guatemala, as the Indians were contented, and had he not always scrupulously carried out His Majesty's orders for the good treatment of the subject nations?

The Archbishop, Ramirez, who at this time was President of the Audiencia of Mexico, receiving the complaint of the royal officers in Guatemala, immediately wrote Alvarado refusing him permission to proceed to Peru, stating that he considered the expedition as ill-advised and dangerous. Tonatiuh, enraged at the letter which he considered due to the intrigues of Cortes (though such was not the case), sent an evasive reply and continued his preparations. The King himself, however, replying to Alvarado's letter refused him permission for the projected expedition and directed him to send the fleet and army to the Isles of Spice or "to discover some new land not already discovered by others." Even Alvarado did not dare override the direct orders of his sovereign, but in the quoted phrase he saw the opportunity to render lip service and still give full rein to his ambition. The pilot, Juan

Fernandez, who had accompanied Pizarro on his first expedition to Peru, arrived in Guatemala at this time and informed Alvarado that the adjoining provinces of Quito (Ecuador) had not been conquered by Pizarro and that, as it was the original seat of the Inca Empire, the missing treasures were doubtless to be found there. Here was the necessary pretext, he would explore and conquer the heretofore unknown kingdom of Quito where he could be within striking distance of Peru.

Preparations went forward with fever-heat lest some other Conquistador arrive in Quito before him. Endless caravans of Indian carriers bore cannon, equipment and supplies for the fleet from the Caribbean ports to Iztapa. The crew and soldiers flocked to take their places, all was forgotten save the beckoning Peru where even kitchen utensils were made of solid gold. The newly formed municipalities hastened to lend arms or foodstuffs for the expedition in return for which they were to have part of the treasure discovered. The City of San Cristobal de Chiapa sent Alvarado two of the five small cannons that guarded that outpost. Indians of the Quiche nation, who heretofore had disdained any manual labour, carried the guns on their shoulders for a distance of over three hundred miles of slippery mountain trails and through interminable flooded lowlands.

The Captain General named his brother Jorge as Lieutenant Governor during his absence. Two other brothers, Gomez and Diego, accompanied the expedition. In the last days of the year 1533, Alvarado left Guatemala City with five hundred well armed Spaniards. Two hundred others who could not secure passage in the vessels remained enviously behind. He had changed his mind in regard to horses, and two hundred and twenty-seven were placed on board. This was one of the most formidable Spanish expeditions ever sent to conquer a portion of the New World. Two thousand Guatemalan Indians were taken as servants, miserable slaves with no exciting illusions of grandeur or wealth, destined to leave their bones in the swamps of Esmeraldas or the snow-clad passes of the Andes. None of them returned to Guatemala.

On January 23, 1534, the fleet sailed, Alvarado leaving a very diplomatic letter addressed to the royal and municipal officials, protesting his affection for Guatemala and begging them to recognize and obey his brother in his absence and promising that the result of the expedition would redound to the glory of the colony. When the fleet was scarcely under way, two vessels were sighted commanded by Gabriel de Rojas, bringing two hundred soldiers as reinforcements to Pizarro. Alvarado seized the vessels without scruple, to the general satisfaction of the newcomers, glad of the opportunity to serve under so famous and successful a Captain. On February 13, the fleet had doubled Cape San Francisco. The commander wished to push on to the settlement of Chincha within the limits of the territory granted Pizarro by Charles V, but as the greater portion of his followers were anxious to set foot in Quito and as strong currents rendered further progress southward dangerous the expedition landed at Puerto Viejo, where the army was organized for the long march inland. Diego de Alvarado was appointed Aide-de-Camp; Gomez de Alvarado, Luis de Moscoso and Enriquez de Guzman, Captains of Cavalry, while the veterans Lazcano and Benavides commanded the foot. The Captain General's guard was under orders of Rodrigo de Chaves, the Attorney Calderon was made Chief Justice with Juan de Saavedra as his bailiff. Francisco Calderon was named Quartermaster. These arrangements completed, Alvarado harangued the soldiers, and dropping the mask of duty and altruism, set forth the expense he had been put to in order to provide the fleet and expedition and appealed to the avaricious nature of his followers to overcome any obstacles between them and the treasures at Quito. The pilot, Fernandez, was sent southward with part of the fleet and a notary public to take possession of any likely harbours not actually garrisoned by Pizarro, while the remaining vessels returned to Panama and Nicaragua for additional recruits.

The army set out in high spirits, having received confirmatory rumours of the immense Inca treasures hidden in Quito. At the outset all went well. In the Province of Xipixaca much placer gold and many emeralds were found. The soldiers threw away the green stones and only the assayer of the expedition, Pedro Gomez, who knew the value of this discovery, profited thereby. Weapons plated with gold and native helmets adorned with precious stones were almost disdainfully collected by the soldiers blinded by tales of vaults packed with gold bars in the capital. Soon, however, the expedition found itself in difficulties. The original guides deserted, leaving the Spaniards without knowledge of the route. Moscoso, sent on a scouting expedition, discovered a town filled with provisions which the Spaniards were greatly in need of, but no gold. He brought back a number of Indians to act as guides but during the night the Guatemalan servants killed and devoured their cousins. Alvarado sent his brother Gomez to search out the route northward and Captain Benavides made an excursion to the east accompanied by both infantry and horsemen. The resistance of several small towns was easily overcome and prisoners taken who agreed to act as guides to Quito. Alvarado selected the route followed by Benavides and arriving at the River Dable found a town empty of its inhabitants and foodstuffs. Again small parties were sent in all directions to look for food, Enriquez de Guzman finding a large town some thirty miles away where dried fish, corn and edible roots were stored in abundance. Alvarado led his army thither where they rested several days, as a large number of the soldiers, especially the infantrymen, were ill and suffering from their long marches and insufficient food. The Captain General placed a soldier suffering from malaria in his own saddle and led the column on foot, his example being followed by the captains and cavalrymen. The region was almost entirely composed of great swamps and had this not been the dry season of the year, further progress would have been impossible. Some neighbouring small towns supplied a quantity of provisions but the inhabitants disappeared into the pathless jungles and the spectre of hunger again haunted the Spaniards. The army moved to a nearby large town where Enriquez de Guzman and a number of others died of their wounds and the climate. The Indian guides professed to be lost and were of no further service. The Captain Garcia de Tovar with forty men was sent to cut his way through the forest, searching for higher ground and food. The jungle was so thick that they were obliged to hack a path with their swords and to sleep at night on hammocks made of vines hung above the endless swamps. After several days' progress northward, Garcia discovered a large town surrounded by cornfields. Corn and deer meat were sent back to Alvarado whose condition by now was desperate. The starving army set out to follow Garcia and while in the midst of the jungle the air was suddenly darkened and the soldiers smothered and blinded by a storm of volcanic ash.[1] The superstitious Spaniards saw in this a forecast of disaster. European and Guatemalan alike died from hunger, climate and fatigue, the former perhaps also from disappointment and the latter from despair. The army reached a very large river covered with a species of water lily whose leaves and branches were strong enough to support the weight of the foot-soldiers. The horses, however, broke through this natural bridge and some days were spent in ferrying them across on rafts. Alvarado divided his force here and set out in advance with the greater part of the cavalry, confiding the command of the remainder to the Attorney Calderon, who was directed to follow the advance guard, taking especial care of the ill. In the crossing of the River Chongo, a large group of Indians in a warlike attitude was encountered. When the Spaniards came within range they shouted in unison and discharged a cloud of arrows, then broke and fled to houses nearby as the cavalry charged. Alvarado occupied the town as temporary headquarters and while waiting for the infantry to come up, sent his brother Diego with a small force toward some hills visible to the northward. The Captain General followed with another group of cavalry, leaving the main force as before to Calderon. Diego de Alvarado found his path winding ever deeper into the volcanic country filled with jagged boulders that tore the feet and limbs of his horses and men and so broken that although they were suffering agonies of thirst under a blazing sun, the Spaniards could not reach a small stream visible a short distance away. Two days were spent in this wilderness, horses and men devouring a kind of cane growing in cracks in the lava for its scarce liquid content. Emerging from the desert the advance guard found a small town where the Indians occupied themselves in making salt and raising sheep, a welcome sight to the hungry adventurers. The inhabitants fled in terror at the sight of these strange beings who they said afterwards must be demons or insane to have traversed the volcanic desert. By a circuitous route shown him by a native, Diego de Alvarado sent his brother a report of his discoveries, accompanied by salt and mutton. It was high time. The Spanish army was dying of hunger, they had already eaten the horses that fell ill, alligators, snakes and even lizards that crossed their path.[2]

While Alvarado was climbing out of the jungle into the desert, one of the great Spanish conquerors, Diego de Almagro, who shared with Pizarro the conquest of the Inca Empire, was at Vilcas, a short distance aside from the route followed by Alvarado. Alarmed by news of the Guatemalan expedition, Almagro had sent two trusted messengers to obtain information but before they returned his fears were rendered fact. Gabriel de Rojas, whose ships Alvarado had seized off the coast of Central America, on landing in the kingdom of Quito (Ecuador) had deserted Alvarado and made his way to Peru with a number of his original followers. As he knew something of the country, he made better progress than Tonatiuh, and arriving in Vilcas, informed Almagro of all details of Alvarado's expedition and plans, not omitting to mention the part played therein by the pilot Fernandez.

Almagro understood the gravity of the situation, confronted as he was by a daring and experienced countryman at the head of a large force and evidently preparing to dispute the conquest of Peru. Ordering Hernando de Soto, who had previously campaigned in Central America and was to find a grave in the Mississippi, to remain in Vilcas and watch the movements of the Inca army, Almagro sent Rojas to Pizarro at Cuzco to advise him of the arrival of Alvarado and to suggest that Pizarro remain in the capital, with all his forces, to prevent a surprise seizure by the newcomer while Almagro himself, with a small force under his orders, would confront Alvarado and if possible reason with him. Almagro set out for San Miguel de Piura where Captain Benalcazar, the Spanish Governor, had recently established his headquarters. On arriving he found the town empty. Benalcazar had apparently deserted Pizarro to join the Guatemalan. This shifting of allegiance by local commanders from one conqueror to another in disputed territory was a commonly practised custom but in this case Almagro was mistaken. Benalcazar, hearing of the arrival of Alvarado, had departed in haste for Quito to seize the treasure for himself if possible. Even under the fantastically rigid laws of the age, the Governor could be convicted only of ambition, not of treason. Almagro followed the traces of Benalcazar. He needed the

Captain's support and there was plenty of time later to discuss the division of spoil.

In the meantime, after resting his exhausted army and restoring many of the ill, Alvarado again took up the march toward the town where his brother had discovered the sheep and salt. Diego de Alvarado had continued his explorations to the foot of a range of very high and steep mountains whose summits were covered with snow. To pass around these mountains would have required a very long and difficult journey, whereupon the Spanish captain resolved to cross over them, a resolution which many of his companions declared insane, as no one knew the road, but nothing was impossible to an Alvarado and the ascent was undertaken on a day marked by a cloudburst and a freezing wind. The Guatemalan Indians and the foot-soldiers suffered greatly before arriving on the opposite slope, where a town of some size was discovered. Their trials were forgotten in finding ample food in the houses. Diego sent a messenger to advise his brother, adding that it was necessary that the whole army cross the mountains. In the meantime Pedro de Alvarado saw his expedition dwindle daily, the wings of the angel of death hovering constantly over the forces commanded by Calderon. Believing that at all costs the deadly low country must be left behind, the Captain General began his ascent of the mountains on a day even colder than that on which his brother had made the crossing. The White soldiers, acclimated though they were to the cold winters of the Spanish highlands, suffered greatly, but their lot was idyllic compared with that of the miserable Guatemalan Indians, accustomed to a daily temperature of one hundred degrees Fahrenheit. The snow burned their eyes, froze their feet, and by the time ten miles had been covered the route was marked by the dead bodies of Indians literally frozen to death. At nightfall the tribulations increased. There was neither fire nor shelter; throughout the night arose the laments of the wretched Indians and at daybreak even the iron heart of Alvarado was wrung by the spectacle spread before him. He regretted then not having undertaken the longer route around the mountains, but it was too late and there was nothing left but to press forward. To animate his soldiers he proclaimed that all of the gold so far obtained by the expedition and now carried by the baggage train, should be the personal property of the soldiers, waiving his rights. On other days this offer would have been received with outstretched hands and shouts of joy. Today the freezing adventurers asked for bread, not gold. So great was their extremity that the baggage train containing all of the gold was abandoned without protest in the snow-clad waste. Alvarado was almost in despair at this evidence of loss of morale, and summoning all his eloquence told the soldiers that they must save themselves, that it was possible to win through the pass, as his brother and his companions had done previously. The march continued but even greater sufferings lay ahead. Fierce cold winds carrying snow and hail swept down upon the column, the sun was hidden and the freezing travellers stumbled blindly across the mountains. The laments of the Indian auxiliaries filled the air, and again the road was strewn with the bodies of Quiche and Cakchiquel. The assayer, Gomez, laden with his emeralds, lost both fortune and life in the storm. A soldier named Huelamo, who had brought his wife and two small daughters with him, seeing them fall exhausted, lay down to die with them. On all sides were scattered jewels, arms, equipment and bodies of the frozen. Overhead the vultures and condors swooped and dove in excited squadrons, falling upon the unexpected feast before the stragglers had passed. Fifteen Spaniards, many Negro servants and two thousand Indians perished in the snow. The survivors were mere walking skeletons. The few Indians who remained alive were snowblind and many had lost their toes and fingers. In the town of Pasi, Alvarado reviewed his wasted troops. Since landing he had lost eighty-five Spaniards, most of the Indians and many of his horses. Nearly all of his followers were ill and none were in condition to undertake a battle with either Almagro or the Incas.

After some rest and leisurely marches through a number of neighbouring small towns, the army reached one of the great Inca roads where the Captain General, to his chagrin, found the marks of horseshoes. Other altruistic conquerors were before him.[3] While the Guatemalan army continued its march toward Quito, Almagro and Benalcazar had joined forces in that city and now turned about to meet Alvarado and dispute his passage. Almagro possessed only two hundred men, cavalry and infantry, but his force was well disciplined and equipped and in good health and thus more than a match for the exhausted followers of the Captain General. En route Almagro fought a battle with one of the yet unconquered Inca armies. The prisoners informed him that the forces of Alvarado were close at hand. To obtain a breathing space for his force which had been severely tried by the battle and the crossing of a river where eighty Indian auxiliaries of the Peruvian force were drowned, Almagro sent Captain Lope de Idiaquez, who at one time lived in Guatemala and knew Alvarado, with four soldiers to watch the movements of the newcomers.

Proceeding incautiously along the Inca highway, the Peruvians turned a corner to find themselves in the hands of Diego de Alvarado who promptly disarmed them and sent them under guard to his brother. Pedro de Alvarado at this time was preparing to attack an Inca chief who had fortified himself close to the highway but abandoned this enterprise to interview the prisoners. He treated them with great courtesy and said he had not gone to Peru but instead had undertaken to discover new lands as he had been commanded to do by His Majesty, the Emperor. The Peruvians were set free and sent back to Almagro bearing a polite and crafty letter, wherein Alvarado veiled his ambitions. He had followed the instructions of the Emperor and at great cost to himself had equipped his army and had carefully remained out of the territory assigned to Pizarro, he wished in no manner to molest the Peruvian commander nor to cause jealousy or discord and that he was en route to Riobamba where he would be glad to meet with Almagro and arrange all things in a friendly manner. Almagro did not credit these friendly intentions and hurried to Riobamba, that he would be found in possession when the Guatemalan army arrived. Subsequently he sent three of his principal captains with an oral message, quite as sincere as the letter of Alvarado, to congratulate the Captain General upon his safe arrival and to assure the Guatemalan that his fame as a Castilian general and loyal servant of the King caused the contents of his letter to be accepted at face value. The emissaries had orders to tell Alvarado that Pizarro was already Governor of the greater portion of these provinces and that he was at that moment expecting a Royal Decree confirming him as Governor General of all parts of the Kingdom of Quito as well as Peru.

Almagro's messengers met Alvarado at the head of his column. Without halting the Captain General answered that on arriving at Riobamba he would send his reply. He did not take the precaution to prevent the Peruvians from talking with his soldiers, which they promptly proceeded to do, keeping pace with the rank and file and enlarging upon the great riches at Cuzco where Pizarro was and pointing out the wisdom of leaving Alvarado for the services of the conqueror of Peru, that it was foolhardy to venture in this wild region in search of possible treasure while gold in immeasurable quantities actually existed in Peru. Arriving at a town fifteen miles from Riobamba, Alvarado sent to Almagro asking for Indian interpreters and a free passage to explore lands beyond the jurisdiction of the conqueror of Peru. Almagro replied that he could not permit so great an army to pass and that there were not sufficient provisions in Quito for Alvarado's force. During all this time his emissaries continued to foment dissatisfaction among Alvarado's troops and the latter sent spies into the Peruvian ranks in turn to seduce Almagro's troops. The first result of this double intrigue was that an Indian, who served as Almagro's interpreter, presented himself to Alvarado giving details of the number of soldiers and their general situation. He said trenches had been constructed around the camp but that he could force the Peruvians to abandon the position by bribing Almagro's Indian allies to set fire to the surrounding woods. His desertion was matched by that of Antonio Picado, secretary of Alvarado, who went over to the Peruvians. The Guatemalan commander, irritated, advanced with four hundred men leaving very few to guard his camp. Diego de Alvarado led the advance with thirty horsemen, the Captain General was close behind with as many more, the Royal Standard was guarded by forty of the best riders, Mateo Lojano commanded sixty archers and musketeers, Rodrigo de Chaves protected the supplies and to Benavides was confided the remainder of the army. Almagro, despite the inferiority of his force, resolved to fight to the end and when the advance guard appeared the Peruvian sentries ordered them to halt.

At this moment a messenger from Alvarado appeared in

Almagro's camp with a message demanding the surrender of
Picado. The Peruvian refused, stating that Picado was free to go
wherever he pleased. Together with this reply he sent the Spanish
Mayor of the newly formed town of Riobamba with a royal
scribe to solemnly warn the Captain General in the name of the
Most High and the Emperor to cause no scandal in the realm nor
to lay violent hands upon the administration of justice nor to
enter the city, ordering him to return to his province of Guatemala and to leave in peace that which the Emperor had granted
to Francisco Pizarro. Almagro, who had literally waded in the
blood of the Incas, protested naïvely that the intrusion of Alvarado
would damage and trouble the latter. Alvarado briskly rejected this
move, declaring that he was Governor and Captain General by
decree of His Majesty, that he held a roving commission to explore
by land and sea, that he could enter into any part of Peru where
no one else was then exercising the powers of Governor and if
Almagro really had made a settlement at Riobamba that he would
do no damage thereto because all that he asked, and for which he
was ready to pay, was that necessary supplies should be given
his army. Almagro's messenger replied that if the Captain General
would withdraw his army a distance of three miles, the necessary
negotiations could be undertaken. The man who had without a
second thought faced almost impossible odds on the field of battle
was confronted by an enemy too subtle for his soldier's mind—
the law. He took counsel with himself, considering that his followers were in great part opposed to settling this difference by
force of arms. He saw the determination of Almagro and remem-
bered that he undertook this expedition against the orders of the
Emperor and the Audiencia of Mexico. He had reason to fear the
wrath of his superiors if he took refuge in force and considered
the possibility of a friendly arrangement, one which would not
damage his reputation. Therefore he sent the Attorney Calderon
and Captain Moscoso to confer with Almagro. But the greatest
concession that the messengers could obtain from the stern old
soldier was that Alvarado might use a small village near Riobamba
to shelter his troops, and that the two chiefs should meet the next
day to arrange their differences. Alvarado counted on his superior
strength as a final card, Almagro on the law.

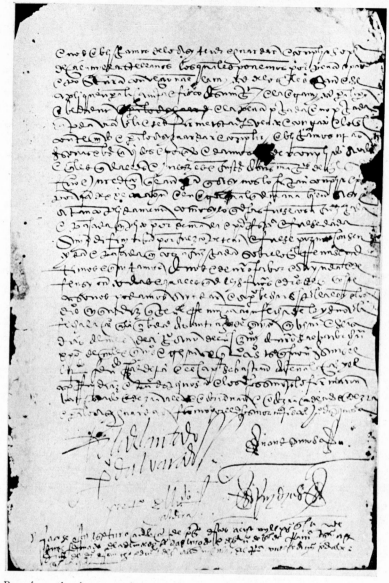

Page from the Agreement between Alvarado and Almagro. Original is in the Harkness Collection in the Library of Congress.
(Translation Given in Appendix "E.")

On the following day Pedro de Alvarado came to Riobamba with a number of his chief captains and was received by Almagro with much courtesy. In the conference, in which the chief supporters of both conquerors were present, various solutions to the situation were considered. Alvarado proposed that a partnership be formed between Almagro, Pizarro and himself to exploit this country and that the arrangement should be sealed as if the high contracting parties were sovereigns by the marriage of Alvarado's daughter[4] with the son of Almagro. The latter declined, wisely pointing out that harmony among three partners is impossible. Finally, after a long discussion it was arranged that Alvarado should return to Guatemala leaving his army and equipment in exchange for a payment of one hundred thousand gold pesos.[5]

This contract having been drawn and signed, Alvarado undertook to explain his action to his followers, stating that he had accepted the arrangement for the good of his army, as the alternative would have been civil war, that the object of all on leaving Guatemala was to find new and richer territories which thus had been accomplished and finally, if they lost him as chief they would gain one with whose valour and liberality he hoped they would be satisfied. Many of the Guatemalan warriors, especially the younger ones, were disgusted to find that after so many trials and sufferings the net result was that they had been incorporated into the army of Almagro when they could have conquered him and made themselves masters of the country, but others rejoiced that they had not been obliged to make war upon their brothers, and as they probably had no great affection for Guatemala they were not displeased to exchange one residence for another.

Alvarado and Almagro departed together to visit Pizarro who had left Cuzco for the coast, anxious to verify reports he had received of the arrival of the Guatemalan Captain General and his people. The two great adventurers met in the old city of Pachacamac where the stocky, swarthy yeoman, conqueror of Peru, appeared at great physical disadvantage with the tall, fair, handsome, smiling Alvarado.

As Pizarro was well satisfied with the arrangement made by Almagro and Alvarado, he received the Guatemalan with much courtesy and feasting. He received the sum agreed upon, and as both Almagro and Pizarro wished to show themselves generous toward the conqueror of Guatemala, they made him a gift of a great quantity of precious stones. A number of soldiers who had taken part in the conquest of Peru, having amassed fortunes which they did not care to risk in the continual strife between the Pizarro family and their enemies, obtained permission from their leader to sail with Alvarado and settle in Guatemala. On his return to Guatemala, the Captain General grumbled that the sum received did not cover the expense of the expedition, while Almagro on his side complained that he had paid three times the value of the ships and equipment.[6]

The expedition to Ecuador was a disaster from all points of view. Alvarado had greatly weakened his colony by the permanent loss of over five hundred of the finest soldiers in Guatemala through death or the incorporation into the army of Peru. His prestige as a conqueror had been sadly dimmed by the anticlimax of the contract with Almagro. His favourable position at court had been lessened by his lack of success. Had he defied the Emperor, discovered and conquered vast new lands rich as Mexico or Peru, his fame on the continent would undoubtedly have surpassed that of Cortes and Pizarro. As it was, while no great harm came to him from this fiasco, his enemies in Spain and in Mexico were able to keep his future ambitions within narrow limits, chafing to the restless spirit of the Captain General. There seems little reason to doubt that if he had overthrown Almagro, Pizarro's enemies in Spain would have gladly used their influence to confirm his possession of Ecuador and the Council of the Indies would have discreetly closed its eyes to the act of violence. In his arrangement with Almagro, Alvarado undertook to emulate the diplomatic traits of Hernan Cortes but with indifferent success.[7]

FOOTNOTES FOR CHAPTER TEN

[1] Milla, *Historia de la America Central.*

[2] Baron von Humboldt, *Vues des Cordillères,* p. 294.
"This highway was formed of great slabs of stone and compared favourably with the finest roads in Italy, France or Spain. The great Inca highway is one of the most useful and gigantic works of man."

[3] Markham, *History of Peru,* p. 88.

[4] Doña Leonor, daughter of Alvarado and the Tlascalan Princess, born in 1520.

[5] $140,000 according to calculation in Chapter VI, but over $1,000,000 according to Prescott.

[6] Milla, *Historia de la America Central,* points out that two of the ships paid for by Pizarro had been seized by Alvarado on the high seas from Pizarro's Lieutenant Rojas.

[7] The text of the letters written by Alvarado to Charles V in regard to the Quito expedition are given in the appendix.

XI

SUNSET

(1535 — 1541)

PEDRO DE ALVARADO returned to Guatemala in April 1535[1] and was received with festivals organized in his honour by the municipal authorities and by much rejoicing on the part of the populace. The Audiencia of Mexico, enraged by his bland ignoring of its decree, no sooner received word of his return than one of its principal members, the Attorney Alonso de Maldonado, was sent to Guatemala to open an inquiry into the acts of the Captain General and to assess a penalty if found guilty. The Audiencia in its own mind had condemned Alvarado in advance, the more so because he had returned empty-handed. Although measures were taken to keep Maldonado's journey and object a secret, the defendant received word in time to prepare his defence. Trusting again to audacity to win for him, he resolved not to wait the arrival of Maldonado and submit meekly to the inquiry but to proceed to Spain and boldly meet all charges against him in the very court of the Emperor. An incident occurring at this time in the neighbouring colony of Honduras furnished a pretext for his absence from Guatemala.

Andres de Cerezeda, Royal Governor of Honduras, was engaged in moving the Spanish capital from the port of Trujillo, founded by Columbus on his fourth voyage in 1502, to the inland valley of Naco, despite the determined opposition of the colonists. Honduras had suffered from continual strife between the Spanish Governor of Panama, who claimed the province as part of Nicaragua, and the Viceroy of Mexico, who, following Cortes, regarded Honduras as the tail of the Mexican dog. The Intendent of Santo Domingo and the clerical authorities there also claimed the territory so that at times three mutually hostile Spanish forces sought to exterminate each other among the dense jungles of the north coast.

Under Cerezeda the misery of the colonists reached such a state that many counselled the assassination of the Governor, but the Royal Treasurer, Diego Garcia de Celis, who while unfriendly to Cerezeda wished to avoid complete disaster, counselled an appeal to Pedro de Alvarado and presently bore the petition to Guatemala. Alvarado accepted the mission eagerly, as the pacification of Honduras would gain him a friendly reception at court. Four months passed before he arrived at Naco, having made a circuitous journey through the region of Santa Cruz in the eastern portion of the present Republic of Guatemala, subduing an Indian uprising and appointing local officials.

The inhabitants of Naco despairing of relief from Alvarado determined to return to Trujillo, taking with them all of the Indian slaves attached to the colony, and when Cerezeda would have disputed their departure they tied him and his few followers to trees in the principal street and set forth. Barely five miles from Naco they were met by Indians who announced the arrival of a large party of Spaniards. Understanding that this was the long-sought relief and fearing that if left alone with Alvarado, Cerezeda would poison the Captain General's mind against them, they hurried back to the village to receive their ally. As soon as he was convinced of Alvarado's motive, the Governor made the best of a bad bargain and renounced his authority in favour of the Guatemalan. Alvarado accepted, named new officials and took measures for pacification of the country. He sent the greater portion of his force under command of the Captain Juan de Chaves to search for a site suitable for the location of a town. The explorers were lost for many days in a wilderness of broken hills and finally coming to a meadow beside a river they exclaimed, "Thank God we have at last found level land!" from which the town was named Gracias a Dios. Another town was founded some distance away with the name of San Pedro Sula. The Captain General made a division of lands among the Honduran Spaniards and donated cattle for the common use of the settlers. Rich gold mines being discovered within a few miles of Gracias a Dios, the town grew rapidly prosperous. Having with so little ceremony become Governor of a province

heretofore entirely independent of Guatemala, Alvarado prepared
to sail for Spain by way of Havana and wrote the municipal
authorities of Guatemala a letter in farewell attempting to leave
a favourable impression, as on his departure from the city he had
stated that his journey was only to Honduras. He sailed from
Puerto Caballos, now Puerto Cortes, Honduras, on about the first
day of August, 1536. Scarcely had he passed beyond the horizon
than the Captain Alonso de Caceres, emissary of the Governor-
elect, Francisco de Montejo, arrived in Gracias a Dios and following an old Spanish custom arrested the officials nominated by
Alvarado and cancelled his land grants. The latter, however, had
been provided with the excuse he sought and could allege spontaneous service on behalf of his sovereign when he arrived in the
presence of Charles V.

The Attorney Maldonado, sent to try Alvarado, arrived in
Guatemala on May 10, 1536, shortly after the Captain General
had left for Honduras. Finding the bird flown, the judge could
not serve his warrant for arrest but contented himself by seizing
all of Alvarado's property and trying him in his absence. Maldonado, being a civilian, was poor, as the treasures of the New World
as yet went to those capable of wielding a sword. Avaricious and
envious by nature, he utilized the power as interim-Governor,
which his mission gave him, to make changes in the government
of the province, ostensibly to lighten the burden of the Indians,
actually to replace Alvarado's friends with his enemies and thus
strengthen his hold upon the property of the Captain General.

In this he was zealously aided by Bartolome de las Casas, Bishop
of Chiapa, whose bitter tongue and venomous pen were dedicated
to the villification of the Spanish conquerors. Hysterical, untruthful and intolerant, de las Casas was a prototype of certain modern
Dissenter clerics who arrogate to themselves those things which
are Caesar's. He was born in Seville in 1474 of French ancestry
and, after completing his education at the University of Salamanca, obtaining the diploma of Bachelor of Laws, came to Santo
Domingo in 1502 in the suite of the Governor Ovando, a relative
and patron of the young Cortes. In 1510 he took Holy Orders. At
this time he was a resident of Cuba, a large slave-owner and
actively engaged in developing a tract of land given him by the

Governor. Although later he professed to hate the institution of
slavery, he was one of the most active proponents of the introduc-
tion of Negro slaves, naïvely alleging that they could do more
work than the Indians. In 1514 giving himself the title of "Protector of the Indians," which was later confirmed officially with
an annual salary of one hundred gold pesos, de las Casas roved
continually throughout the Indies and the Spanish Main, making
frequent trips to Spain to complain of the alleged outrages of the
Conquerors. It may be wondered that these men of iron resolution
permitted their critic to pass thus freely through the realms of
which they were absolute masters. He was protected by his
religious garb and the Council of the Indies which, ever jealous
of the Royal Governors, was delighted to find as unscrupulous a
tool. The strictures of de las Casas were refuted by Don Juan
de Quevedo, Bishop of Darien, Father Olmedo and other brethren
of the cloth, who while not shutting their eyes to the plight of
the Indians, refused to follow him in his fantastic flights of imagination. In 1535 Bishop Marroquin, en route to take over the
diocese of Guatemala, requested de las Casas to accompany him,
bringing a number of Dominican Fathers to occupy a monastery
which had been founded by the Franciscans in 1529.

Arriving in Spain, Alvarado made good use of his influential
connections, so much so that on October 22, 1538, at Villadolid,
Charles V signed a decree restoring the government of Guatemala to Alvarado for the next seven years and nullifying in
advance any sentence that the Audiencia might in the meantime or
in the future pass against him. Great as this evidence of fortune
was, it was succeeded by greater. The distinguished presence and
great fame of the conqueror of Guatemala, undimmed by the expedition to Quito now that royal favour shone so brilliantly upon
him, moved the heart of Doña Beatriz de la Cueva, sister of Alvarado's deceased wife. Charles V looked with pleasure upon this
union and personally interceded with the Pope that a dispensation
for the marriage might be granted. Shortly thereafter, Doña
Beatriz, accompanied by her husband and twenty maids of honour,
set out on the long journey to the New World where death had
overtaken her sister and already lifted its sombre wings in welcome
to the second niece of the Duke of Alburquerque. The Governor

Maldonado was visiting the northern portion of his realm when
he received the news of Alvarado's landing at Puerto Caballos.
Questioning the messenger he learned that the Captain General
arrived, not with the humble mien of a culprit about to hear sentence passed upon him but with the confident bearing of a warrior
high in his sovereign's favour. Not pausing to gather his personal
effects in the city of Guatemala, Maldonado fled to Mexico.

Alvarado wrote the municipal authorities of Guatemala from
Puerto Caballos on April 4, 1539, making a reference to a previous
letter which he had sent from Villadolid immediately upon issuance
of the royal decree, asking that many Indians be sent him as
tlamemes (carriers), stating that in addition to his bride and her
maids of honour he was bringing a great quantity of supplies as
well as three hundred archers and many other Spaniards.[1a] He
modestly announced his wedding and advised his readers that the
maids of honour were of excellent family and unmarried, adding
that he did not believe this latter condition would long continue.
Alvarado was evidently in high spirits, as well he might be for he
was again Fortune's favourite.

Two hundred men of his company were set to work to open a
road from the port to San Pedro Sula with such good results
that in ten days a trail wide enough for two mule trains to pass
was completed. The party remained at the port for twenty-five
days, unloading and preparing for the long overland trip. Many
of the newcomers sickened from the climate but none died. Forty-
five days were required to transport the personnel and baggage
to San Pedro where additional men and mules sent from Guatemala were awaiting them. Needing additional carriers and beasts
of burden, Alvarado had written Francisco de Montejo, Governor
of Honduras, from Puerto Caballos without receiving an answer.
This silence led the Guatemalan to believe that Montejo hoped
lack of provisions would cause his train to disband, but the Captain
General pushed on toward Gracias a Dios. A short distance from
this town they were met by Cristobal de Pedraza, Bishop-elect of
Honduras, another "Protector of the Indians." The Bishop begged
Alvarado to write to Montejo again before meeting him and,
although angered at the previous discourtesy, he consented. Alvarado bore an order from Charles V to Pedraza ordering him to

arbitrate the difference between the Captain General and Montejo originating in the cancellation of Alvarado's land grants three years previously. The Captain General asked Pedraza to undertake this mission immediately but the Bishop counselled delay, knowing that Montejo was willing to cede the government of Honduras to him on certain conditions.

The two Governors met and after much hesitation on the part of Montejo, Alvarado was enabled to write the Emperor from Gracias on August 4, 1539, advising him that, subject to the approval of His Majesty, Montejo had ceded the government of Honduras to him in exchange for that of the Province of Chiapa,[2] Alvarado's estate of Xochimilco in Mexico, and the assumption by him of Montejo's debts amounting to two thousand gold pesos. He did not neglect to point out the economies resulting from the unification of Honduras and Guatemala and estimated an increase in the royal revenue of one hundred thousand gold pesos annually if he were permitted to govern them both. Montejo for his part wrote two long and bitter letters to the Emperor, both dated June 1, 1539, in which he accused Alvarado of seizing his government by force, the Bishop of partiality, denied any previous difficulties in the government of his province and insinuated that His Majesty himself was not above favouring the Guatemalan. He begged the Emperor to disapprove the contract and to punish the Bishop. Charles V, however, saw no reason to change his good opinion of the blond son of Estremadura, and Honduras remained united to Guatemala.[3]

Somewhat carried away by his triumph, Alvarado wrote to the Municipality of Guatemala asking them to send one of the Mayors and two Aldermen to inspect the royal seal and orders which he brought with him as evidence of his renewed and extended powers. Always jealous of its prerogatives, the Municipality declined, alleging that Alvarado had no power to make such a request and stating that it would receive him in the Council Chamber.

In the Annals of the Cakchiquels, but not elsewhere, it is recorded that en route to Guatemala City[4] Tonatiuh with his own sword slew the high priest of the Cakchiquel nation in a dispute over the treatment of an allied tribe.

Alvarado reached the city on the fifteenth day of September

and on the sixteenth the royal officials as well as the chiefs of the municipality were present in the Council Chamber to receive him. Many of those present had been open or secret partisans of Maldonado, witnessing the confiscation of Alvarado's property with expressions of joy and hoping that if he ever returned it would be a prisoner. Now they were unable to restrain their rage and eagerly spread a rumour craftily concocted by Alvarado to identify his enemies, that his powers were not properly drawn and signed. When the Council came to order, he presented a document signed by the Emperor on August 9, 1538, wherein Charles V after recounting the reports which Alvarado had made to him of the state of affairs in Guatemala, promised to appoint him Governor for an additional term of seven years, subject, however, to the termination of the inquisition of Maldonado. Gonzalo de Ovalle, an Alderman who had become an enemy of Alvarado because the Captain General had decided against him in a quarrel with another Spaniard, jumped to his feet saying that the document was not valid in that it constituted only a promise and not an appointment and further that it was subject to the sentence of the Audiencia. A number of the other officials supported Ovalle and declined to recognize Alvarado as Captain General and Governor. Having thus placed his enemies on record, Alvarado smiled grimly and handed the royal scribe a scroll, commanding him to read it aloud. This proclamation dated at Villadolid on October 22, 1538, addressed to Maldonado himself and to all royal and municipal officers in the Province of Guatemala, directly named Alvarado as Governor for an additional seven years and commanded them to obey him as such under pain of incurring the royal displeasure. It further nullified in advance any adverse sentence of the Audiencia.[5] Violators of this ordinance were to be fined 100,000 maravedis.[6] The opposition was thunderstruck and he was unanimously received as Governor and Captain General. Playing his cards carefully, Alvarado publicly fraternized with his enemies making them his most ardent partisans. Several days were given over to rejoicing during which the newly arrived maids of honour received a more favourable impression of this new capital than they had looked forward to in the long dreary overland journey carried on the shoulders of Indians.

Present Appearance of the Abandoned Port of Iztapa, Guatemala, from where Alvarado Sailed for Ecuador and Mexico (in 1540).

Neither Alvarado nor Charles V had forgotten the proposed voyage to the Isles of Spice and immediately upon his arrival at Puerto Caballos, the former sent instructions to Guatemala for the construction of two ships at Iztapa, and when writing to the Emperor in August 1539 he was able to announce the completion of the first. The construction of this fleet, which finally consisted of thirteen small vessels, exhausted Alvarado's personal fortune and left him deeply in debt to many of his countrymen. Diaz del Castillo states that, so great was the cost of equipment including ironwork brought overland from Vera Cruz six hundred miles away, eighty vessels of equal size could have been built in Spain for the sum expended on these thirteen. In addition to the cost of the vessels, munition, equipment and food for one thousand soldiers and sailors and more than two hundred horses, were provided by the commander. [7, 8] While personal ambition played a great part in Alvarado's eagerness, the expedition, if successful, would undoubtedly benefit Spain and was therefore in a much different category than the self-seeking voyage to Quito.

On May 19, 1540, Alvarado appeared before the Municipality of Guatemala and stating that he was about to depart, named as Lieutenant Governor and Captain General in his absence the Attorney Francisco de la Cueva, his brother-in-law. Some of the Aldermen demanded that the interim-Governor post a bond but Alvarado denied the request, exhibiting a royal order which he claimed exempted his substitute from this requirement. When he was about to leave the council chamber, one of the Aldermen detained him stating that some decision should be taken with regard to the Quiche and Cakchiquel Kings who had been prisoners in the city for a number of years. The speaker stated that it would be dangerous to leave them in prison during his absence as they might escape and lead their nations against the colonists. It is a little difficult to see from this distance why the Indian prisoners should constitute a greater danger during this journey of Alvarado than during his previous absence in Spain. Several other Aldermen joined in the petition, asking the Captain General to take the prisoners with him or execute them. He returned a noncommittal answer and the fate of the Indians remains a mystery. All of the Spanish authors, without exception, state that Alvarado carried

the captive kings with him while Brasseur de Bourbourg quotes
the annals of the Cakchiquels to the effect that he caused the
Indians to be hanged two hundred and sixty days after his return
from Spain. The Commander proceeded overland to the port of
Acajutla in the present Republic of El Salvador where the fleet
awaited him.

On June 4, 1540, together with eight hundred and fifty Spanish
soldiers and a large number of Indians including some of the
principal nobles of the Quiche and Cakchiquel nations, he set sail
and, after a voyage shortened by favourable winds, reached the port
of Purificacion in the Province of Jalisco, Mexico, where a stop
was made for water and fresh vegetables. At this time the Viceroy
of New Spain was Don Antonio Mendoza whose desire to conquer
the Isles of Spice had aroused the enmity of Cortes then engaged
on the same mission. The Emperor had directed Alvarado, in
return for a free hand, to give one-third of his personal share of
the profits of the expedition to Mendoza. When he arrived at
Purificacion, the Viceroy was occupied in a search for the fabulous
Seven Cities of Cibola. These mystic cities, said by the Monk
Marcos de Niza to lie somewhere in the region included in the
present Mexican State of Sonora or Arizona, were new Eldorados
where even the doors and kitchen utensils were of solid gold. Marcos de Niza unfortunately had not brought back even a frying-pan
to prove his contention but Mendoza required no further proof
than the word of the wandering friar and promptly sent three
vessels, under command of Hernando de Alarcon, to explore the
western coast of Mexico and penetrate the Gulf of California
while Francisco Vasquez de Coronado with a considerable body of
troops marched overland in search of the seven cities.

Advised of the arrival of the powerful Guatemalan squadron,
the Viceroy sent two officers of his staff to Purificacion to propose
to Alvarado a joint expedition to Cibola, deferring the voyage to
the East Indies. Mendoza followed hard on the heels of his sub-
ordinates accompanied by the same Maldonado who had previously
been sent to judge the Captain General and by the Bishop of
Guatemala, Marroquin. The Governors of Guatemala and Mexico
met at the villa of Tiripitio at the home of Juan de Alvarado,
relative of the Guatemalan. A formal contract was drawn and

signed November 29, 1540, which in its preamble designated
Alvarado as Governor of Guatemala and Honduras and after men-
tioning the powers given by Charles V for the discovery in the
East Indies, the cost of Alvarado's fleet and the expedition sent
by the Viceroy Mendoza to discover the seven cities, contains the
following interesting clauses:

First. The Viceroy ceded to the Captain General the fifth part of
any treasure which up to the date of the contract had been found
by the expeditions of Vasquez de Coronado and Alarcon.

Second. Thereafter, Alvarado was to receive one-half of all treasure
discovered by these expeditions.

Third. Alvarado ceded to Mendoza one-half of his profits from
the projected voyage to the East Indies in place of the one-third
assigned in the contract of Charles V.

Fourth. Neither partner was to make any claim against the other
for the expense he was put to for the formation and maintainance of
expeditions under his command up to date of the contract.

Fifth. Thereafter expenses were to be shared equally.

Sixth. The partnership should last for a period of twenty years and
bind their partners, heirs and successors in the case of death of either
partner. If either partner wished to sell his share of the enterprise
he could do so, the other having the right to purchase on terms equal
to those offered by any other bonafide purchaser.

Seventh. The headquarters and stores should be at Acapulco,
Mexico, and the shipyard at Xirabaltique,[9] in the Province of Guatemala.

Eighth. Hereafter, when ships were to be constructed, Alvarado
would supply sails, riggings, spars and woodwork while Mendoza
should find the anchors, artillery, and iron work, the cost thereof to
be equally divided between the partners.

When the contract had been signed, each party swearing his
faith one hand upon the cross of the Order of Santiago, a decora-
tion both possessed, the Viceroy and Captain General proceeded to
Mexico City where Alvarado remained until the close of May
1541. During this time one of the seven cities of Cibola was discovered and Monk Marcos de Niza proven a colleague of Ananias,
but so great was the spirit of adventure that the partners merely
transferred their imagination to the remaining six cities.

Early in June Alvarado arrived on the coast of Jalisco to undertake the expedition in search of the fabulous cities. Destiny which heretofore had carried him swiftly over obstacles and enemies now tired of her burden. The Indians of the nearby Province of Nueva Galicia revolted and attacked the Spanish settlers in such numbers that resistance was impossible. The acting Governor, Cristobal de Oñate, finding the troops at his command insufficient to crush the rebellion, requested aid of Mendoza and also of Alvarado. The latter was already aboard ship but felt it his duty to aid his beset compatriots and disembarking part of his force set out for Guadalajara. Ten thousand Indian warriors had fortified themselves in the village of Nochistlan, built on a high rocky eminence crowned by pines. Anxious to be off to the Isles of Spice, Alvarado declared for an immediate attack, stating that he was ashamed that four wildcats howling on a hill in the pines could so disturb two provinces.[10] Accustomed to victory no matter how great the Indian army, he heard with disdain the suggestion of the Governor that they await the arrival of the aid sent by Mendoza. Oñate well knew the strong position and fighting qualities of his Indian antagonists. Alvarado harangued his troops, stating that the die was cast and that in the name of God he expected every man to do his duty since that was what they had come for. Oñate spoke to his followers in a different vein, saying, "let us be ready to rescue those who came to rescue us." On the twenty-fourth of June, the Captain General halted his force beneath the towering height of Nochistlan and, reconnoitering the enemy's position, discovered that it was surrounded by seven stone trenches built into the steep hillside and so deep that the Indian warriors therein were completely hidden.

Alvarado could have besieged the Indians and forced them to surrender or starve, but Fabian tactics were not to his liking. Digging his spurs into his horse and followed by every Spaniard, he rushed up the precipitous slope. The besieged, who had apparently expected this move, loosed a landslide of boulders upon the Christians, almost burying them beneath the weight of the rolling stones and forcing them to retreat to the foot of the hill. So great was the volume of rocks thrown down by the Indians, that the lowest entrenchment was literally carried away. On the heels of the boulders the natives descended by thousands, forming two long lines of warriors in the form of the jaws of a pincers which closed upon the small group of Spaniards. Alvarado understood his peril and ordered a retreat. Having thus drawn the enemy some distance from their stronghold, he turned about and ordered a charge, a manœuvre that won many battles for him. But unfortunately the terrain, covered with boulders, swamp holes, scrub pine and cactus, so impeded the movement of the horses that a charge was impossible, and even the infantry were compelled to extricate themselves at every step from the knee-deep mud. Giving the order to retire until a suitable battlefield should be reached, Alvarado placed himself in the rear of the column, performing prodigies with his sword and crushing beneath the hoofs of his horse Indians overanxious to seize wounded and dead Spaniards. The army retreated for ten miles through the swamps, their horses and steel armour an impediment, while hordes of Indians hung on their flanks, picking off the soldiers with lances and arrows and dragging the wounded away for sacrifice. Alvarado gave his horse to a wounded soldier and fought on foot.

When at length they reached level firm ground and turned to take vengeance on their enemies, the Indians fled with derisive howls. The army had been saved, thanks to the heroic example of Alvarado. At this moment when the Captain General had again proven his matchless courage and generosity, Destiny rang down the curtain. A scribe named Montoya, who had taken part in the battle, was panic-stricken and arriving in the open space, though the enemy no longer pursued, set spurs to his horse as if the entire Indian army were at his heels. Alvarado, still on foot, seeing the terrified face of his follower said, "Be tranquil, Montoya, the Indians appear to have left us." Blinded by his fear, Montoya spurred his horse again and the poor beast, at the point of exhaustion, reared on its hind legs, stumbled on the slippery rocks and fell upon the Captain General, whose heavy armour prevented his escape. Captain and soldier ran to his aid and the enemy, seeing the Spaniards disorganized, approached once more. "It is not well that the Indians know my danger," said Alvarado, ordering his distinctive armour removed and given to one of his captains who mounted a horse and turned the Spanish forces toward the natives. Seeing the figure that had caused so much havoc during the day thundering toward them, the Indians broke and fled for the last time. Lying on a stretcher made of lances and a soldier's coat, the Captain General overcame the agony of his crushed body long enough to give orders for the retirement to the village of Aten-guillo, adding "what has happened cannot be helped and it should happen to anyone who takes with him people like Montoya."

One of the captains bent over Alvarado, "Where does Your Lordship feel the most pain?" The bruised lips of the Captain General moved slightly and his aide bent low to hear the murmur, "In my soul." In this final hour of his life Alvarado gazed in despair at his ambitions and plans never now to know fulfilment. As death was a matter of a few moments, the Last Sacrament was administered and a brief will, transcribed by Diego Hurtado and the unfortunate Montoya, provided for burial in the Church of Santo Domingo in Mexico City. Apart from certain specific requests, all of Alvarado's fortune was left outright to his widow whom he ordered to comply with the contract entered into with Mendoza. The Bishop of Guatemala, Marroquin, and Juan de Alvarado should jointly exercise the powers of executor, "and as I am very tired from my wounds and as the said Bishop of Guatemala knows the persons to whom I am indebted, be it little or much, because I have many times discussed my debts with him, I hereby give him full power in order that he and Juan de Alva-rado, resident of the city of Mexico, jointly and not separately, unless one has power of attorney from the other for that purpose, considering the distance from Mexico to Guatemala where the said Bishop resides, shall make and carry out my will according as to them may seem best and in accordance with instructions which I have hereinabove given and may they discharge it so as to clear my conscience [of debts]." Alvarado signed the document in a shaky hand before Luis de Castilla, Fernan Flores, Francisco de Quellar, Alonso de Luxan, Juan Mendez de Sotomayor and the two scribes as witnesses. Scarcely had this formality been com-pleted than a tremor shook his frame and as Luxan rushed to his side, his hand, which had been attempting to point at some unseen object, dropped limply over the edge of the cot. The Captain General was dead.

FOOTNOTES FOR CHAPTER ELEVEN

[1] Milla, *Historia de la America Central*, p. 267, says "toward the end of the year 1535," but the final letter of Alvarado to the Emperor, giving an account of the expedition to Quito is dated at Guatemala, May 12, 1535.

[1a] Milla, *Historia de la America Central*.

[2] Chiapa was equal in territory to the present Mexican State of Chiapas which formed part of the royal Province of Guatemala until after the separation from Spain in 1821.

[3] *Coleccion de Documentos Ineditos del Archivo de Indias*, Vol. II, p. 253.

[4] Not the present site of the city of that name which was founded in 1774.

[5] Milla, *Historia de la America Central*, p. 302, gives the text of this proclamation:

"El Rey. — Licenciado Maldonado, Nuestro Juez de residencia de la provincia de Guatemala, e a todos los Concejos, Justicias, Regidores &a, sabed: que nos hemos proveido de la Governacion de esa dicha provincia al Adelantado D. Pedro de Alvarado, por termino de siete años e mas cuanto fuere nuestra voluntad, segun mas largo se contiene en la provision que de ello le habemos mandado dar, e agora por parte del dicho Adelantado me ha sido hecha relacion que a causa decirse en ella que se la hace la dicha merced no pareciendo de la residencia que vos el Licenciado Maldonado le tomais e habeis tomado, culpas por do merezca ser privado de ella, se teme e recela que no le quereis recibir al dicho oficio, ni dar la posesion del, poniendole en ello algun impedimento, a fin de le hacer dano, en lo cual el recibiria mucho agravio y dano a causa de la mucha gente que lleva para la conquista de las islas e provincias del poniente, cuya conquista e gobernacion asi mismo le habemos encomendado, e me fue suplicado vos mandase que libremente le recibieses a la dicha governacion, conforme a su provision sin le poner en ello impedimento alguno, e como la mi merced fuese, e Yo hubelo por bien: por ende Yo vos mando que luego que con esta mi cedula fueredes requeridos, sin embargo de cualesquiera clausulas que vayan en la dicha provision que asi mandamos dar al dicho Adelantado de la governacion de esa provincia, le recibais al dicho oficio e al uso y ejercicio del, e se lo dejeis e consintais usar ye ejercer libremente por sie e por su lugarteniente, por el tiempo en la dicha nuestra provision contenido, hasta tanto que por Nos otra cosa de les envie a mandar, sin que en ello se le ponga ni consintais poner embargo ni impedimento alguno; e los otros fagais ni fagan ende al, por ninguna manera pena de la nuestra merced e de cien mil maravedis para la nuestra Camara. Fecha en la villa de Valladolid, a 22 dias del mes de Octubre de 1538 años.—Yo el Rey.—Por mandado de S. M., Juan de Samano."

[6] $400.

[7] Milla estimates the cost of a horse in Guatemala in 1539 at from one hundred and fifty to three hundred gold pesos.

[8] Milla locates the Isles of Spice as known to the Spaniards at this time as lying between Celebes and Papua. The neighbouring islands were discovered in 1511 by the Portuguese but claimed by the Spaniards. However, at the treaty

of Zaragosa (1529) Charles V withdraw his claim for a consideration of 350,000 gold ducats. Ramirez estimates this sum at approximately $800,000 U.S. currency. The islands have been Dutch possessions since 1607.

[9] The location of this port is not certain.

[10] Ramirez, *Proceso de Pedro de Alvarado*.

XII

AFTERGLOW

(1541)

ON THE following day, June 30, 1541, the Captain General was buried beneath the altar of the village church. Later the remains were moved to Tiripitio and still later to the Church of Santo Domingo in Mexico City. In 1570, by order of his daughter, Doña Leonor, who had since married Francisco de la Cueva, they were brought to Guatemala and interred in the cathedral at Antigua whither the colonists had moved after the destruction of Alvarado's settlement in September 1541. Milla states that the remains were lost when the church was rebuilt in 1680, but the present author believes that they are resting undisturbed under the great altar of the cathedral at Antigua destroyed by the earthquake of 1773. In 1927 in company with the priest-caretaker of the church, the author descended into the crypt of the Alvarado family, but the remains of the Conquistador were not found. The ground beneath the principal altar had not been disturbed and rings hollow. Close by are several vaults, one now used as a chapel. It was the custom to bury illustrious persons under the great altar and it is reasonable to suppose that the first figure in Guatemalan history would have been interred in the place of honour of the cathedral.

In addition to his widow, Alvarado left only one legitimate heir, Doña Leonor. Juarros[1] speaks of two sons of Alvarado by Doña Beatriz, but no other author mentions these children and Spanish law would have required the inclusion of legitimate male children in the Captain General's will. The existence of five natural children is mentioned by Bernal Diaz del Castillo, one of whom named Pedro was lost at sea with his uncle Juan de Alvarado en route to Spain to petition the Emperor for a grant of lands in recompense for the services of his father. A younger brother,

Diego, sought his fortune in Peru and was killed in battle. The three remaining children by another mother, Gomez, Ines and Anica, were killed in the destruction of his palace at the time of the earthquake and flood.

The Viceroy Mendoza wrote on July 5 to the acting Governor of Guatemala, Don Francisco de la Cueva, advising him of the death of Alvarado. The letter arrived on August 29 but rumour preceded it. The Captain General's enemies forgot their rancour and all joined in the rigorous mourning, lasting nine days. Doña Beatriz became almost insane with grief, and hearing that the place in which her husband had been killed was named in the Jaliscan Indian tongue, Muchitiltic ("all black"), ordered that all the walls of the palace inside and out be painted black. Even the roofs and the stone pavement of the courtyard were darkened with a black emulsion of oil and water found in a nearby spring.[2] This extraordinary proceeding disturbed many of the superstitious inhabitants of Guatemala who, endeavouring to console the widow, stated that the Almighty could have sent even greater disaster. Doña Beatriz, enraged, commanded them to keep silent, saying that there could be no greater misfortune than the death of her husband. These words caused great scandal in the city. Her grief, great as it was, did not supplant calculating ambition in the heart of Doña Beatriz. On the morning of September 8, 1541, the widow of the Captain General called her brother, the Bishop and the municipal officials to the palace and after telling them that she had heard that the Royal Treasurer, Castellanos, pretended to the vacant seat, ordered them to name and accept her as Governor and Captain General. This unparalleled demand left her hearers speechless but, after some hesitation, they excused themselves politely to take counsel. Alone in the Council Chamber a discussion raged between the supporters and opponents of her candidacy. The majority, however, inclined in her favour and on the following day the municipal and royal officers confronted Doña Beatriz in the great hall of the castle. The widow was dressed from head to foot in sweeping robes of black velvet. Great sheets of black cotton cloth lined the walls and covered everything, even the silver candelabra had black shades. The Alderman, Gonzalo Ortiz, speaking on behalf of his fellows, notified the widow of her election to

*Ruins of the Cathedral at Antigua, Guatemala, destroyed by
the earthquake of 1773, where Pedro de Alvarado
and his wife are buried.*

which she replied in a firm voice that she accepted the office, thanking the officials, and would carry out her duties and serve His Majesty as if she were Pedro de Alvarado who was then in glory. Such is an exact translation of her words as preserved in the municipal records of Guatemala.[3] The new Governor then took the oath, presented the bond required of officials not directly named by the King, and in signing the scribe's minutes wrote with a firm hand "The Unfortunate Doña Beatriz." A sudden thought seized her and taking up the pen she rapidly drew a horizontal line through "Doña Beatriz" as if thereafter she wished to be known only as the "Unfortunate One." A number of authors have doubted this incident but the signature is still extant with the last two words carefully crossed out.[4] The widow had another surprise in store for them. Handing the Governor's baton to her brother, she announced her selection of him as Lieutenant Governor, reserving to herself only matters relating to the allotment of lands and Indian slaves. These were the most delicate and incidentally the most lucrative matters with which the Governors of Spanish colonies had to deal and Doña Beatriz wished to reserve this source of income exclusively to herself.

The news of the election of Doña Beatriz was received with general surprise in the city and with rage by the Royal Treasurer, Castellanos, and his followers. Their indignation knew no bounds and they were determined not to recognize the position of the widow and her brother, alleging that the election, contrary to the Salic Law, was null and void. Knowing that simple protest would merely cause them to be thrown into prison, they resolved to seize Doña Beatriz and Don Francisco and make Castellanos Governor until the Emperor should be heard from. It was then seven in the evening of September 9, 1541, and the conspirators separated, arranging to meet at two hours after midnight on September 11 to seize the palace and the Governor. Doña Beatriz, hearing of the conspiracy from her spies, sent in haste for the Lieutenant Governor who came accompanied by his secretary, Robledo, a scheming individual who played each side against the other. Doña Beatriz was all for arresting the malcontents in the act and when de la Cueva protested that without proof such action would be illegal, and dangerous where it concerned the royal officials, Doña

Beatriz replied sharply that she knew no law in such matters, that
it was public and notorious these same men had conspired against
the Captain General during his lifetime and concluded by threatening her brother with the loss of his post if he did not at once
sign the order for the arrest of the conspirators. Robledo drafted
the document which the Lieutenant Governor signed and handed
to the Captain of the Guard, ordering him to take an escort and
seize the conspirators whenever found. Robledo made an excuse to
leave the hall, scribbled "The Lieutenant Governor has just signed
an order for the arrest of you and your friends, hide at once," and
sent it to Castellanos by a trustworthy servant. The conspirators
fled to an underground chamber in an unoccupied house, the last
barely leaving Castellanos' residence by a rear door when the
Captain of the Guard thundered at the front portals.

The city of Pedro de Alvarado, now known as Ciudad Vieja,
was built on the lower slopes of the great Volcan de Agua, a thousand feet above the bottom of the valley where the city of Antigua
was later founded. The streets of Ciudad Vieja are steep and
narrow and the houses appear to be holding on grimly to the
mountainside. The castle built by the Conquistador was large,
of stone and three stories in height, a chapel for the private use
of the inhabitants having been recently erected on the roof. The
principal church was of stone as were the houses of a number of
the leading citizens. The remainder were of sun-dried bricks
(adobe) lined with plaster, while the artisans and Indians possessed shelters of wood and cane. The castle, church and better
houses were roofed with heavy tiles, the huts with palm thatch.
The castle of Alvarado was built high on the mountainside, so as
to command the town, in the mouth of a deep broad arroyo (gulch)
which led toward the crater and was choked with great boulders
and the trunks of fallen trees.

September is a season of heavy rain in Guatemala, but the storm
which began on September 8 exceeded any in the memory of the
inhabitants. The continual downpour was a bad omen in the minds
of the superstitious inhabitants who regarded the deluge as punishment for the blasphemous words of Doña Beatriz. The rain continued unbroken throughout the ninth and tenth. The inhabitants
went gloomily early to bed as the streets were knee deep in water

and the candles flickered and guttered in the drip from leaking
roofs, penetrated everywhere by the weight of the storm. Two
hours after darkness set in[5] a sharp earthquake accompanied by a
great noise was heard. Many of the inhabitants fled in terror from
their homes while others were buried beneath the weight of falling
walls and roofs.

In the crater of the extinct Volcan de Agua, twelve thousand feet
above sea level, a lake of ice and water had collected.[6] The earthquake broke the thin rocky wall to the east and the avalanche
poured down the arroyo leading to the city. On its way the gulch
was blocked here and there by dams of boulders and logs forming
small lakes which added their force to the flood. So great was the
force of the current that huge trees were snapped off like matches
and boulders carried like straws on the churning torrent. The
path of the avalanche is still marked, deeply gouged in the side
of the volcano. The empty crater is well over fifteen hundred feet
in diameter and three hundred feet deep. The ungovernable torrent
swept out of the gulch into the streets of Guatemala, filling them
to a depth of from six to eight feet with a mass of water, ice,
trees, boulders and débris against which none could contend. The
flood swept through the ground floor of the palace of Alvarado,
drowning many of the Indian servants and sweeping the remainder
out through the windows and down the side of the mountain.
Doña Beatriz, who slept on the second floor, awakened by the
earthquake and the roar of the torrent, rushed to the chapel on the
roof, followed by Doña Leonor and twelve of her maids of honour,
bearing in her arms Anica, the five-year-old natural child of Alvarado. Doña Leonor left them to find Alvarado's other children
who were in the care of servants in a lower room of the castle. She
was guiding them toward the stairs of the chapel and safety when
a great rush of water swept through the corridor and carried the
entire party far down the street. Doña Leonor managed to seize
the branches of a tree still withstanding the current and remained
there until morning. The children were drowned.

At the first shock the conspirators left their refuge and leading
their partisans hastened to the palace shouting that they as well
as the earthquake were instruments of the Lord to punish Doña
Beatriz. Don Francisco and the palace guards had just attacked

them when the wall of water swept down and hurled friend and
foe far down the slope.

The storm increased in fury and as Doña Beatriz embraced the
infant Anica with one arm and the crucifix in the other, a second
and more violent shock rocked the town. The frail walls of the
chapel collapsed, crushing her and her suite beneath the weight of
the heavy tiles. When morning dawned the flood had subsided
but the city was in ruins. Few if any of the houses remained standing and the streets were blocked with mud and débris. (At the present time only the upper story of Alvarado's castle projects above
the new level of the ground.) Six hundred Spaniards and a much
larger number of Indians perished during the night.[7] Among the
dead was the Royal Inspector General, Ronquillo, and many of
the conspirators. The afflicted inhabitants set to work to rescue the
wounded and remove the dead from the ruins. Sufficient spirit
still remained to cast the blame for the catastrophe upon Doña
Beatriz and some were for throwing her body to the wild beasts
or placing it upon a raft in the river that it might drift to sea. The
Bishop Marroquin, however, defied them and the woman Governor
was buried in the cathedral, one of the few edifices that withstood
the fury of the flood. In 1580 her body was moved to the cathedral
of Antigua and placed beside that of her illustrious husband. The
unfortunate maids of honour were buried in the church of San
Francisco in Antigua where until 1615 a common inscription proclaimed their fate.

Thoroughly terrified the survivors decided to abandon the city,
Francisco de la Cueva and Bishop Marroquin being elected joint
Governors until Mexico or Spain should select a permanent official.
After some discussion the village of Tianguecillo, near Chimaltenango, was selected as the new site of the capital and the inhabitants ordered to select their lots. Before action could be taken,
however, the Royal Engineer, Juan Antonelli, who was in Guatemala by orders of the Emperor to study the problem of communications, proposed a site in the Valley of Panchoy, about three miles
from the ruined town. On October 22, 1541, the resolution to move
to the new location was adopted and the fourth City of Guatemala,
now known as Antigua, was founded. This capital was largely

Photograph by the Author

Ruins of the Castle of Pedro de Alvarado at Ciudad Vieja, Guatemala, destroyed by the earthquake of September 10, 1541. Only the chapel, where Doña Beatriz de la Cueva, wife of the Conqueror, was killed, is shown, the lower stories of the building being buried beneath the present ground level.

destroyed by an earthquake in 1773, and in 1774 the present City
of Guatemala, forty miles away, was established.

As soon as his urgent duties permitted, Bishop Marroquin, who
had received full power of attorney from his co-executor, Juan
de Alvarado, set himself to the task of liquidating the estate of the
Captain General. The twenty thousand Indian slaves working
in the mines, plantations and other properties of the Conquistador
were set at liberty by the executor with the proviso that they should
continue their present employment as freedmen. It is interesting to note that the good Bishop did not free Alvarado's Negro
slaves. With the laudable ambition of snatching what the hand of
the Captain General could no longer protect, the Audiencia of
Mexico dispatched an emissary to Guatemala bearing a decree
seizing the land and villages possessed by Alvarado and naming
tax collectors who were to apply the revenues to the construction
of roads, bridges and churches. The Council of the Indies appropriated these jackal-like tactics to its own account, promulgating
on October 10, 1542, an order signed by the President, Cardinal
Loaiza, seizing all of the lands of Alvarado, his wife and children
and giving them to the Crown. Spain was at least consistent in
defrauding those who had conquered the New World for her.
The Audiencia of Mexico and the Municipal authorities of Guatemala showed their teeth when the edict of confiscation reached
Guatemala in 1544, but the Governor, the same Maldonado who
fled precipitately from the Conquistador in 1539, gathered courage now that his enemy lay beneath Mexican soil and Alvarado's
property passed to the Crown.

The loss of the slaves and lands left the estate of the Captain General insufficient to pay the many claims. Many if not all of
these debts were contracted in the service of the same Charles V
who, once Alvarado lay cold in death and powerless to win new
lands for the Crown, stretched gluttonous hands for the dead man's
shoes. Marroquin's first step was to pay all debts of less than
twenty gold pesos. A multitude of servants, small tradesmen and
freed Indians were thus compensated for their services but the
greater number of the creditors received little or nothing. In June
1541, after Pizarro and Cortes, probably the richest and most
powerful Spaniard in the New World, fate and the rapacity of his

sovereign so reduced the estate of Alvarado that by the new year his surviving children suffered poverty and the pangs of hunger.

On the bier of Pedro de Alvarado there might well be graven "Sic Transit Gloria Mundi."

FOOTNOTES FOR CHAPTER TWELVE

[1] Part V, Chap. III.

[2] Marroquin, *Documentos Ineditos del Archivo de Indias.*

[3] Milla, *La Hija del Adelantado,* p. 202.

[4] Milla, *Historia de la America Central,* p. 327.

[5] According to the eye-witness testimony of Bishop Marroquin, *Documentos Ineditos del Archivo de Indias,* while Fuentes and other authors say two hours after midnight.

[6] *Anales de la Sociedad de Geografia e Historia de Guatemala,* March 1928, p. 223, mentioned an Indian legend that the body of the Maya Indian King Qencab had been buried in the crater lake and that it had been foretold that when his nation should perish at the hands of foreigners his corpse would take vengeance.

[7] Milla, *Historia de la America Central,* p. 331.

Stephens, *Incidents of Travel in Central America,* describes the Volcan de Agua as follows:

"While I was blowing my fingers and copying the inscription, the vapour cleared away a little, and gave me a view of the interior of the crater. It was a large oval basin, the area level and covered with grass. The sides were sloping, about one hundred or one hundred and fifty feet high, and all around were masses of rock piled up in magnificent confusion, and rising to inaccessible peaks. There is no tradition of this mountain ever having emitted fire, and there is no calcined matter or other mark of volcanic eruption anywhere in its vicinity. The historical account is, that in 1541 an immense torrent, not of fire, but of water and stones, was vomited from the crater, by which the old city was destroyed. Father Remesal relates that on this occasion the crown of the mountain fell down. The height of this detached part was one league, and from the remaining summit to the plain was a distance of three leagues, which he affirms he measured in 1615. The area, by my measurement is eighty-three paces long and sixty wide. According to Torquemada (and such is the tradition according to Padre Alcantara, of Ciudad Vieja) this immense basin, probably the crater of an extinct volcano, with sides much higher than they are now, became filled with water by accumulations of snow and rain. There never was any eruption of water, but one of the sides gave way, and the immense body of fluid rushed out with horrific force, carrying with it rocks and trees, inundating and destroying all that opposed its progress. The immense barranca or ravine by which it descended was still fearfully visible on the side of the mountain. The height of this mountain has been ascertained by barometrical observation to be fourteen thousand, four hundred and fifty feet above the level of the sea. The edge of the crater commands a beautiful view of the old city of Guatemala, thirty-two surrounding villages, and the Pacific Ocean;

at least so I am told, but I saw nothing of it. Nevertheless I did not regret my labour; and though drenched with rain and plastered with mud, I promised myself in the month of February, when the weather is fine, to ascend again prepared for the purpose, and pass two or three days in the crater." (Vol. I, p. 275.)

"The most dreadful calamity that had as yet afflicted this unfortunate place occurred on the morning of September 11, 1541. It had rained incessantly, and with great violence, on the three preceding days, particularly on the night of the tenth, when the water descended more like the torrent of a cataract than rain; the fury of the wind, the incessant appalling lightning, and the dreadful thunder were indescribable. . . . At two o'clock on the morning of the eleventh, the vibrations of the earth were so violent that the people were unable to stand; the shocks were accompanied by a terrible subterranean noise, which spread universal dismay; shortly afterward, an immense torrent of water rushed down from the summit of the mountain, forcing away with it enormous fragments of rocks and large trees, which, descending upon the ill-fated town, overwhelmed and destroyed almost all the houses, and buried a great number of the inhabitants under the ruins; among the many, Doña Beatriz de la Cueba, the widow of Pedro de Alvarado, lost her life." (Vol. I, p. 280.)

FINIS

APPENDICES

Extracts from the Book of Acts of the City of Santiago de Guatemala covering the first six years from the foundation of the city in 1524 to 1530. Copied from the original documents by Don Rafael de Arevalo, Secretary of the Municipality of Guatemala, in 1856.

The author is indebted to Don Victor Miguel Diaz of Guatemala City for the following extracts.

THE BOOK

of the founding of the very noble and very loyal City of Saint James of the Knights of Guatemala and of the acts of its Governors from July 29, 1524, and thereafter.

(Note by Arevalo: The first page is entirely illegible and I could only ascertain that it treated of the election and taking of office by the first Mayors[1] and Aldermen.)

In the said city of Santiago on the twenty-seventh day of the said month of July of the said year before me, Scribe Alonso de Reguera, there appeared the honourable Mayors Diego de Roxas and Captain Baltasar de Mendoza, and the Aldermen, Don Pedro, Hernan Carrillo, Juan Perez Dardon and Domingo de Zubiarreta and on this day, Wednesday, all entered into the Council Chamber together, together with His Excellency, the Lieutenant Governor.

And they ordered that whereas in this town there is much need of an official Crier, for the execution of justice and for other necessary matters, that Diego Diaz, a resident of this town be, and he is hereby elected Town Crier, as he is the person most adapted to this office and he is commanded to accept and perform the duties and he shall receive a salary such as is customary in the Indies.

And they further ordered and commanded that the blacksmith of this town shall receive for every hundred nails, when he supplies the iron, two gold pesos and that his price shall be moderate

[1] In the Spanish custom there were two Mayors serving jointly and possessing equal powers.

on all things which he makes, under penalty of fine. And further that the blacksmith shall receive, for shoeing all four feet of a horse, the customer supplying the iron, even though it be only a question of shaping the shoes, one gold peso, and for a blood-letting one gold peso under penalty of paying four times the excess in case he charged more, half of the fine to be paid to the Fiscal Agent of Their Majesties and the other half to be retained by the Judge hearing the case and in regard to other activities of his profession he is to charge a moderate price.—Pedro de Alvarado, Diego de Roxas, Baltasar de Mendoza, Pedro Portocarrero, Hernan Carrillo, Juan Perez Dardon, Domingo de Zubiarreta.

On this same day the Mayors and Aldermen order the said Diego Diaz to undertake the duties of Town Crier as he had been ordered and commanded and to undertake them immediately under penalty of one hundred lashes and when he replied that he did not know how to undertake his office, he was commanded to do so nonetheless, whereupon he accepted and asked instructions.

Friday, July 29, 1524, the aforesaid honourable Mayors and Aldermen of this city of Santiago being in the Council Chamber it was unanimously ordered that the said Diego Diaz shall receive per year and during the time which he serves as Town Crier the sum of one hundred castellanos as salary which shall be paid from taxes or by liens imposed for reason of public works or from fines.—Baltasar de Mendoza.—Diego de Roxas.—Pedro Portocarrero.—Juan Perez Dardon.—Domingo de Zubiarreta.—Hernan Carrillo.

In the city of Santiago on the eighth day of January, 1525, before me, Alonso de Reguera, Royal Scribe, and Scribe of the city, there appeared the very noble Señor Pedro de Alvarado, Lieutenant Governor and Captain General of these regions by orders of the very magnificent Señor Hernan Cortes, Governor and Captain General of New Spain, by decree of Their Majesties, and said that whereas at the time, that at the suggestion of Their Majesties and of the same Governor, he had founded here the city of Santiago, conforming to the customs and order of other founders and populators of cities in the realms of Castille, he had elected and named for the said city two Mayors and four Aldermen in order that they should undertake the administration of justice and the regulation of the said city and its surrounding country and whereas the said terms of office were about to expire and he wished to renew them on the first day of each year hereafter and to make this a custom. And by so doing to follow the said order and custom and because this well served the purpose of Their Majesties for the good government and population of the said city, now once more in the name of Their Majesties and the said Governor, he elects and names as Mayors that they may take charge of the administration of justice—Baltasar de Mendoza and Gonzalo de Alvarado, both being present, and for Aldermen—Don Pedro Portocarrero.—Hernando de Alvarado.—Diego Holguin and Pedro de Valdivieso, all of whom he commanded in name of Their Majesties to make use of and exercise the said offices during the time stipulated therefor and he gave them such powers as they might require and carry out in all measures the powers, duties and responsibilities devolving upon them, first, however taking the solemn oath required of each of them in such case, being witnesses of said oath, Jorge de Alvarado.—Gomez de Alvarado and Diego de Roxas and all of the other Spaniards present.—Pedro de Alvarado.

And immediately thereafter the said Captain General, Pedro de Alvarado, received the oath from the forementioned Mayors and Aldermen with the solemnity required by the occasion with the exception only that Don Pedro Portocarrero did not take the oath at this time as he was absent through illness.

In the city of Santiago of Guatemala, May 6, 1525. On this said day the Captain General, Pedro de Alvarado, stated: That whereas in name of Their Majesties he had selected Mayors and Aldermen for this city naming among others as Alderman, Diego Holguin, who had departed from this city to reside in the city of San Salvador[2] of which he is Mayor and that at present there is in

[2] This city was founded in 1525 and is still the capital of the Republic of El Salvador in Central America.

Guatemala only one Alderman and as there exists the necessity of holding meetings of the City Corporation in due form to carry out certain pressing duties in the service of Their Majesties for the good government and regulation of this city and because of the absence of Aldermen there is no quorum, therefore, by virtue of the powers reposed in him, he has nominated and elected to that place as Alderman vacated by the said Diego Holguin, Francisco de Arevalo who accepts the position and the said Captain General received from him the solemn oath as required by law and there being witnesses, Baltasar de Mendoza and Hernando de Alvarado.

On this same day the Captain General, the Mayor Baltasar de Mendoza and the Aldermen Hernando de Alvarado and Francisco de Arevalo, met in the Council Chamber and passed the following ordinances : that a pig of thirty areldes and upward shall be sold for twenty gold pesos, and from twenty-five areldes sixteen gold pesos and not for more under penalty of losing the pigs thus sold and a fine of one hundred gold pesos for the Magistrate and Fiscal Agent of Their Majesties. This edict was publicly cried this same day in this same city, there being official witnesses Pedro Jimenez, Gaspar Arias and Gonzalo de Solis as well as many other people.

And on this same day the aforesaid officials ordered that, as it is necessary to guarantee the permanence of the church of this city and to keep the same in repair and in order that the necessary expenditures may be made for the repair and other expenses of the said church, that Francisco Davila be named Custodian of the church and that he should be given power accordingly, and being witnesses to this act Gonzalo Dovalle and Ignacio de Alvarado.

And on this same day the said officials named as Custodian of the public property of this city, that he should guard it and keep it in his possession and that he should expend such sums as were necessary for the proper care of the said property, Gonzalo de Solis who was present and accepted the said office and took the solemn oath required by law, all of the undersigned being witnesses thereto.

On this same day the said officials ordered that eggs shall be sold in this city at the rate of one gold real per egg and shall not be sold at a higher price under penalty of losing the said eggs and fine of one gold mark for the Judge and Fiscal Agent of Their

Majesties, the undersigned being witnesses. This edict was publicly proclaimed by the voice of Diego Diaz, Town Crier and being
official witnesses, Pedro Jimenez and Gaspar Arias as well as many
other persons.

On this same day the said officials being in the Council Chamber
decreed and ordered that it should be publicly announced in
this city that all persons who desire to become citizens and
landowners of this city of Santiago, today and tomorrow in any
hour of the day to appear before the Scribe of the city and lots
in the town site shall be given and assigned to them, all of
which were publicly proclaimed by the voice of Diego Diaz, Town
Crier, and thereafter the following gentlemen stated that they
wished to be inscribed as landowners of the said city.—Pedro de
Alvarado.—Baltasar de Mendoza.—Hernando de Alvarado.—
Francisco de Arevalo.

El. Sr. Captain General
Baltasar de Mendoza, Mayor
Gonzalo Dovalle
Hernando de Alvarado, Alderman
Francisco de Arevalo, Alderman
Gonzalo de Alvarado, Chief Constable
Reguera
Ximenez
Solis, Custodian
Juan Vazquez
Juan Rodriguez
Diego de Roxas
Don Pedro
Don Rodrigo
Franco
Juan Martin
Gaspar Arias
Cristoval de Salvatierra
Juan Moreno
Diego Diaz, Town Crier
Rodrigo Diaz
Francisco Lopez
Andres Lasso

Alonso de Medina
Pedro Moreno
Andres de Ulloa
Pereda
Cristoval de Robledo
Dardon
Cueto
Ulloa
Bezerra
Carrillo
Cepeda
Vicarreta
Monroy
Diego Gonzalez Herrero
Pedro de Mendoza
Diego de Sta. Clara
Salinas
Juan Medel
Juan Alvarez Portuguez
Anton Martin
Calveche
Cristoval Rodriguez

In the city of Santiago, October 4, 1524, the Captain General,
being about to depart for Mexico, stated that as there remained
in the city no Mayor to mete out justice he will name and elect as

Mayor, Pedro de Valdiviseo, a citizen and Alderman of this city who accepted the office and took the oath with the required solemnity and the Baton of Mayor was delivered to him, there being witnesses Gaspar Arias, Hernan Carrillo, Diego de Roxas, Hernando de Alvarado, and all were commanded to obey him as Mayor under penalty of one thousand gold pesos fine payable to the Judge and the Fiscal Agent of Their Majesties, those present being witnesses. Pedro de Alvarado.

I, Pedro de Alvarado, Captain General of these regions by decree of our Emperor and Empress state: whereas at the time that I, commissioned by Their Majesties, came to conquer and possess these lands and the Provinces of Utlatan and Guatemala and others adjoining them under the authority of Spain, in order to better serve Their Majesties, I determined to populate them with the Spaniards under my command and I founded in this Province of Guatemala the city of Santiago, as is well known to all, and wherein in the name of Their Majesties I named and elected Mayors and Aldermen to execute justice both civil and criminal following the ancient custom of the Kingdom of Castile and imitating in everything precedents established by experienced and learned persons. And because conforming to the same regulations and ordinances the terms of the said Mayors and Aldermen have expired and due to expire the first day of the new year I have named and elected to the said posts new officials who shall exercise the said duties as they have heretofore been exercised in this said year of 1526 beginning on the first day of the said year. Therefore, I, in the name of Their Majesties, have elected and named as Mayors of the city, Diego Bezerra and Baltasar de Mendoza and as Aldermen, Hernan Carrillo, Hernando Pizarro, Don Pedro Portocarrero and Diego de Alvarado, citizens who are present and in name of Their Majesties I have commanded them to accept the said posts and to undertake their duties in all matters concerning the government and justice in this city, first taking the oath required in such cases and the said Mayors, having taken the oath, received the Batons of Justice as a symbol of their office and by this act I commanded all citizens and residents of this city, present or absent, to receive the said persons in their official capacities under penalty of one thousand gold pesos to the Judge and Fiscal Agent of Their Majesties. Dated in the said city of Santiago on the thirtieth day of January, 1526. Pedro de Alvarado.

On this same day immediately after the above election had been verified, the said Captain General Pedro de Alvarado received the solemn oaths required by law from the said Diego Bezerra and Baltasar de Mendoza as Mayors, in accordance with the form and manner of the oaths presented by last year's Mayors and as set forth in the beginning of this Book of Acts of the City of Guatemala, there being witnesses Diego de Roxas, Gonzalo Dovalle, Pedro de Valdivieso, Horosco and Hernando de Alvarado and many other Spaniards.

And immediately thereafter the Aldermen, Don Pedro Portocarrero, Hernan Carrillo, Diego de Alvarado and Hernando Pizarro took the oath in accordance with that in use in past years and as set forth by me, the said Scribe, in the Book of the City, the undersigned being witnesses.

In the city of Santiago on January 30, 1526, there being present in the Council Chamber the very noble Pedro de Alvarado, Captain General of these regions, the Mayors, Diego Bezerra and Baltasar de Mendoza, and the Aldermen, Hernan Carrillo, Don Pedro Portocarrero, Diego de Alvarado and Hernando Pizarro, the following ordinances were passed.

1. First, the Mayors and Aldermen stated that His Excellency the Captain General had need of a bodyguard because of the revolts now under way in various parts of New Spain and because lack of such a bodyguard might cause damage to the life or person of His Excellency in that some person or persons who bore him hatred might attempt to kill or wound him to the great loss of this country. Therefore they requested him to guard his person by accepting or selecting as many guards as he deemed necessary and in whom confidence could be reposed. The Captain General replied that the suggestion was one of benefit to Their Majesties and to the Governor of this country and that he would gladly accept such a bodyguard, there being witnesses Juan Peaz, Scribe, Diego

Bezerra, Baltasar de Mendoza, Don Pedro Portocarrero, Diego de Alvarado, Hernan Carrillo, Hernando Pizarro.

Council Chamber, August 23, 1526. In the city of Santiago, twenty-third day of August, 1526, the said Mayors and Aldermen being present in the Council Chamber with the Captain General Pedro de Alvarado, decided to name and elect an ambassador who shall proceed to the City of Mexico and in name of this city negotiate on behalf of this municipality and for its general good, and on the said day the said Baltasar de Mendoza, Mayor of this city and the Aldermen, Don Pedro Portocarrero, Hernan Carrillo, Diego de Alvarado and Hernando Pizarro have themselves and in name of all the landowners and residents of this city absent from the meeting, given full power to Diego Bezerra, Mayor of this city, who was present, to undertake in general manner all business in the City of Mexico with the Governor or with any other person matters which may relate to this city and to the good or general benefit of the landowners and residents thereof in conformity with the instructions that he has received from the Council and anything else that may be of general importance, with a free hand in the amount of the costs of his trip and requiring him to make a formal report of his activities on behalf of this city and granting to him the general power of attorney in the usual form, there being present as witnesses, Gonzalo de Alvarado, Francisco Lopez, Francisco Sanchez, Diego Diaz, Bartholme Bezarro, Don Pedro Portocarrero, Hernan Carillo, Diego de Alvarado, Baltasar de Mendoza and Hernando Pizarro.

In the city of Santiago on the twenty-sixth day of August, 1526, there being present the Mayor, Diego Bezerra and the Aldermen Portocarrero, Carrillo, Diego de Alvarado and Pizarro. On this day there being present in the Council Chamber the Captain General, Pedro de Alvarado, he stated that whereas the Mayors of this city and the Aldermen thereof were going to the City of Mexico with the said Captain General to negotiate certain matters for the benefit of the city and for the common good of the residents thereof and as there would remain in this region no officials that new officials should be elected. Therefore, in name of Their

Majesties he selected in place of the said Mayors, Don Pedro
Portocarrero and Hernan Carrillo, residents of this city and as
Aldermen, Hernando de Alvarado, Jorge de Alvarado, Francisco
Dovalle, and Diego Monroy, who being present were commanded
to accept the said posts to thereafter serve as magistrates and to
take the required oath all of whom accepted immediately.—Pedro
de Alvarado.

TRIAL OF PEDRO DE ALVARADO

1529

LIST OF CHARGES AS DRAWN BY THE AUDIENCIA OF MEXICO.[1]

1. That when the said Pedro de Alvarado came with Don Hernan Cortes to New Spain to conquer and populate the same, that being captain of one of the ships of the fleet of the said Cortes, he came ahead of the fleet to the island of Cozumel where the Indians received him in peace and gave him that which they had and not being content therewith he entered into the country with certain of his people, burning and robbing certain towns without cause or reason. Whereupon the Indians of the island fled to the jungle and the said Pedro de Alvarado made war upon them.

2. And the said Pedro de Alvarado is accused of having on arrival at Villa Rica marched to certain nearby villages with his men and although the Indians did not make war upon him nor commit any hostile acts, that without formally calling for their submission as was required in the instructions from His Majesty, he caused the villages to be burned and goods seized and made war upon them.

3. And the said Pedro de Alvarado is accused: when the Spaniards first came to this city, he being captain of a certain party of them, of seizing secretly large quantities of gold, feathers, jade, cloth, cacao and many other things which in our secret investigation appears to have been proven and of which the gold alone was worth at least thirty thousand pesos, and that of the same he did not pay the Royal Fifth nor give any part thereof to his companions as he was obligated to do.

4. And the said Pedro de Alvarado is accused of: at the time

[1] *Anales de la Sociedad de Geografia e Historia de Guatemala,* March 1931.

that the Spaniards came to this city and captured Moctezuma, they also took one Camazin, nephew of the said Moctezuma and who was in his own right a great Lord in this country and the said Camazin said to Hernan Cortes that if he would send a captain with him to his domain that he would give him all the gold and jewels that he had and the said Hernan Cortes sent with him Pedro de Alvarado to the city of Tuzcuco where the said Camazin lived and because the said Camazin did not give him all the gold and treasure which he wished he ordered the said Camazin tied hand and foot to a pole and being bound thus burning rosin was thrown upon him in such a way that his body was burned in all parts and that he was on the point of death and this was done in order that he should give them more gold and without any other reason or motive whatsoever.

5. And the charge is made against the said Pedro de Alvarado that at the time that the said Hernan Cortes left this city to proceed against Panfilo de Narvaez, he left the said Pedro de Alvarado to guard this city and in his power, Moctezuma, the Lord thereof, together with all of the gold and treasure which up to that time had been accumulated which was a great quantity and at the time of departure, Moctezuma asked permission of Cortes to hold certain feasts and dances which his people were accustomed to celebrate at such time of the year and the said Cortes gave the requested permission, and the time having come for the said feasts and dances, the said Moctezuma ordered them held and there being one day in the house of the said Moctezuma a great number of Indians dancing and celebrating their feast the said Pedro de Alvarado, together with the Spaniards under his command, entered into the fort where the said Moctezuma was prisoner together with many Lords and principal chiefs and their servants, and entering into the patio where all were dancing, without any cause or reason whatsoever, fell upon the Indians and killed all of the Lords captive with Moctezuma and four hundred principal chiefs who were present and a great number of Indians who were dancing to the number of three thousand for which reason the tribes rose in arms because

their fellows had been killed without reason and because of this war, more than two hundred Spaniards died at the hands of the Indians, many horses were lost and more than four hundred thousand Indians were killed in the said war. Much gold was lost, much of which belonged to His Majesty and to the soldiers. All of which is a charge against Pedro de Alvarado because he killed Indians who were dancing in a state of peace by licence of the said Cortes.

6. And the further accusation is made against Pedro de Alvarado that being Captain as aforesaid and commanding the rear guard with many horses and foot-soldiers at the time when the army evacuated the capital, the said Pedro de Alvarado arrived at one of the gaps which existed in the causeway there being one beam remaining across the gap on which the Spaniards must pass, the said Pedro de Alvarado vaulted the gap leaving his people without a Captain while the enemy came behind them. And the said Alvarado on his horse galloped to the head of the column where the said Hernan Cortes was and when he arrived Cortes asked him if all his people had passed and the said Pedro de Alvarado replied that they had which was not true since they did not have a Captain to animate them and encourage them to kill the Indians and because of the absence of the said Pedro de Alvarado, a quantity of gold belonging to His Majesty was lost. All of which is a charge against the said Pedro de Alvarado.

7. And the further accusation is made against the said Pedro de Alvarado that being Captain at the conquest of Tepeaca; that when certain soldiers gambled against orders of the said Hernan Cortes that the said Pedro de Alvarado instead of proceeding formally against them took from them a great quantity of gold which was their property and which he said they had used in gambling and kept it for himself and when one Spaniard argued that the gold had been taken from him illegally, he ordered the soldier given one hundred lashes publicly without any cause or reason whatsoever.

8. And the said Pedro de Alvarado is accused; while he was lieutenant at Villa Rica, of taking from the Indian chief at

Papolo against his will, two handsome women that he had.
And because the chief did not want to deliver them willingly
the said Pedro de Alvarado caused him to be imprisoned
whereupon he died of the treatment received from the said
Pedro de Alvarado.

9. And the further accusation is made against the said Pedro de
Alvarado that at the time of the conquest of this city, he being
captain at Tlatelulco, he as captain should strive to animate
and enthuse the people under his command in as much as they
were in great peril but that he left many nights and went to
the town of Tacuba [Tlacopan] and it was public among all
his soldiers or most of them that he went there to sleep with
an Indian woman whom he kept as mistress using as a pretext that he went to Tacuba to obtain reinforcements and
supplies.

10. And the further accusation is made against the said Pedro
de Alvarado that at the time of the conquest of this city,
guards were placed so that no person should take for himself
gold nor silver nor jewels but that the said Pedro de Alvarado
and the soldiers of his company took much treasure which
they kept for themselves without paying the Royal Fifth and
in the village of Tacuba by authorization of the said Pedro
de Alvarado Indian goldsmiths were employed in melting the
said gold into bars.

11. And the said Pedro de Alvarado is charged of having publicly
said before certain persons, while in the city of Tacuba, that
a certain Tapia was coming from Santo Domingo with
powers as Governor and Pedro de Alvarado said that should
he come, he, Pedro de Alvarado, would have him beaten and
make him eat his powers, and a Spaniard present said to
Don Pedro de Alvarado that as the soldiers were not vassals
of the said Alvarado they did not have to obey his commands. Whereupon the said Pedro de Alvarado said that if
the speaker or ten or a dozen more were hung by Alvarado
for such words, nobody would murmur.

12. And the charge is made against the said Pedro de Alvarado
that at the time that the said Cristobal de Tapia came to New
Spain with powers as governor, he was one of the principal

persons who caused Tapia to return where he had come and because his brother, Gonzalo de Alvarado, then commander at Villa Rica, had received the said Cristobal de Tapia and obeyed his power as governor, the said Pedro de Alvarado quarrelled with him using harsh words.

13. And the charge is made against the said Pedro de Alvarado that while Alonso de Grado, who was then Auditor, was being brought as prisoner to this city by command of Hernan Cortes that the said Alvarado with certain of his followers met Grado two leagues out of the city, speaking harsh words to him and took the books of accounts and the said Pedro de Alvarado being Mayor said that he would save Cortes the trouble of going out of the city to hang Grado which it is presumed he said because the said Grado favoured those things which fostered His Majesty's interests.

14. And the accusation is made against the said Pedro de Alvarado that while going to conquer and populate the Province of Oaxaca that because the Indian Lords of this province did not give him as much gold as he wished, he had them pursued by savage dogs until they gave him certain chains of gold for his dogs and for his horses and especially that they gave him a chain which was worth at least three thousand pesos of gold and that he did not populate the said Province of Oaxaca, but instead went to the city of Tututepeque where he took for himself much gold of which it appears he did not pay the Royal Fifth.

15. And further it is charged against the said Pedro de Alvarado that the Indian chief of the Province of Xalapa, being in a state of peace and vassal of His Majesty and having given much gold to Hernan Cortes for account of His Majesty, had sent to ask aid against a slave of his who had risen in rebellion. Cortes sent the said Pedro de Alvarado with certain infantry and cavalry and instead of going to Xalapa, he went to Teguantepeque where the said rebellious slave was. And arriving there with his men, the said slave exhibited to him a house in which there was much gold and silver and jewels and pearls and feathers and told him to take as much as he wished and the said Pedro de Alvarado took much

treasure and the said slave said that if he would place in his
power the Lord of Xalapa, he would give him as much gold
as he might wish and the said Pedro de Alvarado, having
as his obligation to capture the said slave and deliver him to
the Lord of Xalapa, not wishing to do so because of the
treasure which the slave had promised him, seized instead
the Lord of Xalapa and delivered him to the said slave who
was in rebellion against him which becoming known to the
vassals of the Lord of Xalapa, they rose in revolt and killed
a Spaniard in the said town of Xalapa and much gold that had
been collected for His Majesty at Sonsonunsco and other
parts was lost, all of which was caused by the delivery of
the Lord of Xalapa into the power of the said slave.

16. And the further charge is made against the said Pedro
de Alvarado that after the events set forth in the preceding
paragraph hereof he proceeded against the vassals of the
Lord of Xalapa who were in arms against the Spaniards,
with the White soldiers he had and with twenty-four thousand warriors which the said slave sent to his assistance and
without formally requiring the rebels to surrender as ordered
in the instructions of His Majesty set upon them, killing a
great many Indians and destroying the Province of Xalapa.
Of all the gold given him, he does not appear to have paid
the Royal Fifth.

17. And it is further charged against the said Pedro de Alvarado
that at the time Francisco de Garay came as Governor by
Royal Commission to the Province of the Panuco, having
disembarked in the territory assigned to him with all his
people, the said Pedro de Alvarado went with many soldiers,
foot and horse, to eject them from their territory against
the instructions which they brought from His Majesty and
that while on the road within the limits of the said province
he met certain people commanded by Gonzalo Dovalle, who
was captured with the other Spaniards accompanying him,
took their horses and arms and sent them as prisoners to San-
tistevan which is a village and fort of the Panuco and having
thoroughly maltreated them, the people who came with Garay,
the said Pedro de Alvarado intrigued so that they should leave

the service of their commander and enter the service of
Hernan Cortes and telling them that de Garay could not
settle there, that he would barely be able to sustain himself,
all of which was the cause of many soldiers of the said Francisco de Garay joining the forces of the said Hernan Cortes
and after this the said Pedro de Alvarado with Diego de
Ocampo took prisoner the said Francisco de Garay and sent
him to this city where he died and this was the cause of the
destruction of the fleet of the said Francisco de Garay and
that the Indians killed more than three hundred followers of
the said Francisco de Garay.

18. And the further charge is made against the said Pedro de
Alvarado that coming as captain to the Province of [blank
in text] and Guatemala by command of Hernan Cortes that
the people of these Provinces warred with him and afterwards came to make peace and the said Pedro de Alvarado
seized the Kings and Lords and that they should give him
gold, burned them without any other reason or cause whatsoever.

19. And it is further charged against the said Pedro de Alvarado
that while Captain of the said Province of Guatemala, the
Indian Lords came in peace and gave him presents of gold,
silver and jewels and treated him very well. It being known
by the said Pedro de Alvarado that a Prince of the said
Province had a very beautiful wife, he seized her and kept
her prisoner until the husband offered jewels and gold and
silver and slaves and begged the said Pedro de Alvarado to
give back his wife and take his possessions. The said Pedro de
Alvarado took all of the gold and slaves but kept the woman.

20. And the further charge is made against the said Pedro de
Alvarado that from the said Province of Guatemala he
departed for towns known as Cuscatlan [Salvador] and
Yxcuyntepeque who were at war with the said Province of
Guatemala and without observing the requirements of His
Majesty, entered into and burned the said towns and killed
their chiefs.

21. And the further charge is made against the said Pedro de
Alvarado that he sent messengers to a town called Aquitapec

ordering that they should clean the streets and place food for
him in the houses and other villages of the neighbourhood.
And the Christians came and seized the Indians who remained in the said towns. The remainder fled to the mountains whereupon the said Pedro de Alvarado proclaimed them
all slaves and branded those which he had seized.

22. And the further charge is made against the said Pedro de
Alvarado that in this same war a village named Nacintlan
arose in arms and after pacifying the village, the chiefs
thereof fled and the said Pedro de Alvarado sent to seek
them and kill them and after they had been killed he burned
the town and the people that were in it.

23. And it is further charged against the said Pedro de Alvarado
that in another village named Paxico, noting the bad treatment of the said Pedro de Alvarado, the chiefs sent its women
and goods to safekeeping and the warriors went out against
the said Pedro de Alvarado and the latter without observing
the rules of war in accordance with the orders of His Majesty
and sending them messengers ordering them to return in
peace, fell upon them and killed all the Indians and destroyed
the village.

24. And it is further charged against the said Pedro de Alvarado
that in other villages named Acatepeque and Moquizalco
that as the said Pedro de Alvarado appeared, the people of
the villages went forth to meet him and he demanded that
they bring food and as the Indians did not return, frightened
at the cruelty said to have been done by the said Alvarado,
the Spaniards who came with the said Pedro de Alvarado
seized all of the Indians they could find and made them slaves.

25. And it is further charged against the said Pedro de Alvarado
that in another village named Yocxocil, the inhabitants of the
said village knowing that the said Pedro de Alvarado was
coming cleaned the streets and awaited him in peace but the
chiefs who had heard of the cruelty he had employed toward
Indians both in war and in peace, determined to arm themselves and die on the field of battle and thus they did as the
said Pedro de Alvarado made no demand for surrender but

fell upon them and killed many, and continued the same practice at Talcusqualco.

26. And the accusation is made against the said Pedro de Alvarado that in another principal town which is called Cascatlan the Lords and principal warriors came forward to receive him in peace and had much fruit piled beside the road with food and other things to eat and when the Spaniards arrived in this town the Indians lodged them very well and provided them with food and other necessary things and being thus in peace the said Pedro de Alvarado commanded each Spaniard to take as many Indians as he could as he might take them as slaves with him which the said Spaniards accordingly did and on a certain day he commanded that all the Spaniards should bring the Indians which they had seized from this town and other towns mentioned in the preceding paragraphs and brand them as slaves, and returned to Guatemala destroying each town as he passed.

27. And the accusation is made against the said Pedro de Alvarado that upon his return to Guatemala from the towns hereinbefore mentioned that he stated to the Lords of the country that he desired to found a city which they thought well of and thereupon the said Pedro de Alvarado commanded them to deliver to him within a certain period of time one thousand sheets of gold of a value of fifteen pesos per sheet and the said Lords set to work to collect the gold in order to please the said Pedro de Alvarado and they gave him eight or nine thousand pesos and said that in view of the short period of time they did not have enough to make up for that required by Alvarado because the latter would only take pure gold, and remembering his cruelty such as the time he had taken the wife of the Prince as his mistress, they rose in arms and the war continued for a long time and the same thing occurred in other parts of the Province and the Indian King said that while the said Pedro de Alvarado was Captain of the Province there would be no peace for Christians even though all the Indians died in war, for which reason His Majesty lost much gold.

28. And the accusation is made against the said Pedro de Alva-

rado that in a town called Utatlan in the said Province
of Guatemala he seized five of the principal Lords and had
them tied to poles and demanded that they bring all the gold
which they had, of which they delivered a certain quantity
which he received and of which he gave no account to His
Majesty's Treasurer, and because thereafter the said chiefs
did not give him more gold he had them burned while attached
to poles.

29. And it is further charged against the said Pedro de Alvarado
that having founded in the said Province of Guatemala a
city known as Santiago, Cortes wrote him a letter ordering
him to depart with his men for Honduras to attack Cristobal
de Olid and that he, the said Pedro de Alvarado, wished to
depopulate the said city but that as the Mayor and Aldermen
and other persons thereof would not do so because it would
not be to the service of His Majesty, he removed them from
office and treated them very badly as he did also other Spaniards because they would not go with him and forced them
to flee to this city and notwithstanding all this the said Pedro
de Alvarado continued to be a partisan of Hernan Cortes and
took half of the people of the said city and marched against
Olid in the service of the said Cortes.

30. And it is further charged against the said Pedro de Alvarado
that in the said Province of Guatemala and in other towns
and provinces where he has been the said Pedro de Alvarado
collected great quantities of gold, silver and jewels and also
that he has not paid the Royal Fifth nor given part thereof
to his companions although many have made demands upon
him and several lawsuits are now pending.

31. And the further charge is made against the said Pedro de
Alvarado that in this New Spain he has killed and tormented
many Kings and principal warriors and other Indians that
they might give him gold and other treasures and that this
is public and notorious.

32. And the further charge is made against the said Pedro de Alvarado that in this New Spain, being Captain and Magistrate,
he has treated many Spaniards very badly and has hung some
without any cause or reason whatsoever. In the Province of

Tututepeque he hanged two Spaniards without cause and without formal trial. In Tacuba he caused a Spaniard to be publicly whipped because the latter had gone into the houses of the Indians for food.

33. And the further charge is made against the said Pedro de Alvarado that when he left for Spain he took with him gold, silver, jewels, etc., without paying the Royal Fifth and particularly a large jewel which was worth five thousand pesos of gold and that the Royal Fifth of the value of these treasures was not paid to the Royal Treasurer.

34. And finally it is charged against the said Pedro de Alvarado that not being a Knight of the Order of Santiago [St. James] and having no right to wear the Red Cross that the Knights of the said order wear that with much daring and contempt for the said order he publicly wore the habit of the Knights of Santiago with a red cross thereon in the city of Santo Domingo and on the Island of Cuba as well as in New Spain and to further injure the order he wore the cross turned inside out and when the Admiral [Diego Columbus] saw this and asked him why he wore the cross in such a manner, the said Pedro de Alvarado said to him that although a Knight of the Order of St. James he was ashamed to wear it openly because he was poor, whereupon the said Admiral reprimanded him and told him not to be ashamed of wearing it in public, and thereafter he signed himself falsely as a member of this order.

Nuño de Guzman   Juan Ortiz Matienzo
              El. Lic. Delgadillo

LETTERS FROM PEDRO DE ALVARADO TO CHARLES V

Sacred Imperial Catholic Majesty:

With Gabriel de Cabrera, Attorney General of this Province, and Juan de Galvarro, I sent Your Majesty a long statement of the state of affairs in this Province and of the ships and fleet which in Your Royal service I have made for the discovery and conquest of the Indies and the mainland in the South Seas asking assistance from Your Majesty which I now return to beg of you and with urgency because I have spent all that I possessed in this enterprise and am now in debt for very large amounts and because my principal attention has been to spare Your Majesty the expenses of this journey which has for its object, the discovery of the Isles of Spice, because in addition to being very costly there are involved much risk and labour and I have attempted the impossible. And as the Lord protects Your service and You, matters have so come about, Most Catholic Majesty, so fortunately that nothing required for this voyage is now lacking, neither in regard to the fleet nor to the persons who are to accompany me nor necessary equipment and supplies; the only present obstacle is that having completed the fleet and being ready to sail many days ago, I had not received an order from Your Majesty from which I would learn if You were pleased with this project for discovery and the route which I propose to take, in order to better satisfy Your Royal desires that they may be crowned with success; and as the instructions from Your Majesty were so late in coming I have been forced to maintain the fleet and expedition at a cost as great as that of the construction of the fleet and since in the construction I spent all my capital and became indebted for fifty thousand gold pesos, now I have spent more than one hundred and thirty thousand as set forth in the accounts which I enclose, and I believe it well spent considering the quality of the affair and the prospects of success.

At this time being in the port of Possession in the Province of
Nicaragua with the fleet, Gabriel de Cabrera arrived with orders
and commission of Your Majesty and he came at a most opportune time because with so much delay the Spaniards began to lose
interest in the venture, the ships became heavy with barnacles and
the supplies dwindled while salaries and expenses mounted to a
great total so that I had spent all which I had saved in the previous
years and in reading the instructions from Your Majesty I find
that Your Highness obligates me to provide a fleet of twelve
ships and four hundred Spaniards and while this requirement
might be considered as impossible due to the fact that men and
ships are so scarce in these new and distant countries, I found it
a mark of royal favour that I should be asked to do what no one
else would be able to do and as my desire is to comply with everything that Your Majesty commands in the forwarded instructions
and preferring to do rather more than less than that which may be
required of me, Sacred Majesty, I am sailing on this day, if God
be pleased, with twelve ships of from three hundred to forty tons
burden of which eight are not less than one hundred tons each, as
well equipped with munitions and supplies as they could be in
Seville. I am taking with me four hundred and fifty Spaniards of
whom two hundred and sixty are horsemen, one hundred musketeers and crossbowmen and the remainder armed with swords
and lances, in addition I have one hundred and forty Spanish
sailors to man the ships and two hundred Negro slaves belonging
to my people. Your Majesty may be sure that never until this day
has there been seen in these parts an expedition so equal to any
demand that may be put upon it because many of my warriors and
noblemen are accustomed to these countries and to the fatigues
of war, an experience which I value very highly as having such
they are vastly more valuable than newcomers from Spain. I am
also taking very good pilots, expert navigators, the most advanced
in their art and whom I am paying very high salaries.

As the principal aim of Your Majesty is the service of God, and
after that exploration, in accordance with your instructions I have
made inquiry hereat for clergymen and thus I am taking with me
two approved by the Order of San Francisco, very religious persons of good character, Your Majesty may have no doubts on this

point. I am taking two others of the Redemptionist Order of no less worth and in order to comply in all ways with the service of the Lord and of Your Majesty, having received word regarding Pedro Bravo who is a Bachelor of Laws and very good reports regarding his ability and manner of living, I have done everything possible to induce him to come with me and in order to serve Your Majesty he has left his house and comfortable life and has accepted the enterprise which has greatly pleased all of my company, and the Spaniards are very content, and because he has all the necessary requirements I beg Your Majesty to bestow upon him the dignity of Bishop of the territory under my jurisdiction which would be of much advantage to me and of benefit to all concerned. I am also taking five other priests who are very worthy persons because the True Faith will have to be celebrated in any territory which we are about to discover and explore and our consciences will be eased with the presence of these religious persons.

My route will be in accordance with the instructions of Your Majesty, and from the 13th to the 20th degree on the other side of the line I shall discover all the secrets of the ocean, its islands and the mainland and where it may appear best I shall conquer and settle. I trust in God that in the happy days of Your Majesty's reign I shall be so fortunate that I may perform for Your Imperial Crown the greatest service that yet have been undertaken in these countries because in addition to my present expedition I have sent two ships which I had built for that purpose to navigate and measure the Strait [the imaginary passage to the Indies which the Spaniards continually sought] that this route may prove the means of communication to these parts in order to establish commercial relations which is the most important matter for Your kingdom. [Alvarado is apparently referring to commerce with the East Indies.]

When I wished to absent myself from the government of Guatemala which is my principal care and to conserve and protect the conquered territories as well as to acquire those as yet unknown and which is one of the principal and richest countries of the New World it appeared to me well that in order for it to remain the state in which I leave it, rich, peaceful and with a contented population, I should entrust my position to a person who will well sustain it and for that reason I sent to Mexico for Jorge de Alvarado, my brother, taking him from his family and peaceful life whom I leave as Your Majesty's representative because in the conquest of this country he was my principal assistant, and in my absence from these countries he conquered and pacified a great part thereof and for that reason he is feared by the Indians and loved by the Spaniards. I am sure that in all that relates to the service of Your Majesty and the good of these countries no other person would do as well and because Your Majesty already has reports regarding him and his previous services which have been many, I beg Your Majesty, because he has suffered from the labours and great danger which he has encountered in New Spain as in these provinces, that he be remunerated by giving him the government of these countries and if any services are necessary on his part in order that he may merit such honour at the hands of Your Majesty I beg that my services may be applied to make up the deficit, and in so doing I have no doubt that my account is in the hands of Your Majesty and for the security and protection of this land and in this way also he and I are protected from the loss of the Indians and villages which in the name of Your Majesty have been given us for our services both in Mexico and Guatemala because in the present enterprise we are so far in debt that this protection is necessary to us.

As the ports in the Province of Guatemala are not good and as I have lost two ships in them I have brought my fleet to this place in the Province of Nicaragua from whence to start my voyage, and as the inhabitants of this Province have been benefited by the opportunity to sell me their labour and supplies of which there is an abundance and by approval of Your government and officials of this Province I remained here for several days making ready for the voyage which by the grace of Your Majesty has been conferred upon me; I kiss the Sacred hands of Your Majesty, being aware that since you have been so good as to confer this honour upon me I am therefore the more obligated to perform services worthy of Your Most Catholic Majesty and may God our Lord lengthen and prosper the reign of Your Majesty for many years with increment of many other lands and kingdoms.

From this port of Possession, January 18, 1534, Your Sacred Majesty's vassal who kisses Your Royal Hands.

EL ADELANTADO PEDRO DE ALVARADO

Sacred Imperial Catholic Majesty:

While I was in the port of Peru to take ship for this Province about two months ago I wrote to Your Majesty all that had happened to me and my fleet since I left the Province of Leon in Nicaragua until that time and as the messenger, Lope de Idiaquez, carried letters from the Adelantado Pizarro, it may be that mine have not been delivered, I am setting forth herein the contents of the previous letters and also some other matters that Your Majesty may be informed up to the date of my return to this Province.

I described to Your Majesty, the ships, soldiers, artillery and munitions that I had ready when about to leave the Province of Leon to undertake a voyage of exploration in the South Seas in accordance with the instructions of Your Majesty and I sent accounts covering everything. After we had set sail I gave the pilots of my fleet the route to be followed and the destination conforming to Your Majesty's commission and thus they did, always sailing westward, and when we were at sea almost four hundred leagues the currents were so strong and the winds contrary that although we did everything possible to continue our voyage until we were in great danger, I was forced to put about for the territory of Peru and I was obliged to throw overboard more than ninety horses and it would perhaps have been necessary to lose all the others and even perhaps some of the expedition for lack of water if we had not landed in Peru without knowing what country it was on a beach named Curaqua more than three hundred leagues from where Pizarro was. There I received notice of a town called Quito beyond the limits of the government of Pizarro and not wishing to continue along the coast to where he might be I decided to enter directly into the country because it seemed to me well to depart from any place where there already might be Spaniards and I encountered the most difficult country of mountains, rivers, swamps and thick and unhealthy jungles that those in the New World have encountered to date. I believe that there is not its equal

in any part of the world and through this country I continued my
journey opening roads by the sword and manual labour for a distance of more than one hundred and sixty leagues which required
seven months and in this time many of my people became ill and
the sickness was so severe that the day after they were stricken
they died and some who recovered lost their wits so that I was
obliged to make inquiries daily as to who had become ill and if he
was a foot-soldier he was thereafter placed on a horse and if
through sickness or insanity he was not able to sit in the saddle
he was tied on the horse and immediately that they became sick
the priest heard their confession and we gave them such medicines
and treatments as we had and if they died we gave them Christian
burial and carefully gathered their belongings for their heirs and
although in this way more than eighty men died, many others
recovered. I myself was so ill that I was unconscious for two days
and in a critical condition for ten more.

At the end of this time we arrived in a more level country where
we found some small villages of a very savage people although
they appeared to be rather wealthy as the men and principal women
wore jewels of gold and silver and from them we took some and
the food which they had which was very little because the neighbourhood is a poor one of small population and of such quality that
although in that country there are villages not more than ten or
fifteen leagues apart no one knew of nor had communication with
the others nor was there a road through this country nor did they
speak each other's language and they had different customs so that
all this part of my journey was without knowing exactly where
we were nor were we able to obtain the secrets of the land and we
had no information from them regarding any Christians that they
might have seen or heard of. Thus I continued through this
country until I arrived at the point where a great windstorm of
snow and hail came upon us with tremendous ice and cold so that
nine Spanish men and women and almost all of the Negroes and
other servants and some of the horses died of cold and such was
the torment and suffering that we had to endure that in order to
escape from this place no one of us was able to retain extra
clothing nor the gold and silver which he had collected from the
Indians and all that we had brought with us I left in the road that

anyone who wished might take because it was all that we could do to save ourselves and each other. If we had tried to bring our belongings with us no one of us would have escaped and because we had in this way lost all which we had carried, we suffered much from hunger as our only food was cooked pieces of palm. So hungry were we that a horse killed on the journey was sold for two thousand gold pesos as food.

I sent in advance a captain with some soldiers to seek some place or town that we might learn where we were and with the remainder I followed slowly after and God directed us to a very wide and smooth road and following this we saw the mark of horseshoes recently made and followed them and found eight horsemen who were brought to me. I learned that they were people of Marshal Almagro who had come some few days before with some of his men to the town called Quito which was within two days' journey of my location and after learning something of this country and their arrival therein and other matters I let them go free and wrote by them to the Marshal advising him of the manner in which I had come and as I desired to continue my expedition and to discover and conquer wherever I could in accordance with the powers given me by Your Majesty without in any way interfering in any way with the government of Pizarro I begged him in order that I might continue my expedition give me free passage to his camp and provide me with some supplies and on my part neither from me nor my people would he receive any molestation or animosity. He received my letters and replied to them but with the messengers he sent secret letters containing many offers and promises to my captains and soldiers in order that they might leave me and serve him. As we were so exhausted from our recent experiences the temptation was too much for some of my people and they murmured among themselves. Some departed secretly from my camp to go to his and some of them killed the Indians and to put an end to all these things I determined to interview Almagro who it seemed to me was somewhat afraid of me and did not wish to see me. I assured him that my arrival would be only to interview him and Pizarro and that I was following the instructions which Your Majesty had given me and if it would serve Your Majesty I would assist him with very good will because all of us were serving Your Majesty and I did all possible to impress this upon him because I had no other desire and asked him on his part to provide me with necessary food to continue my expedition and both parties appointed certain friends to settle these matters and draw up and sign a convention before a notary.

In the meantime he acted in a most treacherous way both personally and by means of his captain giving all of my people gifts and offers which were so great that they were overcome in this manner and talking between themselves said that if I wished to continue my conquest not more than thirty men would follow me of the one hundred and fifty horsemen and two hundred and fifty foot-soldiers under my command. When Almagro saw the state of affairs he did not wish to sign the agreement drawn and I therefore made him many concessions greatly to my prejudice and to his advantage wherein I lost greatly and since I could do nothing else I sold him all my ships with all they contained and my slaves and horses and my own belongings in the sum of one hundred thousand pesos according to a calculation of their worth which we made there although this scarcely paid me for the cost of the ships themselves. This I did because I did not want to lose everything and because with this money I could fit out another expedition to continue the search for new lands which Your Majesty ordered me to undertake. The ships alone with the arms, artillery and supplies and the advances which I made to my soldiers cost me more in Guatemala than I received from Almagro. Of all of the foregoing I wished to make a formal record and of the requirements which I made of him which he would not consent to and he said that I should prepare no written document in order that I should not be able to show Your Majesty what he had done to me which was a very bad decision, and as I did not wish to have so bad an act upon my conscience since we are all mortal I instructed that this be done in the service of Your Majesty although it was not accomplished without much complaint on the part of Almagro and those that were with him because I firmly believe that if they had been permitted to have their way Your Majesty would have lost very much as I believe that the Royal Fifth of this conquest of Quito will surpass two million pesos of gold which they will now be able to undertake with the soldiers and horses which I brought with me for this purpose in addition to my desire to conquer and place beneath the Crown of Your Majesty all these new lands. In addition to all this I have particularly received much damage because so signal a matter [conquest of Quito] has been taken from me and in which I could have served Your Majesty very greatly so that I have lost more than half of what I spent taking no account of what I might have obtained in this expedition.

In order to receive payment in gold for my ships and supplies it was necessary to go with Almagro to Jauja where Pizarro was whom I asked once more to return my ships to me together with everything which I had brought and to aid me in passing through his territory to the task which Your Majesty had sent me which he did not wish to do nor would he consent that I should take testimony thereof before a notary and seeing that so long as I was there he could not follow his own designs gave orders that a ship be placed at my disposal to return me to Guatemala together with the gold for the payment of my ships and even then he refused to pay all that had been agreed to and Your Majesty knows that this was not deserved, and he gave me a ship, one of those which I had sold to him, that I might come here and then he would not permit the ship to stop at Panama because he knew that I came from Peru with the intention of going immediately to kiss Your hands and ask for justice and punishment for those who done such a great disservice and so much damage to Your Majesty. He stated beforehand that he would not give me passage unless I returned immediately to this Province and in secret commanded the captain of the vessel to leave me in the port of Leon in Nicaragua without consenting that there should come with me one single Spaniard of my expedition who wished to return with me so I should leave with strangers and without witnesses as to his conduct.

In addition to the above Your Majesty will know that when I arrived with my fleet in the said country of Peru on the beach where I disembarked seeing that it would be impossible to continue my journey because of the contrary currents and winds which always blow that I sent two of the best ships to continue the journey along the coast of Peru to learn the ports and shape and size of the country and as the place on which I landed would not be suitable as a port in the service of Your Majesty, that some other more suitable location might be discovered without prejudicing in any way the government of Pizarro. The ships followed part of the coast and they were at a port where the people of Pizarro had established themselves they would not permit my ships to enter nor would they sell them food or supplies but on the other hand by the orders of Pizarro, money and promises were secretly sent to the master and the seamen that they might desert the vessel which those of one ship did and went over to Pizarro and for lack of a sufficient crew this ship could not continue its voyage returning with much danger because of the handful of men. The other ship went forward several leagues beyond Chincha which was a point where no other ship had ever arrived, and the people of Pizarro were in the port and by commands and threats to the sailors and giving them gold won them over and they also won over the master with presents they gave him and took possession of the ship for Pizarro with all that it contained, so that I was compelled to sell them everything and for this reason I was unable to explore as far as the Cape which otherwise would have been possible as the ships were very good and provided with all other necessary things.

In order for me to form and complete another fleet as powerful as that which I took on this voyage as I wrote to Your Majesty it is evident that this is not the proper place from which to undertake an expedition to the South Seas. Although my desire to serve Your Majesty is very great, my resources do not permit me to do all things necessary and in order to provide for the people who came with me it was necessary for me to pay off many of their debts and to purchase for them from merchants and other people many things which they stood sorely in need of such as clothing for themselves as well as arms and other necessary things and the merchants seeing the need in which I stood sold them to me at excessive prices and the total was so great I was obliged to obligate myself to many both for the general expenses of the fleet and for account of those persons who accompanied me. Although as I have told Your Majesty all of my people remained with Marshal Almagro, if I had been allowed to retain my ships I would soon have been in position to continue my voyage and discover with them some great thing and territory. It was for this purpose that I might thus enhance Your Majesty's position in the South Seas that I acquired so great obligations and debts and that it was necessary to sell them in order to obtain something with which to repay my obligations and although I did everything possible to evade this it was necessary for me to take this step. Now with all of the equipment and supplies and the horses and foot-soldiers that I brought to this country, Almagro has departed without any licence of Your Majesty to conquer the territory which I was to discover and populate in accordance with Your Royal instructions. I do not know how he will fare nor what success his expedition will have because of the small experience that he has in such matters; but I say to Your Majesty that upon my arrival in those parts peace was assured and lastingly, for given the small number of Spaniards both horse and foot that he had at his command and the position they were in and the war then under way they should have all perished but with the people that I brought with me, all of this has been changed very much and Almagro's position was so improved that I fear that the arrival of orders from Your Majesty to Pizarro which he said were en route will foment some great discontent between them in which all will be lost.

I am satisfied that Your Majesty has faith in me and in my desire to serve you to the increase and prosperity of your Empire and therefore believe me in what I say, since I was no party to their refusal to permit me to take testimony of all of these acts before a notary nor would they permit me to draw any other instrument satisfactory to Your Majesty lest it show the great disservice which they are doing to Your Majesty and that they might hide the damage which they had done to me and the complaints which I might make against them. I understand that they have now in my absence drawn up documents using as witnesses persons whom I have had to punish for crimes because no one could have been more just in governing such a multitude of all kinds of persons and there not failing those who wish me ill especially the principal soldiers who left me for the promises and presents given to them and now wish to blame me and thus excuse their own conduct. I beg Your Majesty in consideration of all the

foregoing that I may not be blamed without being heard because
I expect to present my explanations in such a manner that Your
Majesty will punish them for the damage done me and restore
the money which I have lost. I expect this because of my faith in
Your Majesty who knows that I have acted only by my desire to
serve Your Majesty and I have avoided all quarrels and scandals
with others [other conquerors] as I might of in disputing the
possession of newly found lands but on the contrary I have lost
all of my fortune and that which in the service of Your Majesty
I hoped to gain. In addition to the foregoing I know that Your Majesty has been told that at the time I left the port of Leon in Nicaragua with my fleet that I took two ships which I found against the
wills of their owners and even if this were true having so great
a mission my voyage was in the service of Your Majesty this
would not have been a matter of great moment, but I had nego-
tiated with the owners to buy their ships which they begged me to
do and thus it was done as appears by the copies of letters and bills
of sale which I enclose herewith and when they delivered the said
ships to me a formal document was drawn before a notary of the
price which I paid for these ships and I paid that which they asked,
all of which appears in the documents attached hereto.

I know that Almagro is writing to Your Majesty asking the
government of the Province that I was to conquer and populate. I
beg Your Majesty, if this has not already been done that it may
not be, for his experience is not sufficient, that I should be deprived
of the right given me in the royal commission under authorization
of which I formed the fleet and spent so much of my fortune and
received so much damage and since I still possess the desire and
ability to render all the service that Your Majesty may require, I
repeat therefore my supplication that the government of this
Province not be given to Almagro but that on the contrary Your
Majesty may give me permission to come to kiss Your royal
hands because having arrived there Your Majesty will learn
in detail the merits of the case and that Your Majesty may see
how You may best be served in the discovery of the lands along
the South Seas wherein the Lord may be served and our Sacred
Catholic Faith exalted and Your Majesty and all of Your realms
benefited as may be shown by the results.

In the letters which Lope de Idiaquez carried I wrote to Your Majesty that on arriving in Guatemala I would make arrangements to leave as soon as possible to come to Spain and to give Your Majesty a detailed account of all that had happened to me and other matters in connection with these realms and to beg You to see that justice is done me for the damages caused me in Peru and I arrived in this city of Santiago on April 20 and found the Indians somewhat restless and some few days before they had killed a number of Spaniards for which they were punished. Now on my arrival they are in a better frame of mind because they know that I take special care to see that they are well treated and take pains to inform myself of the actions of those Spaniards who are set in control over their villages and all else which is necessary for the government of this country and the protection of the natives thereof. For this reason and in order to acquaint myself with other matters concerning Your Majesty's service either in this Province or in Mexico the officials of this city and the royal officials situated here believe that I should not now leave these Provinces and have even given me to understand that if I do not remain here voluntarily they will complain to Your Majesty and they believe that if I remain here now this Province will be benefited and therefore I have delayed my departure until Your Majesty sends me formal licence that I may come to kiss Your Royal hands and to inform You of matters. I believe that my trip to Spain will bear fruit and that Your Majesty will be greatly pleased thereat. I have thought many times that as in the South Seas there must exist many islands and mainlands with great wealth and population and since in the days of Your Majesty's reign the discoveries have commenced may God grant that we may also continue to discover lands where His Sacred Name may be praised, the Faith increased. Having considered the best manner in which to undertake that which should be done, I find that to undertake such a voyage from the coast of New Spain and these Provinces is a very great risk for the Spaniards and the Indians accompanying them and brings no worthwhile result because the great currents and contrary winds which prevail in these oceans prevent exploration as I have learned by experience and as also the Marquis of the Valley [Cortes] has sent two ships to discover which have been thrown back by the great currents as well as the two ships which I sent before my departure. Although they left in very good weather and followed the route laid out for them neither one nor the other could make progress on the high seas against the winds and were forced to turn back and mine by the force of the currents were carried to the shore of Peru and the same happened to me with the fleet under my command which was so well equipped and supplied as Your Majesty knows from my letters and since the ships that can be made here are neither very large nor strong and the timbers are not as durable as those of Spain and principally because the teredos of the warm water here attack and ruin the timbers of the ships in a short time so that they fail when most needed. As these repairs cannot be carried out at sea but require delay until the ship can arrive in some place where it may be careened, and to know all that remaining unknown of the South Seas, and for so great an undertaking, and because of such interest in the discoveries that may be made in this sea, it appears to me at the outset that we should consider a very much larger fleet constructed in Spain. Six or seven large ships well equipped with artillery, supplies, sailors and food for many days and there should be at least seven hundred soldiers on them and these should be brought by their captain through the Strait of Magellan until they reach some island or mainland on the other side of the Isles of Spice. Having arrived there ships should be sent from the fleet to this coast and these provinces to advise You how the newly discovered lands are populated and to take back with them horses, as there will be by that time a great quantity of animals available here, and up to two thousand Spaniards as settlers, and supplies and even ships. With all this they may return to where the remainder of the fleet is and from there follow a general plan, setting out in this manner to discover and locate all of the islands of that sea because thus coming and going they will not fail to find whatever is as yet unknown and with the news of these discoveries they can then return to Spain or come here. As the route by the Strait of Magellan is very long they could return this way if they prefer to do so and in this way the enterprise could be consolidated and the greatest possible benefit derived therefrom. If Your Majesty is pleased to consider what I have said and the same is suitable, I hope that Your Majesty believes I am sufficiently able to undertake this work and I beg Your Majesty to call me to Spain and I will come at my own cost. I will place seven hundred crossbowmen and archers on the shores of the Isles of Spice and I will sustain myself there until the arrival from this Province and New Spain of two thousand horsemen for as I have said there will be an abundance of horses and supplies such as meat, vegetables and fish as well as ropes and other equipment and some ships which are available on these coasts. With all of these people it will be possible to conquer islands and mainlands in the South Seas. If Your Majesty thinks well of this I beg of You to send me permission to come to Spain because I believe this is something that will greatly serve Your Majesty's interest. I am prepared to leave immediately upon receipt of licence leaving the government in good hands so that nothing may happen during my absence. I have provided many cattle and pigs in the suitable portions of these countries that they may increase so that food will be available when the ships which shall come for the men and horses may require it and return promptly to where I shall be with the remainder of the fleet. Since I wrote to Your Majesty from Peru that I was very far in debt and although I have paid some part of the latter I still remain owing various amounts. I have sixty thousand ducats which I wish to keep. I wish to defer this payment until I see what Your Majesty wishes to do and since my creditors may be paid from the proceeds of my granaries, receiving each year one-third of the amount due them, I beg Your Majesty to order that these debts be paid in this manner although owing to the excessive prices of which I have already told you many of them have already really been paid. Thus I may be able to take these sixty thousand ducats to Spain to begin spending them on the fleet to be constructed there because if Your Majesty wishes to give me charge of this enterprise in continuation of the contract made with Your Majesty before I should desire to sail from Spain for the Isles of Spice within a year from this day and I expect such good fortune that within a short time Your Majesty will know all of the South Seas and upon advising the Spanish settlers of my discovery the lands may be populated very quickly. I beg Your Majesty to order this undertaking without the loss of the least possible time if You approve of my idea because in my opinion this is the only feasible manner in which this expedition can be carried out and any time that is lost in placing it in execution is a great loss to Your Majesty from the point of view of the wealth that may be encountered. I hope that in undertaking this expedition to render You greater service than any other of Your vassals ever has.

And if Your Majesty will send me licence to proceed to Spain I trust that you will accompany this with another permitting me to take with me six residents of this Province that they may be captains with me in the expedition. I will select those who by experience and ability are deserving of such positions. I will give orders that during my absence no one shall interfere with the Indians which by Your Majesty's command have been confided to their care.

In the meantime I have heard that while I was away from these Provinces several letters have been sent from here to Your Majesty and to the Council of the Indies stating that in order that my fleet might be well manned I have taken many settlers of this city and from the other towns of this government so that some of them remained without inhabitants. This is exactly to the contrary of the truth because Your Majesty will learn that of the Spanish settlers in this government I did not take more than ten and in place of these many newcomers have taken up land and become settlers. So many persons have arrived from Spain before and after the sailing of my fleet who were desirous of going to Peru that there is not food enough in this country to sustain them all. Every day so many pass here that I marvel that the City of Mexico is not deserted even with the great population that it possesses.

In order to give land and employment to these people we have just founded the City of San Miguel on the River Serapa and we are undertaking to conquer and populate the adjoining Provinces which since their territory is rugged we have not as yet distributed among the Spaniards. With so many mouths to feed and as there are already so many Spaniards in Peru and little chance for all to gain a fortune and the great need of footstuffs together with the risk of the life of those who desire to continue from here to

Peru that many of those who have come here with the intention of proceeding will settle in these Provinces because there is no other territory as fertile as this. It has always been my intention, which I have never lost sight of, to continue the settling of these Provinces so that if Your Majesty may be pleased to send for me everything will be in order in these Provinces and Your Majesty's interests will be well served.

May God extend the life of Your Most Sacred Catholic Majesty for many years.

From this city of Santiago of the Province of Guatemala on the twelfth day of the month of May, 1535. Of Your Sacred Catholic Majesty humble vassal and slave who kisses Your Most Royal hands.

EL ADELANTADO PEDRO DE ALVARADO

CONTRACT BETWEEN
PEDRO DE ALVARADO AND
DIEGO DE ALMAGRO

August 26, 1534

KNOW ALL TO WHOM THESE PRESENTS COME, that I, the Adelantado, Don Pedro de Alvarado state: that of my own free will I do hereby sell to you, the Marshal Don Diego de Almagro, all of the fleet of ships and supplies therewith which I at present own and possess in the South Seas as follows: one galleon *San Cristobal* and one ship *San Clara,* and another ship *Buenaventura* and another *La Concepcion,* and two sloops *San Pedro* and *Santiago;* which I sell to you as I have said with all of their supplies, anchors, ropes, iron work, arms, artillery, munitions and anything else connected with and on board the said ships in order that you may hold and use the same as your personal property; and regarding the said fleet I state that I sell it to you in the form in which it is for the price and amount of one hundred thousand pesos of good gold at four hundred and fifty maravedis per peso. And I, the said Marshal Don Diego de Almagro, state; that I recognize and ratify my willingness to pay to you, the said Adelantado, Don Pedro de Alvarado, the said one hundred thousand pesos in gold in the form and fineness stated which I will give and pay to you in the Province of Jauja upon your demand, or on demand of persons bearing sufficient and satisfactory powers from you for that purpose, in the town of San Miguel or any other town of that Province which you, the said Adelantado, may select with the understanding that if the payment is to be made in the said town of San Miguel, you will give me three months' time during which I may arrange for the transportation of the said gold to the place of payment, with the further condition that if during the said three months any part of the gold then in transport shall be lost, such loss and risk shall be for my account and I shall be obliged to give and pay you the said one hundred thousand gold pesos. And in the same manner, all of the said ships from the date of this agreement, or from today forward, shall be and remain my personal property. All of the foregoing in the manner therein set forth we ratify and oblige ourselves to carry out and comply with as we have agreed under penalty of one hundred thousand pesos for violation of this agreement, which sum we fix and agree upon as the conventional penalty; in case of violation of this pact and the application of the penalty, one-half of the fine shall be paid to the injured party and the remainder to the Royal Treasurer and whether or not the contract be violated and the penalty paid, none-theless this contract and all therein contained shall remain in force and in order to submit ourselves to this contract and carry out the obligations thereof, we pledge our personal fortunes and possessions of any nature whatsoever as subject thereto and we give full power to any competent authority of any jurisdiction or power whatsoever, in order that they may force us to comply with this contract or pay the penalty herein provided in the same manner as if the penalty had been assessed by a court of competent juris-diction. For this reason we renounce the favour and shelter of any defence or the protection of any laws or rights which in such case we might have the right to make use of.

This agreement is dated in the City of Santiago de Quito, the twenty-sixth day of the month of August, of the year of Our Lord, 1534, in the presence of our witnesses, Fernando Calderon, Cap-tain Sebastian Benalcazar, Captain Ruy Diaz and Juan de Espinosa and the signatories El Adelantado Pedro de Alvarado, Juan Espi-nosa as witness—Fernando Calderon, Ruy Diaz, and I, Domingo de la Presa, Royal Scribe and Notary Public, empowered to prac-tise in the Court and all portions of the Realm, attest that I was present as one of the witnesses and I affix my signature hereto in testimony of the truth of the matter.

DOMINGO DE LA PRESA

BIBLIOGRAPHY

Acosta, José de, *Historia de Indias,* Madrid, 1894
Anales de la Sociedad de Geografía y Historia, Guatemala, 1927-1928-1929
Annals of the Cakchiquels, paleographed in narrative form about the time of the Conquest. (A translation was published in Philadelphia, 1885)
Arevalo, and Diaz, Victor Miguel, translation of the manuscript "Actas del Ayuntamiento de Guatemala 1526-1534," Guatemala, 1856

Bancroft, H. H., *Annals of Early Mexico,* New York, 1883
——*History of the Pacific States,* San Francisco, 1883
——*A Popular History of the Mexican People,* San Francisco, 1887
Barcia, Andres de, *Historiadores primitivos de las Indias Occidentales,* Mexico, 1749
Bourbourg, Brasseur de, *Histoire des Nations Civilisées de l'Américique Central,* Paris, 1854

"Coleccion de Documentos Ineditos del Archivo de Indias" (manuscript). (Squier published a translation in Albany, 1860)
Cortes, Hernan, *Cartas de Relacion de la Conquista de Mejico,* Madrid, 1922
Cortes Society, The, *Documents and Narratives Concerning the Discovery and Conquest of Latin America,* New York, 1925

De Landa, Diego, Bishop, *Relaciones de Yucatan,* Madrid, 1898
de las Casas, Bartolome, *Historia de las Indias,* Madrid, 1559
Del Mar, Manuel, *Historia de Mejico,* New York, 1828
Diaz, Victor Miguel, *Narraciones,* Guatemala, 1918
Diaz del Castillo, Bernal, *Conquête de la Nouvelle-Espagne,* Paris, 1877
——*Discovery and Conquest of Mexico,* London, 1928
——*Historia Verdadera de la Nueva España,* Madrid, 1632

Duran, Diego, *Historia de Indias,* Mexico, 1867

Folsom, George, *Despatches of Cortes to Carlos V,* New York, 1843
Frejes, Francisco, *Historia de la Conquista,* Mexico, 1839

Genet and Chelbatz, *Histoire des Peuples Mayas-Quiches,* Paris, 1927
Gunther, Siegmund, *La Epoca de los Descubrimientos,* Barcelona, 1926

Herrera, Antonio, *Historia General,* Madrid, 1750
Humboldt, Baron von, *Vues des Cordillères,* Paris, 1811

Jimenez, Francisco, *Historia de la Provincia de San Vicente de Chiapa y Guatemala,* edition of Villacortes, Guatemala, 1929
Juarros, Domingo, *History of Guatemala,* Guatemala, 1808

" La cuarta relacion q' Fernando Cortes . . . envio al muy alto y muy potentissimo invictissimo Señor Don Carlos" (manuscript), Toledo, 1525
Lonchay, Henri "La Valeur des Ducats et des Ecus Espagnales," *Bulletin des Lettres,* Académie Royale de Belgique, Brussels, 1906
Lorenzana, Francisco Antonio, *Historia de Mejico,* New York, 1828

Markham, C. R., *History of Peru,* New York, 1892
Marroquin, Lorenzo, *Documentos Ineditos del Archivo de Indias,* manuscript
Milla, José, *Historia de la America Central,* Guatemala, 1879
———*La Hija del Adelantado,* Guatemala, 1898
Municipality of Guatemala, *La Romantica Ciudad Colonial,* 1928

Navarrete, M. F. de, *Viajes de Cristobal Colon,* Madrid, 1922

Oviedo, G. Fernandez de, *Historia de las Indias,* Madrid, 1851

Pelleport-Jaunac, J. P. A., *Histoire de l'Empire du Mexique,* Paris, 1845
Prescott, W. H., *History of the Conquest of Mexico,* Boston, 1856
———*History of the Conquest of Peru,* New York, 1847
"Proceso de Pedro de Alvarado y Nuño de Guzman," Mexico, 1529

Ramirez, J. F., *Proceso de Pedro de Alvarado,* Mexico, 1847
Rodas y Villacorta, Antonio, *Manuscrito de Chichicastenango,* Guatemala, 1927

Sentenach, Narciso, "El Maravedi—su grandeza y decadencia," *Revista de Archivos, Bibliatecas y Museos,* Madrid, 1905

Solis, Antonio de, *Historia de la Conquista de Mejico,* Paris, 1889

Squier, E. G., *Collection of Rare and Original Documents and Relations concerning the Discovery and Conquest of America,* New York, 1869

Stephens, J. L., *Incidents of Travel in Central America,* New York, 1841

Subercaseaux, Guillermo, "The Origin of the Hispanic-American Peso," *Inter-America,* New York, August 1923

Torquemada, *Historia de la Inquisicion,* Mexico, 1870

Vargas Machuca, Bernado de, *Milicia y Descripcion de las Indias,* Madrid, 1599

Vignaud, Henry, *The Colombian Tradition,* Oxford, 1920

Vines Escudero, Antonio, "Evalucion de la Moneda España," *Revista Nacional de Economio,* Madrid

Willard, T. A., *The City of the Sacred Well,* London, 1928

INDEX